Louise Lecavalier

Louise Lecavalier

Dance, Labor, Culture

MJ Thompson

methuen | drama
LONDON • NEW YORK • OXFORD • NEW DELHI • SYDNEY

METHUEN DRAMA
Bloomsbury Publishing Plc, 50 Bedford Square, London, WC1B 3DP, UK
Bloomsbury Publishing Inc, 1385 Broadway, New York, NY 10018, USA
Bloomsbury Publishing Ireland, 29 Earlsfort Terrace, Dublin 2, D02 AY28, Ireland

BLOOMSBURY, METHUEN DRAMA and the Methuen Drama logo are trademarks of Bloomsbury Publishing Plc

First published in Great Britain 2025

Copyright © MJ Thompson, 2025

MJ Thompson has asserted her right under the Copyright, Designs and Patents Act, 1988, to be identified as Author of this work.

For legal purposes the Acknowledgments on pp. xv–xviii constitute an extension of this copyright page.

Cover design: Ben Anslow
Cover images: At top, © Linda Dawn Hammond/IndyFoto.
At bottom, © Claude-Félix Blanchard.

All rights reserved. No part of this publication may be: i) reproduced or transmitted in any form, electronic or mechanical, including photocopying, recording or by means of any information storage or retrieval system without prior permission in writing from the publishers; or ii) used or reproduced in any way for the training, development or operation of artificial intelligence (AI) technologies, including generative AI technologies. The rights holders expressly reserve this publication from the text and data mining exception as per Article 4(3) of the Digital Single Market Directive (EU) 2019/790.

Bloomsbury Publishing Plc does not have any control over, or responsibility for, any third-party websites referred to or in this book. All internet addresses given in this book were correct at the time of going to press. The author and publisher regret any inconvenience caused if addresses have changed or sites have ceased to exist, but can accept no responsibility for any such changes.

Every effort has been made to trace copyright holders and to obtain their permission for the use of copyright material. However, if any have been inadvertently overlooked, the publishers will be pleased, if notified of any omissions, to make the necessary arrangement at the first opportunity.

A catalogue record for this book is available from the British Library.

A catalog record for this book is available from the Library of Congress.

ISBN:	HB:	978-1-3501-9520-2
	ePDF:	978-1-3501-9522-6
	eBook:	978-1-3501-9521-9

Typeset by Integra Software Services Pvt. Ltd.

For product safety related questions please contact productsafety@bloomsbury.com.

To find out more about our authors and books visit www.bloomsbury.com and sign up for our newsletters.

For all those who work and dance

Contents

List of Illustrations   x
Acknowledgments   xv

Introduction: Moving Force: On the Cultural Work of the Dancer Louise Lecavalier   1

1   Dancer as Relay: Fragments for a Phenomenology of the Dancer   23
2   *Non Non Non*: Material Labor and the Excess of the Virtuoso   75
3   Punk Neo-Expressionism in the Early La La La Repertoire   113
4   Hybrid Body, International Cyborg: Rehearsals Against Purity   147

Conclusion: Dancing, Glorious Expenditure   181

A Partial Timeline: Fragments for a Life in Dance   200
Bibliography   210
Index   225
About the Author   230

Illustrations

Inside cover
0.1   Lecavalier, Godin, and Lock, Cooper Building Studio, 1984. Photo: Jack Udashkin

Inside back cover
0.2   Lecavalier, White Wall Studio, 2024. Photo: François Blouin. Retouch: Luc Lavergne. Image courtesy Louise Lecavalier/Fou Glorieux

Introduction

I.1	Photo shoot for *Businessman in the Process of Becoming an Angel* (1983). Photo: Jack Udashkin	2
I.2	Édouard Lock and Louise Lecavalier at Metropolis (1994). Photo: © Linda Dawn Hammond/IndyFoto	4
I.3	In performance, *Human Sex* (1985). Photo: © Linda Dawn Hammond/IndyFoto	6
I.4	Portrait of the artists (1985). Photo: Édouard Lock	13

Chapter 1

1.1	Louise Lecavalier, photo shoot for *Businessman in the Process of Becoming an Angel* (1983). Photo: Jack Udashkin	24
1.2	Lecavalier, Parc Lafontaine, July 29, 1990. Photo: © Linda Dawn Hammond/IndyFoto	44

Zine section

1.3   Montréal and Laval.

1.4   Lecavalier with Groupe Nouvelle Aire, c.1980. Photo: Claude-Félix Blanchard. Image courtesy Louise Lecavalier/Fou Glorieux
1.5   Louis Guillemette and Miryam Moutillet in *Oranges: ou la recherche du paradis*, December 1981. Photo: Ron Diamond
1.6   Poster for *Oranges*, design by Michel Lemieux. Courtesy: Michel Lemieux/Bibliothèque de la danse Vincent-Warren
1.7   Louise Lecavalier and David Bowie, London, July 1, 1988. Photo: Anton Corbijn/Getty Images
1.8   Façade of the Cooper Building, 2016. Photo: Étienne Tremblay-Tardif
1.9   At the Cooper Building Studio: Claude Godin and Louise Lecavalier, 1983. Photo: Jack Udashkin
1.10 Façade of the Rialto Theatre, Montréal, June 14, 1981. Photo: Allan Raymond/Courtesy Allan Raymond Collection, Jewish Public Library
1.11 Édouard Lock and George Skalkogiannis, final show of *Businessman*, at the Rialto. Photo: Jack Udashkin
1.12 Carole Courtois, Louise Lecavalier, Marc Béland, *Human Sex*, 1985. Photo: Édouard Lock
1.13 Lock and Lecavalier, *Human Sex*, 1985. Photo: Édouard Lock
1.14 Crowd at the Spectrum, Montréal, August 3, 1983. Photo: Robert Nadon/Archives La Presse
1.15 Louise Lecavalier, Marc Béland, Claude Godin in *Human Sex*, 1985. Photo: © Linda Dawn Hammond/IndyFoto
1.16 Lecavalier, Godin, Béland, in *Human Sex*, 1985. Photo: © Linda Dawn Hammond/IndyFoto
1.17 Program, *Businessman in the Process of Becoming an Angel*, Front. Courtesy: © Linda Dawn Hammond/IndyFoto
1.18 Program, *Businessman in the Process of Becoming an Angel*, Back. Courtesy: © Linda Dawn Hammond/IndyFoto
1.19 Poster, *New Demons* (1987). Photo: Édouard Lock/Courtesy: Édouard Lock/Bibliothèque de la danse Vincent-Warren

1.20 Sarah Lawrey, Louise Lecavalier, Sarah Williams, *Infante, c'est destroy* (1991). Photo Wolfgang Kirchner. Image courtesy Louise Lecavalier/Fou Glorieux
1.21 Performing with Donald Weikert, Post-Sex Garage/Love-In Protest, Parc Lafontaine, July 29, 1990. Photo: © Linda Dawn Hammond/IndyFoto
1.22 Lecavalier and Montréal street artist Zilon (Raymond Pilon), Post-Sex Garage/Love-In Protest, Parc Lafontaine, July 29, 1990. Photo: © Linda Dawn Hammond/IndyFoto

Chapter 2

2.1 Flyer for *Non Non Non je ne suis pas Mary Poppins*. Photo: Jacques Perron. Image courtesy Louise Lecavalier/Fou Glorieux   79
2.2 A portion of the contact sheet for *Non Non Non je ne suis pas Mary Poppins* (c.1982). Photo: Jack Udashkin   90
2.3 Lecavalier in *Non Non Non* (c.1982). Photo: Jack Udashkin   95
2.4 Lecavalier in *Non Non Non* (c.1982). Photo: Jack Udashkin   106
2.5 Lecavalier in *Non Non Non* (c.1982). Photo: Jack Udashkin   107
2.6 Working together: La La La Human Steps in *Human Sex* (1985). Photo: © Linda Dawn Hammond/IndyFoto   107

Chapter 3

3.1 Miryam Moutillet and Louise Lecavalier in *Oranges*, December 1981. Photo: Ron Diamond   117
3.2 Miryam Moutillet and Michel Lemieux in *Oranges*, December 1981. Photo: Ron Diamond   117
3.3 Photo shoot for *Businessman*. Photo: Jack Udashkin   119
3.4 Louise holds Édouard. Photo: Jack Udashkin   120

3.5	Developing *off-axis*, Claude Godin and Louise Lecavalier. Photo: Jack Udashkin	127
3.6	Signing work: Claude Godin and Louise Lecavalier. Photo: Jack Udashkin	130

Chapter 4

4.1	Blurring the body. Photo: © Linda Dawn Hammond/ IndyFoto	171
4.2	Photo: Greg Gorman for l.a. Eyeworks	175
4.3	Poster for *Strange Days*. © 1995 20th Century Studios Inc. All rights reserved	176
4.4	Production still, *Strange Days*. Photo: Merie W. Wallace/ Courtesy: Fou Glorieux/20th Century Studios Inc.	178

Conclusion

5.1	*2* (1995) Louise Lecavalier. Photo: Édouard Lock	184
5.2	Louise Lecavalier and Frédéric Tavernini in *So Blue* (2012). Photo: Carl Lessard. Image courtesy Fou Glorieux	189
5.3	Louise Lecavalier and Frédéric Tavernini in *So Blue* (2012). Photo: Carl Lessard. Image courtesy Fou Glorieux	190
5.4	Louise Lecavalier and Frédéric Tavernini in *So Blue* (2012). Photo: Carl Lessard. Image courtesy Fou Glorieux	191
5.5	*Delusional World* (2023). Photo: François Blouin. Retouch: Luc Lavergne. Image courtesy Fou Glorieux	195
5.6	*Delusional World* (2023). Photo: François Blouin. Retouch: Luc Lavergne. Image courtesy Fou Glorieux	196

Timeline

6.1 *Fantasie sur quatre notes*. Choreography by Louise Latreille, Lecavalier at right. Photo: René De Carufel/ Bibliothèque de la danse Vincent-Warren 201
6.2 At the Rialto after the final performance of *Businessman*. Photo: Jack Udashkin 203
6.3 Extending the body: Louise Lecavalier and Rick Tija. Photo: Édouard Lock 206
6.4 Photo: Carl Lessard. Image courtesy Fou Glorieux 209
6.5 Photo: Dieter Wuschanski. Image courtesy Fou Glorieux 209

Acknowledgments

This book starts at the place where work, time, and space have met for me: my dad's woodshop; my mom's sewing room; my grandfather's lumber yard, as an employee of Barrett's in Ottawa; my grandmother's swivel chair, connecting voices as an operator for Bell Telephone. It starts with work, manual and otherwise: not as a practice on which to project romantic notions or, worse, abstracted reflections of dignity. Instead, I aim in this research to honor the ways that everyday people acquire and transform skill, making and remaking their bodies, through directed effort. It starts, too, in dance studios, makeshift or otherwise—mirrored and sprung. It starts with dancing—and the hours of sweat and labor, repetition leading to technical know-how; aesthetic, embodied, and intellectual discovery; adrenalin, communion, failure, and, on occasion, exhilarating, marvelous joy.

It also begins twenty-five years ago, as a graduate student in the Performance Studies department at New York University. The extraordinary dancer/performer Louise Lecavalier had just retired from Montréal-based dance-theater company La La La Human Steps and was in New York teaching a class in the Experimental Theatre Wing at Tisch School of the Arts. I attended her class: crowded, mostly students too young to know the 1980s, a few of us older fans, all jittery, stretching, watching ourselves and others in those weighted moments before class starts. Afterwards, we met for coffee and I inquired about a possible writing project related to her work. Since then, and between moves to different cities—short stints in New York and Paris before returning to Montréal—and following the birth of her twin daughters Romie and Janne, and the founding of her own company *Fou glorieux*, Louise has been a generous contributor and interlocutor, sharing her thoughts and the dance history as she lived it, in informal conversation and recorded oral history interviews over twenty-five years. My enormous thanks and appreciation to her for the time and insight, without which this book couldn't have been written. More, I'm thankful for the movement and imagery she presented through dance—they continue to inspire and offer alternative views of what a body can do. In considering her singular contributions and long-term presence and commitment to dancing, I hope to shine love by extension on the many dancers and workers who make performance possible and whose critical contributions often remain unmarked.

Dance is tricky to write about, and I am indebted to a number of photographers who accompanied me along the way. My thanks to the irrepressible Linda Dawn Hammond, artist, activist, and scenester in 1980s Montréal; and someone whose documentation of pivotal historic moments—including the 1991 Sex Garage assault by local police officers on Montréal's queer community; and the Kanesatake resistance and road blockade at Oka in 1997—have indelibly shaped the historical record. Her performance images track the earliest days of La La La, when the company was small and finding its way; and testify to the energy and power of the movement. Images by rebel performance curator and producer Jack Udashkin, Executive Director for multiple companies, including Margie Gillis, La La La, Fortier Danse-Création, and Marie Chouinard, as well as Executive Director of dance at the National Arts Centre (1988–2000) and Artistic Director at Theatre Lachapelle (2007–15), provided a crucial glimpse of Lecavalier's 1981 choreography, *Non Non Non je ne suis pas Mary Poppins*, as well as evidence of rehearsals and behind-the-scenes material conditions. Numerous other photographers contributed over the years—including René De Carufel, Ron Diamond, Édouard Lock, François Blouin, Luc Lavergne, and Étienne Tremblay-Tardif. I am hugely indebted to the artists, journalists, producers, and friends who spoke with me about these histories, with special thanks to Édouard Lock, Louis Guillemette, Miryam Moutillet, Michel Lemieux, Jackie Gallant, George Skalkogiannis, Philip Szporer, Dena Davida, and John O'Neil for their recollections. Special thanks to designer Pata Macedo, for her imaginative work on the zine-like insert. Equally, I thank the many people who spoke informally with me over the years, in bars and coffeeshops, at gallery openings and grocery stores, sharing stories of encounters with Louise onstage and off but consistently attesting to the depth of her impact.

My deepest thanks to Peggy Phelan, who read a version of Chapter 2 at a critical moment and whose writings and teachings have provided inspiration over many years. Dance scholar Kate Elswit read a draft of Chapter 3, offering helpful feedback on the clusters of projects gathered under the name of German expressionism. Marcia Siegel generously shared an unpublished manuscript about one of Lecavalier's recorded dances, *Human Sex* (1985)—her eye was a helpful reminder of the power of material observation and description. Finally, Felicia McCarren's course, "The Cultural History of the Dancer," in 1998 at Tisch in New York began this work and offered critical frameworks for thinking that I return to again and again. Her gifts as a thinker and teacher continue to shape my work.

Three friends, colleagues, and mentors have guided my work since the earliest days: Anne Flynn, Penny Farfan, and Lisa Doolittle, each of them fierce advocates for dance, the body, and the importance of writing history. Extra thanks go to theater scholar Penny Farfan, who commented on different drafts and proposals and offered encouragement over many years; her insight into queer modernism and women's performance, along with her excellent eye as a reader, kept me going through pivotal moments. During the first summer of the Covid-19 shutdown, my friend Michelle Dent convened a group of Performance Studies alumni and friends to meet weekly on the subject of writing and teaching during the pandemic. These conversations centered on the practice of writing and offered a balm of connection during a very difficult time: my thanks to Michelle Dent (New York University), Claudia Brazalle (University of East London), Blagovesta Momchedjikova (New York University), Jason King (USC Thornton School of Music), Toni Sant (Salford/Manchester University), Jo Novelli-Blasko (Independent Artist/Scholar), and Javier Serna (Autonomous University of Nuevo Leon). My thanks to York University theater and performance scholars Laura Levin and Marlis Schweitzer;

and to Brynn Schiovitz, of Chapman University, who published early versions of some of this work and provided important editorial feedback. The librarians at Bibliothèque de la danse Vincent-Warren in Montréal and the New York Performing Arts Library in Manhattan provided key resources and support; special thanks to Marie-Josée Lecours, Chief Librarian at the Vincent-Warren. At Concordia, Pamela Caussy at the Visual Collections Repository provided extraordinary support in digitizing photographs. Finally, my friends and colleagues performer/dramaturge Angélique Willkie and filmmaker Liz Miller bolstered my work through critical conversations during walks across the Plateau, Montréal, on myriad subjects including art, the academy, writing, and feminism.

Many research assistants, all of them extraordinary, contributed to this project in different ways since I first began teaching at Concordia in 2011: my thanks especially to Tristan Clairoux, a thinker of uncommon dexterity and a tenacious researcher, transcriber, and data manager. Thanks too go to Fréderic Gagnon, Katerina Kurtola, Allison Peacock, Jennifer Quintanilla, David Rose, and Vincent Viezzer. This project was funded by the Social Sciences and Humanities Research Council and benefited from a residency at the Leighton Colony at the Banff Centre in 2022.

Lastly, my love to Mark Sussman, whose editorial comments and epic breadth of performance knowledge made the work of writing all the more fun. His humor and inversive, chiasmatic thinking continues to vex, turn, stir, and enliven all things every day. Thanks, finally, to Sam and Finn, whose indelible gifts in motion as drummers, skaters, doers, and thinkers keep helping me see the world anew.

Introduction

Moving Force: On the Cultural Work of the Dancer Louise Lecavalier

I'm like a construction worker with a house to build—he's not going to build it in his mind.

—Louise Lecavalier

During the 1980s, I worked as a waiter in Ottawa, then a modest capital city of 800,000 people, mostly employed in the Civil or other services. Everyone I knew was either a waiter, a bartender, or a cook. Some found government jobs, working on the census or processing tax returns. A friend of my roommate's worked at the foundry of the Canadian Mint, literally making money, but his real job was bass player in a band. The tidy government city felt strange to us; on the one hand, closed off and closed by midnight. On the other, strangely alive, with a small scene driven by live music, street busking, vegan squat-cafés, and late-night dance clubs across the river in Hull, Québec—where the DJs were excellent, and the rules were different. It was fun against the odds, and the odds were many: flat economies, boring jobs, the waning ideal of government-as-service-provider, the HIV-AIDS pandemic. This was the context in which I first saw the company La La La Human Steps perform. I remember talking with friends about Lecavalier's stage presence: she was a giant, he was a god. We'd say now that they revised our understandings of gender, through muscle and movement all tangled up in a liberating punkwave, rockwave, shockwave. Back then, it was just shitty jobs and cool friends and after-hours dancing.

Figure I.1 Photo shoot for *Businessman in the Process of Becoming an Angel* (1983). Photo: Jack Udashkin.

We looked to Louise, to move and move differently, and the world felt wide open.

It's hard to remember now. When Lecavalier rose to prominence in the early 1980s, she did so alongside a world still enthralled by all manner of hardened category: men, women; white, black; straight, gay; avantgarde; and popular. Judith Butler's pivotal work on gender as no more, no less than the patterned repetition of behaviors over time had yet to be published;[1] and other key works of the period such as Benedict Anderson's *Imagined Communities* (1983), with its understanding of nation as narrative and construct; and Gayatri Spivak's translation of Derrida's *Of Grammatology* (1976), offering deconstruction as critical method, were only just beginning to circulate in academic discourse. As principal dancer with La La La Human Steps from 1981 to 1999, Lecavalier raised a fist to the norms of dominant categories and binary thinking, and she did so at a cultural moment ready to respond in sheer

---

[1] Judith Butler, "Performative Acts and Gender Constitution: An Essay in Phenomenology and Feminist Theory." *Theatre Journal* 40, no. 4 (1988): 519–31.

relief to the expansive qualities of body and genre that emanated from her presence. Lecavalier, along with dancer/choreographer Édouard Lock and the founding members of the company,[2] figured a new kind of concert dance: revised and uncodified movement vocabularies that played with strength, speed, body language, and the tension between ground and air. The work was brashly spectacular with its rock band aesthetic, pounding live music, varied use of film and video, and embrace of the club and the image as performance spaces.

Lecavalier, I argue, stood at the center: a powerful mover and committed artist whose ambiguous presentation and ability to lift and move her partners challenged patterns of gendered labor in dance. Alongside the rise of performance art, with its use of the body as overt political marker, the kinds of dance and theater vocabularies she developed with Lock and friends through the 1980s dovetailed with a more widespread blurring of the disciplines, perhaps best exemplified in the fields of Women's and Performance Studies, fields that map my own learning trajectory. Her charismatic presence on stage and off fueled urgent discussions in the media and in the cafés around thematics of feminism, gender, cultural innovation, and international mobilities. Performing at a small yet dynamic (sub)cultural scene in Montréal, Lecavalier's career arced in tandem with enormous changes in socio-political life, notably the performativity of gender; the rise (and fall) of Québec nationalism and the middle-class; and the arrival of the neoliberal economic model (Figure I.2).

This book reflects on Lecavalier's early career, beginning in 1981 with her first choreography, *Non Non Non je ne suis pas Mary Poppins*; and continuing through that decade into the early 1990s, tracking key moments in the La La La Human Steps repertoire. Lecavalier, driven by inquiry and artistry by all accounts, stayed focused on the body— its abilities, its malleabilities, its material facts, and the effects of its stylization. She remained sharply attuned to its position as an always

---

[2] Louis Guillemette, Michel Lemieux, and Miryam Moutillet.

Edouard Lock & Louise Lecavalier
LA LA LA HUMAN STEPS Montreal, 1994

Figure I.2 Édouard Lock and Louise Lecavalier at Metropolis (1994). Photo: © Linda Dawn Hammond/IndyFoto.

politicized and political entity, yet her day-to-day work centered on artistic research and dancing. Long before she started dancing, she played with a difference; as a young child, her heart's desire was to be awake and outdoors, roaming the Ste-Dorothée neighborhood northeast of Montréal while others slept. The eldest and only daughter in a working-class family of six, she loved sports and imagined growing up to be a superhero or an astronaut. At 15, when she first thought of dancing, she recalls:

> My chances were slim. I had an idea of what it would be like as a girl, romantic etc—and I knew I couldn't do that. When the guys danced, there were a lot of jumps …. I wanted to do that. I thought, "If I were a guy, I'd like to dance."[3]

Entering the CÉGEP Bois-de-Boulogne, she studied biology and registered for pre-med requirements but was most drawn

---

[3] Lecavalier in St-Raymond (2017), *Louise Lecavalier: Sur son cheval de feu*.

in by *parascolaire* dance classes. Later, her strong body and high-speed performance would be met with astonishment and love by audiences around the world, while at the same time being read as manic, hypersexualized, even anti-feminist by contemporaries, scholars and critics alike. But while feminist scholars of the period[4] tended to emphasize extreme body practices as only another kind of disciplining and compliance, my time with Lecavalier in formal and informal conversation and as a viewer showed extremity to be a function of where on the stage you stand—that is, often dependent on performative readings, unrelated to the technical and physical achievements developed by the dancer. I argue that her contributions have been driven by a deep skepticism regarding power and a resistance to the disciplining effects that recur across Western forms of concert dance training. This is not to say that awareness always precludes investments in the status quo; her tireless commitment to dancing, however, writ through daily practice, gathering huge audiences, over many years, stands as a relentless kind of questioning—kicking against forms of enclosures that aim to constrain bodies in motion.

Dance scholar Randy Martin writes that "what gets concentrated on stage as an apparent purity of movement is an abstraction of techniques and kinesthetic sensibilities from an entire historical corporeality."[5] Martin's work bats away notions of purity in dance and takes the moving body as social, cultural, and political mix as a given; more, he names dance's core superpower as its ability to gather people together in relation in shared time and space, underscoring its political dimension. By his account, and in spite of the pervasive and totalizing pressure and logic of the markets, dance allows "people to gather to reflect

---

[4] See Sandra Lee Bartky, *Femininity and Domination: Studies in the Phenomenology of Oppression* (New York: Routledge, 1990); and Susan Bardo, *Unbearable Weight: Feminism, Western Culture, and the Body* (Berkeley, Los Angeles, London: University of California Press, 2004/1993).
[5] Randy Martin, "Dance and Its Others: Theory, State, Nation and Socialism." In *Of the Presence of the Body: Essays on Dance and Performance Theory*, ed. André Lepecki (Middletown, CT: Wesleyan University Press, 2004), 47–63; 62.

Figure I.3 In performance, *Human Sex* (1985). Photo: © Linda Dawn Hammond/IndyFoto.

on what they can be together."[6] Whereas for Martin, this gathering capacity is emblematic of a popular desire and possibility for socialism, by my account (writ with love and hope through the following pages), Lecavalier's dancing opened a crack in the walls of embodiment, labor, and culture as these have played out in Québec and farther afield. For those of us watching, swaying in the crowd, we simply said, Wow. And stepped through the crack (Figure I.3).

Situating the writing of dancing

To paraphrase Marx, dancers make dance and they make their bodies too, but they make them under conditions that are never entirely their own. Written from the perspective of a fan and longtime observer, and feeling the work as an homage to the often invisible labor of the dancer,

---

[6] Ibid., 62.

I aim to understand Lecavalier's singular role—and by extension, that of the dancer as a figure in history—as a creative force in shaping company aesthetics and history as well as the public discourse on dance, labor, and identity as it unfolded during the 1980s.

Whereas the role of the choreographer is well documented, often the first element of dance committed to historical record, the dancer often slips from view, as does the shared nature of dancemaking. With ontologies challenged in all manner of directions, from pernicious histories of mind/body dualism to perceived associations with the "feminine," from ephemeral aspects of the form that can challenge sight and visibility to the way the form engages the body, ever a volatile political site, dancing can present challenges for historians seeking stable artefacts and categories of understanding.[7] As dance critic and historian Roger Copeland noted in his 1983 anthology, fixed definitions of what separates dancing out from other forms of movement remain limited, despite productive theories of expression, imitation, and form.[8] More recently, infused by the protocols of performance studies, scholars have tended to focus on dance as a series of actions and effects; for example, dance scholar Gabriele Klein understands dance as a "specific physical-sensual way of accessing worlds."[9] Noting the slippage between dancing and choreography, she writes,

> the once close link between dance and choreography gradually loosened. Choreography as an arrangement of movement, as work and as notation was in itself challenged and the previous dualisms of composition and improvisation, work and process were called into question.[10]

---

[7] Helen Thomas, *The Body, Dance and Cultural Theory* (New York: Palgrave Macmillan, 2003), 10–11; and Lynn Matluck-Brooks, *Women's Work: Making Dance in Europe Before 1800* (Madison, WI: University of Wisconsin Press, 2007).

[8] Roger Copeland, "What Is Dance?" In *What Is Dance?* ed. Roger Copeland and Marshall Cohen (Oxford, New York: Oxford University Press, 1983), 1–9; 2.

[9] Gabriele Klein, "Dancing Politics: Worldmaking in Dance and Choreography." In *Emerging Bodies: The Performance of Worldmaking in Dance and Choreography*, ed. Gabriele Klein and Sandra Noeth (Bielefeld: Transcript Verlag, 2011), 23.

[10] Ibid., 21.

Klein affirms the slippage between the roles of dancer/choreographer, interpreter/author that have come into play since the 1980s, a slippage that sits at the heart of Lecavalier's career. More, she situates this shift within a landscape of economic precarity, wherein dance's political potential resides in its ability to "grate against the reigning order."[11]

Building on that understanding of politics, and taking dance as a way of living, working, producing, and resisting enforcements of sociocultural habit, this study asks, What can be learned in close dialogue with the dancer and through careful thinking with the dancing? What can consideration of an exemplary performer over many years offer in terms of understanding the role of the dancer in making and circulating new ways of being for possible worlds? Popular accounts in the media and biographies have tended to focus on the individual and/or personal lives of the dancers, risking mythology and canonization.[12] Feminist performance critics of the period, however, looked to material and political aspects of content and form, emphasizing radical forms that stood outside the mainstream practices of the performing arts—at least initially—and diving deeply into feminist and post-structural theory.[13]

My approach began first with listening. In interviews and conversations since 1998, Lecavalier offered accounts of her work that were serious, funny, and rigorously focused on dancemaking. Her voiced recollections, told to me in English, as an oral tradition seemed an excellent mirror to dance, circulated via body-to-body knowledge and rendered in time, with all the pauses, shapes, timbre, and sound that shade live performance generally. More, and following queer and performance studies scholars Ann Cvetkovich and José Esteban Muñoz, it tipped the terms of historiography towards the body and to story, rooted in "an evidence that has been queered in relation to

---

[11] Ibid., 25.
[12] A point well made, for example, in Hanna Järvinen's *Dancing Genius: the Stardom of Vaslav Nijinsky* (London, New York: Palgrave Macmillan, 2014).
[13] Jill Dolan, "Feminist Performance Criticism and the Popular: Reviewing Wendy Wasserstein." *Theatre Journal* 60, no. 3 (2008): 433–57. http://feministspectator. princeton.edu/articles/feminist-performance-criticism/

the laws of what counts as proof."[14] This book builds from Lecavalier's oral histories, understood not as "truth," last word, or the really real but instead as partial, incomplete reflections. Memories on their way to becoming something else: fragments, stories, discourse, performance.

Lecavalier's role as interlocutor over many years form the spine of these essays, offering what I hope is a critical assessment of the work of the dancer. Alongside the extraordinary dancing and critical eye, she offers an important vantage point for study because of her longevity and fame; as an internationally recognized figure, generating a kind of mania of attention and fandom on par with historical figures like Isadora Duncan, Loïe Fuller, and Anna Pavlova, her performances offer an important relay between dance specialists and everyday fans, and a useful shorthand for readers who are likely to have seen her perform, whether live or on TV. As I wrote this work, people often described the first time they saw Louise ("It was all her, and she was burning, burning hot …!"[15]) or else told me about encounters they had had with her in and around the Plateau, Montréal. In these essays, the singularity of Lecavalier may help us to see how all dancers shape the ricochet between art and discourse; and how they labor to re/produce the form, though under different conditions and towards distinctive ends.

Focusing primarily on the 1980s and early 1990s, I argue that this decade constituted a radically formative period of production for Lecavalier, within the context of La La La Human Steps under the choreographic leadership of Édouard Lock. Scrappy and still in formation, the company pulled together disparate forms and materials in order to find their repertoire: elements of dance, theater, athletics, performance art, film and video, and popular music, cobbled together along the Main and the former manufacturing neighborhood of Montréal's Plateau. This amid intense socio-economic shifts at local

---

[14] Ann Cvetkovich, "Introduction." In *An Archive of Feelings: Trauma, Sexuality and Lesbian Public Cultures* (Durham, NC: Duke University Press, 2003), 1–14; and José Esteban Muñoz, *Cruising Utopia: The Then and There of Queer Futurity* (New York: New York University Press, 2019/2009), 65.

[15] Benoît Chaput (2010).

and global scale. For art historian Maurice Berger, the 1980s was a time of "reactionary self-enrichment ... driven by the politics of greed, fear and self-interest." Yet that claim is balanced by a progressive drive in the era, towards shared authority, revised canons, and "the need to transcend the mythical objectivity of official history in order to achieve a broader, inclusive and more accurate view of the past."[16]

Across culture writ large and material culture specifically—from the ground-breaking arrival of hip hop to the image and sound overlay of music television—new forms of movement and motion were being imagined. New York-based curator Dan Cameron remembered the time as a unique period when the "artworld" and the "club scene" came together, each one shaping the sensibilities of the other and ultimately pulling apart hierarchies; he found that culture became in the 1980s a "refuge for the disenfranchised," necessitated by an increasingly indifferent society.[17] From the deregulation of broadcasting under American president Ronald Reagan to the devastating appearance of a new illness, AIDS, in 1981, new forms of politicized discourse and injustice came into view. Internationally, Glasnost (1986–91) and the fall of the Berlin Wall (1989) appeared to mark the end of communism and oppressive dictatorships. Poland's trade union Solidarity and global movements to end apartheid in South Africa and nuclear armament in the United States and Russia suggested powerful new forms of solidarity. By the end of that decade, the culture wars had begun, starting with the conservative outcry against Nan Goldin's 1989 exhibition *Witnesses: Against our Vanishing* at Artists Space in New York.

In Québec, the 1980s began and ended with activism and apocalypse, grounded in feminist innovations and the fear thereof. Whereas as Québec feminism of the 1960s and 1970s was strongly aligned with nationalist goals, organized by radical, generative groups like the *Front de libération des femmes du Québec* (1969–71) and its successor le *Centre*

---

[16] Maurice Berger, *The 1980s: A Virtual Discussion. Issues in Cultural Theory, 10*. Georgia O'Keefe Research Centre/Santa Fe and Centre for Art, Design and Visual Culture/University of Baltimore Maryland (New York: Distributed Art Publishers, 2007), 15.
[17] Ibid., 72.

des femmes, that alliance had all but faded by the late 1970s.[18] After the so-called "Yvette incident," in which Lise Payette, the first Québec Minister on the Status of Woman, pointed the finger at conservative women as a bar to winning independence, the Parti Québecois shifted its stance on feminism to support the nuclear family as key to Québec strength. Some scholars attribute this shift as a starting point to an antifeminist movement that scapegoated women rather than economic policy.[19] The decade began and ended with ambivalence. On the one hand, there were real achievements including affirmation of abortion rights; on the other, the decision was left open to lawmakers to review and re-litigate. On the one hand, there was a loosening of a focus on national oppression and a turn towards the intersectional, perhaps best evidenced in AIDS activism. On the other hand, far more dire, there was École Polytechnique, where a male shooter targeted women, murdering fourteen as the province and nation debated whether the incident could be read as a political assault rather than that of a single bad actor.[20]

In Québec and internationally, the 1980s were extreme, marked by radical transformations in our understanding of bodies, labor, politics, and economies. Fredric Jameson, discussing poles of nostalgia or recrimination when describing the past, points out the illusory sense of unity often assigned to a decade. In his classic essay on periodization, he writes:

> the 80s will be characterized by an effort, on a world scale, to proletarianize all those unbound social forces which gave the 60s

---

[18] Sean Mills, "*Québécoises deboutte!* Nationalism and Feminism in Quebec, 1969–1975." In *Contemporary Quebec: Selected Readings and Commentaries*, ed. Michael D. Behiels and Matthew Hayday (Montréal: McGill-Queens University Press, 2011), 319–37.

[19] See Melissa Blais and Francis Dupuis-Déri, "Masculinism and the Anti-Feminist Countermovement." *Social Movement Studies: Journal of Social, Cultural and Political Protest* 11, no. 1 (2011): 21–9; and Jeffery Vacante, "Liberal Nationalism and the Challenge of Masculinity Studies in Quebec." *Left* 11, no. 2 (2006): 96–117.

[20] Denyse Baillargeon, *A Brief History of Women in Québec* (Waterloo, ON: Wilfred Laurier Press, 2014); Chantal Maillé, "Intersectionalizing Gender Policies: Experiences in Quebec and Canada." *French Politics* 16, no. 3 (2018): 312–27; and Chantal Maillé, "Transnational Feminisms in Francophonie Space." *Women: A Cultural Review* 23, no. 1 (2012): 62–78.

their energy, by an extension of class struggle, in other words, into the farthest reaches of the globe as well as the most minute configurations of local institutions (such as the university system). The unifying force here is the new vocation of a henceforth global capitalism, which may also be expected to unify the unequal, fragmented, or local resistances to the process.[21]

Global capitalism did indeed come to pass, bringing the turn to financialization and shifts in the nature of work; transforming time and space through new technologies; and generating careening mobilities that open for some and shut down for others. Under Thatcher (1979), Reagan (1980), and, in Canada, Brian Mulroney (1981) and, in Québec, Bourassa (1985), economic downturns bookended the decade: the Volcker shock in 1980 and the Savings and Loans crisis and junk bonds crash in 1990. By the early 1990s, in Montréal, the collapse of its industrial past was complete, and the turn toward neoliberal policy was well on its way. More broadly, the mood of the time was suggestive of what Italian Marxist Franco Berardi, referring specifically to economic policy, has described as "the law of the strongest."[22]

Berardi's diagnostic offers an important backdrop for the reception of Lecavalier's dancing, which toured internationally at the time and continues to circulate widely. As a signature performer, with La La La and independently since the early 2000s, public fascination with her strong body and athletic, high-speed dancing has been deemed at once defining of the zeitgeist and often through the lens of strength. In 1985, *New York Times* critic Anna Kisselgoff noted that Lecavalier's "difference in attitude defines our times."[23] Deborah Jowitt, writing in the *Village Voice* about *Businessman in the Process of Becoming an Angel* (1983)—the title registering Lock's sardonic take on the idea that business will save us—describes the dancing as an "all-out storm":

---

[21] Fredric Jameson, "Periodizing the 60s." *Social Text* (Spring/Summer), no. 9/10 (1984): 178–209; 209.

[22] Franco Berardi, "Communism Is Back but We Should Call It the Therapy of Singularization" (Generation online, 2009). https://www.generation-online.org/p/fp_bifo6.htm

[23] Anna Kisselgoff, "Dance: Edouard Lock's Punk Style." *The New York Times*. October 6, 1985, Section 1, 73.

Despite the intimacy and daring handling of one another's bodies, the performer's encounters carry little charge of eroticism, aggression, or affection. They're like business transactions in which power and manipulativeness have become so ritualized that they come into play even when there is no need for them.[24]

More recently, writing about Lecavalier's independent choreography *So Blue* (2012), Jowitt finds her dancing to have "remorseless intensity … we should be so strong."[25] Yet all dancers are strong, building material

Figure I.4 Portrait of the artists (1985). Photo: Édouard Lock.

---

[24] Deborah Jowitt, "Honk if You Love Dogs." In *The Village Voice*, October 9, 1984.
[25] Deborah Jowitt, "Step Quickly, Don't Fall Off the World." *Arts Journal: Arts, Culture, Ideas.* September 15, 2015: https://www.artsjournal.com/dancebeat/2015/09/step-quickly-dont-fall-off-the-world/

strength in contrast to pressures, judgments, precarities, and injuries. Lecavalier fearlessly showed that strength, deemed unimaginable for women and within concert dance, but to see only the strong in the work is to mirror the anxieties of the socio-cultural moment (Figure I.4).

Is this a dance? Performance/Labor

Writing in the wake of the 1980s, feminist scholar Peggy Phelan wrote persuasively about the potential of live performance to generate difference. In 1993, writing amid the enormous cultural loss associated with the AIDS crisis and in the aftermath of the American Right's (ongoing) attacks on the arts and arts funding,[26] she notes,

> Performance, insofar as it can be defined as representation with reproduction, can be seen as a model for another representational economy, one in which the reproduction of the Other *as* the Same is not assured.[27]

Paying close attention to the relationship of performer to viewer, between the "looker and the image of the other," Phelan points to how representation always shows more (and less) than it intends, while performance hovers in a present that though bound to forms of repetition—from training to rehearsal to the archive—resists exact repeatability. Since then, many authors have instead sought to emphasize the durability of performance, particularly through embodied forms of knowledge passed along through oral traditions and ephemera.[28] My own study of Lecavalier develops from oral histories, narrative accounts, video documentation, live performance, photography, and

---

[26] Peggy Phelan, *Unmarked: The Politics of Performance* (New York, London: Routledge, 1993), 135.
[27] Ibid., 146.
[28] See especially José Esteban Muñoz, "Gesture, Ephemera and Queer Feeling: Approaching Kevin Aviance." In *Cruising Utopia: The Then and There of Queer Futurity* (New York: New York University Press, 2019/2009); and Rebecca Schneider, *Performance Remains: Art and War in Times of Theatrical Reenactment* (New York, London: Routledge, 2011).

various kinds of ephemera that function not as decisive accounts of a stable original or past but as authentic remnants that offer speculative access to the "what" (when, how, and why) of what happened.

Phelan's thinking guides the essays that follow in two key ways; the first challenges the "truth effect" of vision—that is, the sense that sight makes fully available the contours of reality and thus makes real—which feels especially significant given Lecavalier's own ability to generate questions about the status, contour, and identity of the moving body. The second emphasizes covert powers—that is, the value of the unmarked, of receding from view, of the ephemeral—which feels once again important in light of the contemporary rise of the Right, across multiple nation states, with ongoing attacks on education, equity, and reproductive rights. Here, I return to the potential of Phelan's work and, indeed, the meaning of the term performativity circa 1980, understood not as a pejorative, suggesting the inauthentic as it is often used today, but rather as an invitation to work the gaps between performance and image, sign and act, within specific socio-political contexts.

Performance studies, and its neighbor phenomenology, shape my approach, aiming for material accounts of what dance *does*, and what dancers *do*. How is it that the presence of the dancer comes to be seen? And what are we to make of material contributions that are unseen, masked by roles such as "muse" or "principal," rather than as author or agent? Lecavalier might respond by saying simply, "work"—that is, her experience in dance has meant returning, again and again, to the studio, to the gym, to the theater, and to life in order to stay with and in the dance. That is, training, rehearsing, researching, and landing— however briefly—the elusive shapes, rhythms, kinesthetics, and imagery that appear as dance. Lecavalier, in interviews with media and myself, over many years has stayed uniquely focused on the work of dance as a practice of inquiry: "I'm always trying to find something: searching, searching to see what is in the move, to find the small things."[29]

---

[29] Louise Lecavalier (2011).

The status of work, broadly conceived, remains contested in 2024, as state support recedes; deregulation and privatization remain the norm; the gap between pay and cost of living widens; and the digitized forms and spaces of bureaucracy and the workplace extend the limits of the workday. New categories appear, among them the knowledge and gig economies, material and immaterial forms of labor, "meaningful" work and "decent" work, to name just a few. David Graeber's bracing indictment of "bullshit jobs" focuses on meaningless forms of employment that "force you to keep busy even though there is nothing to do."[30] In contrast to precarious work, such jobs are well paid but soul-destroying to the extent that they are known by those who do them to be useless. A proliferation of recent studies on the nature of work circa 2024 include Daniel Susskind's *World Without Work* (2020), wherein the robots replace us; and Matthew Crawford's *Shop Class as Soul Craft* (2009), wherein manual know-how saves by building self-worth through valued acts of doing. My focus on the work of the dancer builds on this renewed attention to labor and stems from the potential of work as a fusion of the manual and intellectual, while emphasizing creative acts of doing.

Dance Studies, of course, has long understood this, with scholars like Mark Franko, André Lepecki, and Ellen Graff grappling with dance as work through philosophical, critical, and social history analyses. More recently, Bojana Kunst has argued that the qualities of artistic labor have come to define precarious labor; she writes, "the essential qualities of life after work (imagination, autonomy, sociality, communication) have actually turned out to be at the core of contemporary labour."[31] Elsewhere, Gabriele Klein in a search for what might constitute political resistance at this point in time links the figure of the dancer to notions of liquidity in the neoliberal economy; she writes, "the new societal

---

[30] David Graeber and Loretta Leng Tak, "Bullshit Jobs: A Conversation with David Graeber." *Built in China Journal*, no. 2 (Acton: ANU Press, 2019).

[31] Bojana Kunst, "Dance and Work: The Aesthetics and Political Potential of Dance." In *Emerging Bodies: The Performance of Worldmaking in Dance and Choreography*, ed. Gabriele Klein and Sandra Noeth (Bielefeld: Transcript Verlag, 2011), 48.

model of the flexible, geographically unattached and vagabond kinetic self-recursive subject has found its prototype in the freelance dancer."[32] Work of this order offers insight into the labor of dance as exemplary of widespread problematics circa 2024.

My argument regarding the work of the dancer, as evidenced in the career of Lecavalier, moves in another direction, aiming to show how embodied forms of labor endure across time, with profound effect and, what's more, how they bring together and breach the manual/intellectual divide and resist other kinds of categorization. Aiming to avoid romantic, glamorized, and universalizing idealizations of physical work, I argue that Lecavalier revealed the muscle that scaffolds all dance and indeed so many of our performative categories. Working within the La La La family and continuing on today with longtime collaborators, she keeps raising hard questions about making dance, embodiment, and agency, against the safety of readymade categories. Returning to Graeber, he notes that, "artists and those drawn to them have created enclaves where it has been possible to experiment with forms of work, exchange, and production radically different from those promoted by capital."[33]

1980s/2020s: women as unruly category

I start from the position that "women" as a category is highly problematic: old-fashioned within the intersectional, hybrid world of today, wherein new identities proliferate working gaps between nature/culture, body/mind, being/doing: and certainly old-fashioned alongside the volatile understandings of the body as danced by Lecavalier. Conceptions of gender have been radically rethought, and the category of "women" has expanded. Yet the term is still necessary within a

---

[32] Klein, "Dancing Politics," 20.
[33] David Graeber (2008), "The Sadness of Post-workerism, or Art and Immaterial Labour Conference—A Sort of Review." https://theanarchistlibrary.org/library/david-graeber-the-sadness-of-post-workerism

global economy that inscribes and divides bodies according to gender and access to reproductive rights, healthcare, labor, and labor equity, as well as protection from gender-based violence. It's still necessary amid the rise (again) of the Conservative Right, with their attacks on reproductive rights, voter rights, affirmative action, and more. And it remains helpful for understanding Lecavalier's impact circa the 1980s within the performing arts in Québec and internationally—her radical presentation of the body on stage shifted understandings of what a body might be. And that shift was all the more dramatic, given received ideas of gender and the feminine that circulated at the time.

In the 1980s and 1990s, the term "women" remained a focusing site for feminist thinking and activism, as did the [feminized] body as the matrix of lived experience and a repository of surface imagery. Feminist theory generated robust critical approaches, critiquing difference and universality; representation and the visual field. Theories of feminine subjectivity, anchored in the disciplines of phenomenology and psychoanalysis, were newly established; and the feminist project was actively engaged in the dismantling of identity taken as biological or visual fact, excepting where strategies of strategic essentialism could afford political impact.[34] The debates of the time focused on the social construction of the category and the limits of pornography, censorship, and white feminism—and the increased visibility of queer, trans, and post-human scholarship were yet to come. The radical solidarity proposed by the coalition activist group ACT-UP in response to the AIDS crisis was emergent, and much was about to change.

As accounts of Lecavalier were beginning to circulate in the popular press—often emphasizing her androgyny or else assigning her dancing machine-like qualities—Donna J. Haraway produced her decisive call for a cyborg feminism that understood "women" as profoundly interwoven with the material, technological, and socio-political fields that surround and constitute them. She noted:

---

[34] Shatema Threadcraft, "Embodiment." In *The Oxford Handbook of Feminist Theory*, ed. Lisa Jane Disch and M. E. Hawkesworth (Oxford, UK: Oxford University Press, 2018), 207–26.

A cyborg is a cybernetic organism, a hybrid of machine and organism, a creature of social reality as well as a creature of fiction. Social reality is lived social relations, our most important political construction, a world-changing fiction. The international women's movements have constructed "women's experience", as well as uncovered or discovered this crucial collective object. This experience is a fiction and fact of the most crucial, political kind. Liberation rests on the construction of the consciousness, the imaginative apprehension, of oppression, and so of possibility. The cyborg is a matter of fiction and lived experience that changes what counts as women's experience in the late twentieth century.[35]

Haraway called for a revised sense of responsibility, critiquing white feminism for its universalizing "fiction" and reflecting on the need for a feminist solidarity to counter massive problems of racism, inequity, violence, and poverty. More, she offered an account of the subject as hybrid, multiple, and embedded; and suggested the strategic model of affinity as a mechanism towards solidarity.

Yet, before the writing and circulation of the theories, people working in the terrain of everyday life had given material form to such understandings. On stages in North America, the UK and Europe, situated squarely within Western concert dance and performance, clear challenges to naturalized accounts of the sexed/gendered body were riveting audiences. Australian performance artist Leigh Bowery (1961–94), for instance, performed an extravagant model of queer theatricality that would be taken up by the Scottish dancer/choreographer Michael Clark, known for his punk style, arch play with gender and sexuality, and always exhilarating dancing. By 1984, Clark had made over a dozen dances and was touring internationally with work such as *New Puritans* (1984) that blended ballet's formalism with camp sensibilities, theatrical costuming, and a profound musicality. American Karole Armitage, with whom Clark danced, also figured at this moment, generating

---

[35] Donna J. Haraway, *Simians, Cyborgs and Women: The Reinvention of Nature* (New York, London: Routledge, 1991), 149.

attention as the "punk ballerina" with *Drastic Classicism* (1981), which integrated live rock music and high-speed movement. Simon Leung, for example, saw in Armitage's dancers "the loss of faith in a discourse of the authentic ..., their gaze fracturing into an endless series of quotational looks of women—not unlike a television ... screen."[36]

Armitage and Clark were extraordinary dancers who exemplified the radical critique of the 1980s, yet they stay firmly within the ballet lexicon, avoiding the scrappy athleticism and DIY sensibility of early La La La vocabulary. On stage, Armitage remained a prima ballerina, a virtuosic, feminized *etoile*; and Clark—who imagined a wildly multidisciplinary dance, steeped in fashion, art, and music alongside a host of friends and collaborators—largely stayed within the technical clarity of ballet. Within modern and so-called contemporary forms, American choreographers Mark Morris (see *Championship Wrestling After Roland Barthes* 1984) and Ishmael Houston-Jones (see *Them* 1985) offered important contemporaneous critiques of the nature of concert dancing and gender in everyday life. Taken together, these evidence a generational shift, wherein new and revised subjectivities sought to counter on stage the patterns and enforcements of social history. Yet all held the title of choreographer and were thus more legible for first-draft histories as figures of authority, agency, and authorship.

Lecavalier's performances endure, in my mind, as a kind of proto-abundance, a material opening up of the post-structural, postmodern intersticiary. As a heterosexual, white French-Canadian woman from a working-class background, she nonetheless presented ambiguously, aspiring to more than the social categories could contain. As a dancer, her performances of intensity and speed, and her ability to create illusions of weightlessness, horizontality, and inversions dovetailed with Lock's aim to create doubt about the contours of the body and what indeed a body was. In the early years, her labor stood outside the more fully reasoned category of the choreographer, with its claims to authorship and authority. Instead, her dancing functioned to generate

---

[36] Leung in Berger, *The 1980s*, 111.

inquiry regarding aesthetics and identities in multiple. Amid brutish discourse and square categories, Lecavalier's dancing gave room to breathe.

In what follows, I focus on the material specificity of Lecavalier's dancemaking, prioritizing her movement and recollections while gesturing to the entwined and enabling contexts in which she worked to extrapolate a claim for the recognition of danced labor. Following materialist approaches that perhaps anticipate feminist scholar Sara Ahmed's "sweaty concepts"[37]—that is, the understanding that conceptual work is practical work and vice versa, my own material description affords, I hope, a glimpse of the bodily effort that anticipated shifting discourse through language, image, and movement. As Ahmed reminds us, "concepts are at work in how we work, whatever it is we do."[38] Taking seriously the contributions of the dancer as artist/worker, without universalizing mythologies or reinforcing notions of the singular sovereign subject, is the line I attempt to walk in the writings that follow (Figure 1.4).

The essays that follow trace her work with and alongside La La La Human Steps, primarily through the 1980s and into the 1990s, when the company was to my mind at its most intimate and innovative: small-scale, interdisciplinary, relatively uncodified. More, they trace the production of critical subjectivities and distinctive kinds of dancerly labor: discursive, cultural, material. Briefly, the book unfolds as follows: Chapter 1 stages an encounter between image and text to consider the discursive exchange generated by Lecavalier's dancing; Chapter 2 describes Lecavalier's 1981 choreography *Non Non Non je ne suis pas Mary Poppins* (1981) and discusses how that work theorized labor and anticipated her contributions to La La La; Chapter 3 discusses the punk aesthetic of the early repertoire and links it to the circulation of expressionist traditions in Montréal; and Chapter 4 considers the power of Lecavalier's performance as/of hybridity, in relation to Black

---

[37] Sara Ahmed, *Living a Feminist Life* (Durham, NC and London: Duke University Press, 2017), 13.
[38] Ibid., 13.

and Jewish aesthetics in the repertoire. Finally, I end with a short reflection on throughlines of critique, virtuosity, and labor in her career, discussing recent work since the forming of her production house, *Fou glorieux*.

Today, Lecavalier is, at 65, still performing and making new work, most recently dancing the avatar in Shanghai artist Lu Yang's live anime techno-nightmare, *Delusional World* (2023). And me and my friends, we are mostly scattered: in different cities, with different jobs, and time moving fast in the spaces between work, relationships, life, bureaucracy. Dancing may come less frequently now, attending a dance concert at the theater; or else dropping in to one of our kids' multi-band, all-ages gigs, out by the tracks in the Mile End. There, the punk youth are still doing it for themselves, still going all out, still kicking against the pricks. At a recent show, the band screamed, "Fuck, yeah!" as the crowd jumped onstage to share the mic and sing along, risking crushing the platform of the makeshift stage. All the while, a mass of undifferentiated bodies dove and swam across the mosh pit. Amid the sea of green hair, dark fashion, goth make-up, and freaky message buttons, a tall figure glided through, blowing bubbles over the surrounding crowd.

If today we understand the self as unbounded and plural, and agency as shaped by the collective, to return to Lecavalier's dancing circa the 1980s is to witness emergent ways of being and culture on the move. *What do dancers do, finally?* They move. Through air and ground, leap and fall, in thrill and injury, effort and sweat, they keep moving and, as they go, they move us, too; moving towards the phenomenal comings and goings, never arriving, that make up culture. Lecavalier recalls, "dancing rooted me to the ground, it put my feet on this earth."

> I think doubting is important ... Back then, I was full of contradiction, full of doubts. A weird balance between insecurity and this strongness ... Still, I was undaunted .... I had lots to learn and lots to observe. I still do. And when it's time to work, I work .... Dance gave me the body. And more. It gives me all my thoughts, everything.[39]

---

[39] Lecavalier (2020).

1

Dancer as Relay

Fragments for a Phenomenology of the Dancer

The world enters language as a dialectical relation between activities, between human actions; it comes out of myth as a harmonious display of essences. A conjuring trick has taken place; it has turned reality inside out, it has emptied it of history and has filled it with nature.

—Roland Barthes

No power without an image.

—Marie-José Mondzain

We were sitting on the back patio on a late May afternoon, talking about the possibility of writing a history about her dance. I was saying something about the deadness of language for me once it's left my body and landed on the page. Lecavalier speculated, "Maybe reading the words is a bit like watching dance in the mirror":

> I don't like to rehearse in front of the mirror. When I do, I see someone who's not really me, and this person annoys me. It seems like it's definitive. Which is bizarre, since supposedly it's just showing me something I'm doing. But every time I look in the mirror, I see the end …. For me, everything is porous. The world doesn't start at my skin, and at the same time I'm exploding out of my skin into the world—the dividing line isn't clear …. A mirror can't show that, and the eyes see better.[1]

---

[1] Louise Lecavalier (2012); Lecavalier notes, however, that today she works with both film and mirrors to create and track movement during periods of creative research. The change came with the turn to choreography and with her arrival at the White Wall studio space in the Plateau in 2014, where a partial mirror (from ceiling to mid-wall) afforded a different kind of depth of field and drew the attention away from the floor and background.

Figure 1.1 Louise Lecavalier, photo shoot for *Businessman in the Process of Becoming an Angel* (1983). Photo: Jack Udashkin.

It was an everyday beckoning of the power of process over form, the phenomenology of experience and post-structuralist discoveries of word as performance and trace. More, it was an instantiation of the peril in any relay between movement and representation, idea and word. Thomas DeFrantz and Philipa Rothfield, in their reading of Foucault and Deleuze, usefully bring the term relay to dance studies in the following way:

> The relay does not follow a predetermined pathway. It moves between theory and practice, without privileging either term. The relay is not a structural concept. It is, rather, a form of movement, a manner of thought which enters into and engages a dynamic terrain.[2]

Whereas Lecavalier prioritized movement and practice throughout her career, representation through word and image and equally as material knowledge also figure in the story of her dance; and the relay

---

[2] Thomas F. DeFrantz and Philipa Rothfield, *Choreography and Corporeality: Relay in Motion* (London: Palgrave Macmillan, 2016), 1–2.

between the two, I argue, generated considerable cultural impact. Highly celebrated and frequently written about, Lecavalier didn't read criticism or reviews; and avoided the hype wherever possible. In the 1980s, showing up for press interviews was not a priority, a fact she shudders to think of in recollection:

> I don't want to waste anyone's time, or say things that were irrelevant or idiotic and I didn't want to kill the work ... It was a huge effort back then to do interviews ... the words didn't come easily.[3]

But that changed as the repertoire developed; and, over many years, working with longtime publicist Annie Viau, she has been steadfast in responding to media queries and representing her work in French and English; and she has met with me repeatedly, with great generosity, over twenty years to discuss her work. Yet representation remains "Other" for her.

Performance Studies scholar Peggy Phelan has described representation as that which is "given to be seen,"[4] an evocative wording that underscores the generosity of artists as makers of images— understood here as a relay between action and representation—as well as their intentionality and agency in the production thereof. Lecavalier is profoundly uncomfortable with the image of herself, a phenomenon I've noticed in interactions across multiple contexts. She would rather not talk about herself; nor does she want attention, even after a stellar performance, when crowds await. Always polite, and quite shy, she nonetheless gives us through dance an abundance of imagery and remains committed to doing so, living in the Plateau quartier in Montréal, despite brief sojourns in bigger centers like New York and Paris where anonymity is more readily sought and where she lived briefly after retiring from La La La in 1999. For Phelan, following Lacan, the magic of that relay may reside in the "reciprocal gaze" that, within psychoanalysis, at once defines the production of subjectivity

---

[3] Louise Lecavalier (2012).
[4] Peggy Phelan, *Unmarked: The Politics of Performance* (New York, London: Routledge, 1993), 3.

and readily elides felt divides between live performance and the performance of art objects and images, since they too activate in viewers a desire to be seen.[5] Phelan observes, "The potential for a responding eye, like the hunger for a responding voice, informs the desire to see the self *through* the image of the other."[6] But whereas Phelan will study the psychic trajectory of the exchange as it relates to subjectivity, I linger here over the relay itself: between artist and view, movement and image, as a sign of the cultural work of Lecavalier, who channels an emergent hybridity during the heady transformations of Montréal and the larger cultural shifts of the 1980s.

Whereas the popular press has tended to lionize her physicality and question her gender, dance historians have tended to focus on choreographic meaning, typically situated in the hands of others or, alternately, kinesthetic meaning drawn in musculature and put to work in theorizing dance and gender. If the history of dance representation is full of false starts and red herrings, screen dreams and misfires, consider especially early European and twentieth-century concert dance history, wherein brutal accountings of the feminized dancing body and its ongoing instrumentalization repeat in the journalism and biographic literature associated with the dancer. I'm thinking here, for example, of American dancer Loïe Fuller, whose ambitious theatrical projects and stellar dancing generated fandom, copycats and commentary on, among other things, the gap between her evocative stage appearance—a flower, a flame!—and her everyday body—a middle-aged woman.[7] The significance of the dancer's work has typically lain elsewhere, in the choreography as meaning, produced via the creative intellect of others, often men. Historically, the choreographer is cited, the dancer remains mute.[8]

---

[5] Ibid., 4.
[6] Ibid., 16.
[7] Loïe Fuller, *Fifteen Years of a Dancer's Life, with Some Account of Her Distinguished Friends* (Boston, MA: Small, Maynard and Co., 1913).
[8] Susan Leigh Foster, *Choreography and Narrative: The Staging of Story and Desire* (Bloomington, IN: Indiana University Press, 1988).

Writing the cultural work of the dancer remains difficult, troubled as much by the phenomenon of gender as performative and the body as floating signifier,[9] as by the ephemeral qualities of theatrical performance and the strong character of Lecavalier's work particularly. Many historians have noted the pattern whereby gender conflates with sexuality in the repertoire in ways that diminish understanding.[10] In her book on Isadora Duncan, with whose iconic stature Lecavalier is often compared, Ann Daly writes,

> By the turn of the century, the dancer (implicitly female but with little distinction between the trained ballerina, the entertaining skirt dancer and the dancer-cum chorus girl) was constructed as a highly paid, empty-headed, blond soubrette of ill repute.[11]

Tracy C. Davis, meanwhile, in her study of working actresses, writes that

> Women performers defied ideas of passive middle-class femininity and personified active self-sufficiency. Their visibility and notoriety in the public realm led to persistent and empirically unfounded prejudices and very real sexual dangers in their work places.[12]

But these scholars are writing about women artists from the Victorian period, you might well argue. The world has changed, and the term "woman" is no longer relevant. But by the early the 1980s, as Lecavalier's dance emerged, the discourse had not shifted far enough; Judith Butler's formative work on gender as a sedimentation of behavior had yet to be

---

[9] See José Gil, *Metamorphoses of the Body* (Minneapolis, London: University of Minnesota Press, 1998).

[10] See Tracy C. Davis, *Actresses as Working Women: Their Social Identity in Victorian Culture* (New York, London: Routledge, 1991); Ann Daly, "Theorizing Gender." In *Critical Gestures: Writings on Dance and Culture* (Middletown, CT: Wesleyan University Press, 2002), 277–339; and Susan Leigh Foster, *Reading Dancing: Bodies and Subjects in Contemporary American Dance* (Berkeley, Los Angeles, London: University of California Press, 1986).

[11] Ann Daly, *Done into Dance: Isadora Duncan in America* (Middletown, CT: Wesleyan University Press, 2002), 157.

[12] Davis, *Working Women*, xiv.

published, and the revelations of the trans body were yet to come.[13] The early writing about Lecavalier simultaneously fetishized her, speculated openly about her identity, and devalued her work. Less innovator, more muse,[14] the work of the dancer remained a surface vision, mired by assumptions around the limits of gender and divisions of labour in dance.

In pivotal works from the early 1980s through the La La La Human Steps canon and continuing today with her independent work with her company *Fou glorieux*, Lecavalier invites seeing and yet remains hard to see. Countering such histories, I argue for the significance of the dancer as cultural interlocutor and shaper of discourse; in the writing and zine-like insert that follow, I aim to stage relays between movement and image towards a performative history or phenomenology of the dancer—incomplete, fragmentary yet invoking perhaps the time, feeling, and effects of Lecavalier's performance. In the zine section to follow, images of the dancer, related representations, and the city of Montréal as a productive scene are set against oral history accounts from colleagues and fans, shifting the gaze off the surfaces of the performing body to focus on the discourse generated by the dancer. Taken together, this chapter testifies to the cultural work of dancer—as told through Lecavalier's early work—whose centrality to a shifting narrative of nation was vividly illustrated in the abundance of discourse generated.

"Everyday discursive practices"[15]

When Lecavalier burst into national and international consciousness in the early 1980s, she did so alongside a contemporary world still very

---

[13] I am indebted to scholarship from the following collections: Susan Stryker and Stephen Whittle, Eds., *The Transgender Studies Reader* (New York, London: Routledge, 2006); and Susan Stryker, Ed., *The Transgender Studies Reader 2* (New York, London: Routledge, 2013).

[14] Lecavalier noted that she actively fought the use of the term "muse"; she rejected its passivity, yet, if taken in the best sense of the word, Édouard's choreography could be seen as muse and inspiration for her dancing.

[15] Leonard C. Hawes, "Becoming-Other-Wise: Conversational Performance and the Politics of Experience." In *Text and Performance Quarterly* 18, no. 4 (1998): 273–99; 293.

much enthralled by category as closure and binary as divide: men, women; white, black; straight, gay; avant-garde and popular. Whereas the status of nation was shifting amid the promise of post-colonial societies, following the election of the Parti Québecois in Québec on a platform of independence, the idea of nation remained dominant, still understood as a kind of bounded singularity, rather than as a set of representations aiming to construct a collective imaginary as per Stuart Hall's account.[16]

As a dancer with La La La Human Steps from 1981 to 1999, Lecavalier circulated indelible imagery at the local, national, and global levels via her stage performances and media representation. With its astonishing physicality, compelling presence and androgynous presentation, her dance challenged gendered expectations of what a body could do and what a dancing body could do. Highly muscled, and lifting up her male partners, Lecavalier offered a powerful revision of gender and the body on stage. Whereas the classical ballet structured the *pas de deux* as a male dancer lifting a ballerina *en pointe*, Lecavalier offered a counter-view—and it was a counter-view that sat largely on her alone within the company. And though contact improv and an emergent breakdancing had, as social forms, zeroed in on imaginative floorwork, the dynamics of exchange and the potential of weight sharing, Lecavalier's dance situated itself within the spectacular frames of 1980s concert dance and popular music and, in doing so, laid image to an emergent political shift and expansion of identities.

Language proliferated around Lecavalier, in descriptions and conversations that followed her performances and presence around town. It's a phenomenon noted by dance scholar Ann Cooper Albright, who reads it as a sign of "unease" around Lecavalier's corporeality.[17] As my research developed, I saw an abundance of imagery circulating

---

[16] Stuart Hall, *Modernity: An Introduction to Modern Societies* (Malden, MA: Blackwell, 1996).

[17] Ann Cooper Albright, *Choreographing Difference: The Body and Identity in Contemporary Dance* (Middletown, CT: Wesleyan University Press, 1997), 28. See too Nikki Sheppy, "Out of Body Experience." In *FastForward Weekly*. Calgary: March 2, 1996.

in the popular press and elsewhere: sometimes the movement was the focus, as in various descriptive phrases collaged from different sources: "human projectile,"[18] "violent,"[19] "manic,"[20] "frenzied,"[21] "kinetic rage,"[22] "self-abusive athleticism,"[23] "bound up … with no spatial intention."[24] Elsewhere, her artist's identity becomes fused with her stage roles: "athletic and aggressive,"[25] "semi-punk,"[26] "a flame on legs,"[27] "a soiled angel,"[28] "a renegade angel,"[29] "half-fiend, half goddess,"[30] "androgynous yet feminine,"[31] "a mere slip of a woman,"[32] "wild thing,"[33] "a veritable dervish."[34] Much of the imagery was confusing to the extent that it moved seamlessly between body, movement, and performed character; and Lecavalier as an individual and subject. One could dismiss these as the residue of outdated attitudes, evidence of habitualized and gendered thinking. Or else one could argue that many images simply resemble the content of a given choreography, as when she is referred to as a "mean little animal" in a review of *Businessman in the Process of Becoming an Angel* (1983), with its dog cut-outs for props and its invocation of a

---

[18] Anna Kisselgoff, "Mixed Media for Rock Music Lovers." *The New York Times*. October 2, 1991, C21.
[19] Steven Durland, "The Wooster Group/La La La Human Steps." *High Performance* 10, no. 3 (1987): 9.
[20] Cooper-Albright, *Choreographing Difference*, 48.
[21] Kirsten Gunter, "New Demons." *Metropolis*. Toronto, ON: October 26, 1989, cover.
[22] Jenny Gilbert, "How Do They Do That?" *The Independent*. London, UK: November 9, 1994.
[23] Nadine Meisner, "Superwoman." *The Sunday Times*. London, UK: October 20, 1996.
[24] Cooper-Albright, *Choreographing Difference*, 48–9.
[25] Jochen Schmidt, "Thoughts of Old Age and Death." *Ballett International/Tanz Aktuell*. Berlin, 1995, 32–5; 34.
[26] Editorial staff, "Best Stage Performer." *Montréal Mirror*. Montréal, QC: May 14–21, 1987.
[27] Chris Roberts, "Let's Dance! David Bowie with La La La Human Steps." *Melody Maker*. London, UK: July 9, 1988.
[28] Deborah Jowitt, "Honk if You Love Dogs." *The Village Voice*. New York: October 9, 1984.
[29] Author Unknown, "Super Human." *Time Out*. October 26, 1988.
[30] Allison Mayes, "La La La's Louise Gets Emotional." *The Calgary Herald*. Calgary, AB: March 6, 1996.
[31] Alasdair Steven, "Whirlwinds of Dance, Not a Tutu in Sight." *The Sunday Times*. Scotland: October 20, 1996.
[32] *What's On*, "Let's Get Physical," October 1996, 19.
[33] Liz Warwick, "Wild Thing." *The Montreal Gazette*. Montréal, QC: October 2, 1995.
[34] *What's On*, "Let's Get Physical," 19.

dog-eat-dog economy.[35] The descriptors were alternately openly hostile or a measurement of the gap between language and dance.

I noted, too, many comparisons of Lecavalier to Anna Pavlova and Isadora Duncan, often with little explication. Given the difference in style, it was hard to know what writers were seeing: her authoritative stage presence; her international stature; comparable themes of death and transcendence in the content of the dance; or something else? On the one hand, these testify to the ready assimilation of women of excellence into signs of nation—Anna as the great Russian artist, Isadora as uniquely American, Lecavalier a kind of Québécoise Maryanne.[36] On the other, the iconic nature of these three dancers suggests a genealogy for the popular forms of devotion generated by extraordinary performance and presence. Less about "unease," I see this proliferation of tellings and describings as a sign of how Lecavalier's dancing drew viewers in, in ways that elided available language, in ways that rehearsed unfamiliar attitudes for the body.

Something about Lecavalier as a constellation of performer/subject in particular generated a strong urge to describe, to reproduce, to copy, or to borrow cultural anthropologist Michael Taussig's phrasing, "to yield into and become Other."[37] Taussig has written about "mimetic vertigo"; that is, the dizzying reproduction of imagery wherein "the interpreting self is grafted onto the object of study," confounding access to any objective original and affirming the mirror-like nature of seeing and knowing.[38] Taussig's words—nonetheless a caution to writers of history—offers a pathway out of perceiving this excess as "unease" or in otherwise pathological terms.

Part of desire to represent might be rooted in the ancient idea that, through mimesis, and following Tausssig's work and the discourse of

---

[35] Amanda Smith, "Eye on Performance." *Dance Magazine*. New York: January, 1986: 24–97; 24.
[36] Erin Hurley, "Introduction," *National Performance: Representing Quebec from Expo 67 to Celine Dion* (Toronto, Buffalo, London: University of Toronto Press, 2010).
[37] Michael Taussig, *Mimesis and Alterity: A Particular History of the Senses* (New York: Routledge, 1993), xiii.
[38] Ibid., 237.

anthropology, the speaker may somehow take hold of the power at work in Lecavalier's dance itself. Over many descriptive accounts of Lecavalier, veering from angel to cyborg, monster to man, thematic clusters emerged around hybridity and power, as if through vernacular speech we were rehearsing the order of bodies and, by extension, nations in flux. Here, we might return to Phelan's cautionary work around identity formation as an economy of exchange grounded in vision. If seeing and being seen are key aspects of subjectivity, fostering a kind of recognition and internalization of values, perhaps this accounts for the largesse of descriptions in the press and in everyday life; in naming, we get a little closer and "become what we behold."[39] But representation always does more and less than it sets out to do, as Phelan reminds us, and kinesthetic imagery throws another curve ball to underscore the malleability of our readings.

Risking understatement, dancers give us something to talk about. Foucault offers the immediate take-off point, in *The Archeology of Knowledge*, noting that discourse is "not a slender surface of contact, or confrontation, between a reality and a language [*langue*]" but rather "the loosening of the embrace, apparently so tight, of words and things, and the emergence of a group of rules proper to discursive practice." He writes,

> These rules define not the dumb existence of a reality, nor the canonical use of a vocabulary, but the ordering of objects. "Words and things" is the entirely serious title of a problem; it is the ironic title of a work that modifies its own form, displaces its own data, and reveals, at the end of the day, a quite different task. A task that consists of not—of no longer—treating discourses as groups of signs (signifying elements referring to contents or representations) but as practices that systematically form the objects of which they speak.[40]

---

[39] Adage paraphrased from the original, "Terrified Los stood in the Abyss & his immortal limbs Grew deadly pale; he became what he beheld." William Blake, "Milton: A Poem in 2 Books." In *The Poetry and Prose of William Blake* (Garden City, Doubleday/Random House, 1804/1965), 96, E28–9.

[40] Michel Foucault, *The Archeology of Knowledge and the Discourse on Language*. A. M. Sheridan Smith, Trans. (New York: Pantheon Books, 1972), 49.

Foucault turns us to discourse as practice, as much as order, and here the imagined pre-discursivity of dance pressures language further to reach for "sayability," in the midst of excess speed and bodily imagery slipping from view.[41] Whereas journalism and media accounts lean towards the mythic, my hope is that the fragments that appear alongside this chapter and indeed throughout my book suggest the subversions and heterogeneities in the work of the dancer as a critical producer of imagery and idea, a catalyst in the collective working out of culture. Here, the material work of the dancer—physical, sensorial, and kinesthetic—moves off the stage and into the everyday, off the individual body and into the collective lives of the community and the quartier.

To situate oral history as fragment may seem haphazard, even arbitrary, or worse, another way to avoid the challenge of meeting head-on the full power of moving bodies. Yet these accounts push in different material directions, avoiding mythmaking and ushering forth thicker descriptions of Lecavalier's work. In the ricochet between dancer, image, and viewer, and the accrual of impressions, perhaps the everyday discursive practice of the community may slip into view; and, what's more, the dancer's status as a producer of culture.

Scenes/Zines

Cultural historian and music studies scholar Will Straw has noted the ambiguous nature of scenes, at once highly productive as "laboratories for cultural citizenship" and potentially conservative, "asserting the values of diversity dispersed across space over those of regularized obsolescence and renewal in time."[42] Within the downtown neighborhood of Plateau-Mont Royal during the late 1970s and early

---

[41] Boris Traue, Mathias Blanc, and Carolina Cambre, "Visibilities and Visual Discourses: Rethinking the Social with the Image." *Qualitative Inquiry* 25, no. 4 (2018): 327–37; 329.
[42] Will Straw, "Scenes and Sensibilities." *Public*, No. 22/23 (2002): 245–57: 255.

1980s, a robust creative scene emerged, energized by punk, new wave, and a raucous do-it-yourself attitude. New forms of expression powered by the handmade and self-taught and the particular energy of subcultures emerged, less a function of the Quiet Revolution than a function of slow reform and an emergent neoliberalism that powered the 1960s. The policies implemented by Premier Jean Lesage (1960–6), whose election had ended the period of the ultra-nationalist Duplessis years, effectively modernized the province, detaching education from the control of the Church; and thus ensuring the production of a skilled labor force. Whereas the Quiet Revolution "legitimized the accession to power of a new technocratic class in Quebec,"

> This class created its own unique identity and history which came to be conflated with that of the collectivity as whole, ie. the francophones of Quebec.[43]

By the end of the 1970s, Montréal had successfully stepped onto the international scene, hosting the 1967 world's fair and the 1976 Olympics. Yet a renewed rift was opening between people and state. By the 1980s, with the No vote on independence, the profound gaps between progress, politics, and opportunity were palpable in the decline of neighborhoods and the emergent youth subculture.

Lecavalier and company were among the creative youth who gathered, figured things out, and created new forms along St-Laurent, or the Main, historically a key artery of industry and commerce that ran north/south and separated the city's French community to the east and English to the west. A former manufacturing space in the Cooper Building, built in 1932 by Russian immigrant and clothing maker Morris Cooperberg, provided cheap, expansive room for La La La's studio. Nearby, artists, workers, immigrants, elites, shoppers, and youths encountered one another along the intersecting streets of St-Laurent

---

[43] Following Jocelyn Létourneau in Donald Cucciolletta and Martin Lubin, "The Quebec Quiet Revolution: A Noisy Evolution." In *Contemporary Quebec: Selected Readings and Commentaries*, ed. Michael Behiels and Matthew Hayday (Montréal: McGill-Queen's University Press, 2011), 182–96; 182.

and Ste-Catherine. Nearby, too, new queer cultures emerged in late-night clubs along St-Denis.[44] Whereas gay creativity had long been a part of Montréal's character, alive in the cabarets and drag performance shows that dominated nightlife along Ste-Catherine in the early part of the twentieth century, a queer political consciousness began to emerge in the early 1980s—following the displacement of the city's gay village around the 1976 Olympics and with the emergence of the HIV-AIDs pandemic. It was in this context of new emergent political realities and the heterogeneity of the city scene that Lecavalier constructed her dancing body; and it was in this particular neighborhood that La La La sought to transform the available materials of dance, popular music, and expressive style towards something new.

In flux then as now, St-Laurent was a mix of fripéries, dépanneurs, empty storefronts, take-out shops, bars, and cafés, a kind of social platform and sidewalk theater poised on the edge of decline and gentrification. In dialogue with other urban centers—artists were traveling between New York, Paris, and Berlin, often supported by state arts funding—many new ideas circulated within the cultural sphere. A thriving music scene included punk and new wave acts that garnered local devotion and occasionally international appeal, for example Men Without Hats. Taking root in empty warehouses as the city's industry shifted and many of the clothing manufacturers relocated to the North of the city or left, artists in the Plateau found low rents and state-funded social programs that allowed for the creation and participation in the scene. The compressed geography, available space, and diverse scenes of the neighborhood fueled and were fueled by the hybridity of La La La's collective vision, which gathered a range of materials to create new dance.

---

[44] See Julie Podmore, "Gone Underground? Lesbian Visibility and the Consolidation of Queer Space in Montréal." *Social and Cultural Geography* 7, no. 4 (2006): 595–625; and Carl F. Stychin, "Queer Nations: Nationalism, Sexuality and the Discourse of Rights in Québec." *Feminist Legal Studies* 5, no. 4 (1997): 3–34.

Montréal has long been understood, according to cultural historian Geoff Stahl, as bound by two overlapping narratives comprising the city's cultural imaginary:

> one of economic decline and weakness marked indelibly by language tensions and sovereignty debates, and the other, a narrative of resilience as expressed through the mythical character of its enduring cultural life.[45]

Yet, as he and others point out, far more diverse sets of projects were unfolding in the city, in ways elided by the dominant narrative of English/French divides.[46] Literary scholar Sherry Simon characterizes the period as passing from "an ideal of a homogeneous, collective identity to a more problematic and heterogeneous conception of social and symbolic union."[47] Historian Sean Mills finds a diverse range of political projects unfolding, inspired by the discourse of decolonization.[48] For example, his study of the Haitian deportation crisis in 1974 shows how Québec-based Haitian migrants rallied for broad support from church groups, unions, activists, and artists, in ways that profoundly shifted the province's sense of itself. He writes, "If the period was marked by the everyday realities of racism, it was also simultaneously shaped by the growth of international solidarity, with Haiti, Latin America, Africa, and elsewhere, which became increasing central to the expanding world of political opposition."[49] To situate Lecavalier's dance within the Montréal of the 1980s is to mark the city's shifting composition and values, and complex political alliances. Taking up the highly flexible forms of identification engendered by the

---

[45] Geoff Stahl, "Tracing out an Anglo Bohemia: Musicmaking and Myth in Montréal." *Public: Cities/Scenes* 22–3 (2001): 100.

[46] Geoff Stahl, "The Quest for Metropolis." *City* 5, no. 2 (2000): 257–9.

[47] Sherry Simon, "Culture and Its Values: Critical Revisionism in Quebec in the 1980s." In *Canadian Canons: Essays in Literary Values*, ed. Robert Lecker (Toronto, Buffalo: University of Toronto Press, 1991), 167–79; 167.

[48] Sean Mills, *The Empire Within: Postcolonial Thought and Political Activism in Sixties Montréal* (Montréal: McGill-Queens Press, 2010).

[49] Sean Mills, "Quebec, Haiti, and the Deportation Crisis of 1974." In *The Canadian Historical View* 94, no. 3 (2013): 405–35.

music, club, and social scenes allowed for distinctive modes of being and solidarity at the core of the neighborhood and the company.

More recently, Straw and colleague Nathalie Casemajor have turned their attention to the visuality of the scene, in part for its "world-making" powers to shift and remake culture. They write,

> the scene is a form of ordering, gathering actors, forces, and materials around a particular cultural object (a musical style or cultural practice, for example), or arranging these elements through the operations of an "optical machine" that serves in the production of knowledge. In these conceptions, scenes become intelligible through their ordering in the realm of the visual.[50]

The visual mattered deeply to La La La, perhaps especially to Lock as a filmmaker as well as a choreographer; Lecavalier was interested in the visual to the extent that it was in the service of the dancing, rather than as décor. An early promotional poster for *Oranges: ou la recherche du paradis* (1981), for example, features two orange figures in silhouette wherein the defining features of the head and face are replaced with an orange for the figure in the skirt and a glass of juice for the figure in the pants, in what I read as a tongue-in-cheek marking of gender stereotypes. Created by company member Michel Lemieux, the poster invokes the culture/nature divide—women as raw material for creation, man as producer. Figured in orange (rather than pink or blue), the work equally elides the human face as a marker of identity. Such imagery—cheaply produced, easily distributed, and papering the city— participated in an ethos of self-production and insider knowledge that was analogous to an emergent do-it-yourself culture associated with punk and new wave. More, it is emblematic of the company's strategic use of visual imagery in dance and in its promotion, which figured Lecavalier at its centre.

---

[50] Nathalie Casemajor and Will Straw, "The Visuality of Scenes: Urban Cultures and Visual Scenescapes." *Imaginations: Journal of Cross-Cultural Image Studies* (2017). http://imaginations.glendon.yorku.ca/?p=9152

Adjacent to this work were fanzines, emergent during this period in the visual aesthetic locally and in punk and feminist politics internationally, conveying information about gigs and more through handbills, flyers, stickers, comics, and other kinds of ephemera. First associated with radical movements of the 1930s, and the availability of cheap technology that allowed for small print runs, including mimeographs and xerox machines, the rise of the fanzine during the punk era offers a useful reference point for the early visual culture inherent in La La La's work and key to the production of Lecavalier's image.[51] At different points in my research, people remembered the visual universe of *Oranges, or the Search for Paradise* (1981), with its graffiti-like writing on giant paper walls—and of *Businessman in the Process of Becoming an Angel* (1983), wherein dog-imagery reappeared on armbands, stage props, flyers, and markings on the street leading to the theater.

The visual discourse generated was at once ambiguous and highly productive. Whereas Lecavalier has been taken up as a national heroine for Québec—gaining international stature and winning Europe's Leonide Massine Dancer of the Year (2013), the Order of Canada (2008), le Grand Prix de la danse de Montréal (2011)—this was not a given circa the 1980s. Like the downtown quartiers of the Plateau and Ville Marie themselves, the dance of La La La included the rock 'n' roll energy of the music clubs that enlivened the streets; the androgyny proposed by punk, new wave, and an emergent queerness; and the aesthetic legacies of migration and immigrant labor. Lecavalier, as a French-Canadian child of a transitioning working class, and La La La as an assemblage of performing artists—"more like a hockey team than a dance company"—challenged audiences around received patterns of aesthetics, gender, and nation in ways that dovetailed with national and international movements. Before she was universally beloved, her

---

[51] Teal Triggs, "Alphabet Soup: Reading British Fanzines." *Visible Language* 29, no. 1 (1995): 72–87. See too Teal Triggs, "Scissors and Glue: Punk Fanzines and the DIY Aesthetic." *Journal of Design History* 19, no. 1 (2006): 69–83; 77.

performed presence was a sledge hammer to established rules for dance and identity more broadly. Within the quartier of the Plateau, sightings of Lecavalier were news. There is Lecavalier, buying groceries at *Soares et Fils* on Duluth, in black leather jacket and dreadlocks. There she is, getting coffee at les Gateries on St-Denis. Stories of encounters with the dancer haunt this work as they haunt the city and quartier, but she was always too hardworking, too shy, and too different to be a scenester per se. Instead, her danced labor and the images it produced became a significant anchor point for neighbors and viewers alike to generate emergent discourse.

Are saints punk rock?
Between icon and (moving) image

Returning to the 1980s and scenes of Lecavalier's dancing, through various recollections and oral histories, theories and cultural histories, a minor flare in my thinking occurred. Rereading notes from various interlocutors, I realized that nearly all the oral history fragments mentioned places that were on streets or neighborhoods named for saints: Sainte Catherine, Saint Denis, Saint Laurent, Sainte Dorothée. Not unusual for a city anchored in French Catholicism, and yet. Whereas I had set out to resist the turn to myth, understood as the erasure of history's materiality, and the canonical placement of Lecavalier within Québec dance, here I risked a return to mythology as a kind of fixicity or flattening in time. Yet, within the context of the city, wherein the names and figures of saints hover in churches, schools, streets, and in the imaginary, the phenomenon of the saint seemed an apt vehicle for reflecting on the reception to Lecavalier, returning us to the realm of devotion as an exchange between icon and image.

Critics often described Lecavalier as a saint or demon. In fact, these kinds of extreme characters repeat across the La La La repertoire. With *Infante, c'est destroy* (1991), for instance, Lecavalier created imagery through her live dancing and Lock's projected film imagery that shifted between the abject and the heroic. On stage, she appeared as if in flight; her spectacular leaps and falls, taking the air, then falling to ground or caught in the arms of a partner, were a defining feature of the work and the repertoire more broadly. On film, writ through projected light, she appears as pure myth: dressed in chain mail as a warrior from Medieval times, attacked by dogs, pierced by a sword in battle. Or else falling, in slow-motion, her body naked and powdered white in a darkened space: "a fallen angel." Such imagery aligns with the repetitive, hypnotic aspects of the work that are suggestive of trance, faith, and heightened states of perception. Contrasting her danced materiality against the film's mythic narrative, *Infante* scopes a mid-path, marking the gap between live presence and history as representation. Across the La La La repertoire, the characters of saints and angels reappear, ambiguous figures that consistently appeared striking to observers and that reverberated with interpretations of Lecavalier as hero.

Understood to straddle the threshold of the human and spirit world, saints are mythic figures thought to accompany us through difficult passages. Whereas angels are imagined as reaching down from the heavens to influence human activity—think Wim Wenders' *Wings of Desire* (1987)—saints were historical people, whose phenomenal actions lead toward the heroic and the mythic. Saints once did things, they were bound to human agency and seen to collapse polarities such as the sacred and profane. Recent scholarship has looked to the performative aspects of the icon as representation, from its lifelike visual qualities to its gestural elements to its efficacious impact.[52] Increasingly, it seems it is the doing of the icon—that is, agency of the encounter between saint and follower—that counts. For historian Robert Maniura, the saint emerges on, in, and through ritual acts of worship. He writes,

---

[52] Bissera Pentcheva, "Performing the Sacred in Byzantium: Image, Breath, and Sound," *PRI Performance Research International* 19, no. 3 (2014): 120–8; and Bissera Pentcheva, "The Performative Icon," *The Art Bulletin* 88, no. 4 (2006): 631–55.

Locating the saint in the actions of devotees doesn't trivialize the category. These performed relationships are weighty things, not least because they also, at least in part, constitute the devotee.[53]

Placing the power of the icon squarely in its encounter with a viewer, Maniura points to the role of contact with the saint in the construction of self. The icon—and here I blur the saint and the saint's image, performance as always already connected to sight and speech—serves to make the invisible visible through its use as devotional medium.

French historian Marie-José Mondzain goes farther in helping us understand the function of visual imagery and discursive practices as they play out within contemporary life. Grounded in her understanding of the Byzantine world's distinction between the image, as an idea and thus able to circulate freely, and the icon, as visible and more readily put to use in the interests of the church, Mondzain writes, "The image and the icon lie at the heart of all considerations of the symbol and the sign, as well as their relation to the problematic of being and appearing, seeing and believing, strength and power."[54] Images function as "crack[s] in being," unfixed and indeterminant—ideas on their way to being perceived. Mondzain, too, emphasizes the viewer of the image; she notes that, whereas the image may or may not come to serve the "iconocracy,"[55] what matters more is its generative aspects—"its operations of continual displacement"[56]—and the "relationship it has with the gaze of the subject, at the crossroads of the gaze and the exchange."[57] Here, the image's power lies not in any documentary "truth" but rather in the powers of exchange they enable. As she argues,

---

[53] Robert Maniura, "Persuading the Absent Saint: Image and Performance in Marian Devotion." *Critical Inquiry* 35, no. 3 (2009): 629–54; 654.

[54] Marie Jose Mondzain, *Image, Icon, Economy: the Byzantine Origins of the Contemporary Imaginary* (Stanford, CA: Stanford University Press, 2005), xiii.

[55] Ibid., 152.

[56] Marie-José Mondzain, "Image Wars: An Interview with Marie-José Mondzain." Briankle G. Chang and Nefeli Forni Zervoudaki, Trans. *Journal of Communication Studies* 46, no. 4 (2022): 329–41; 339.

[57] Marie-José Mondzain, "Image, Subject, Power: An Interview with Marie-José Mondzain." Briankle G. Chang and Nefeli Forni Zervoudaki, Trans. *Inter-Asia Cultural Studies* 22, no. 1 (2019): 83–99; 90.

"It is not because it is true that it has power. It is because it has power that it becomes true."[58] Mondzain's chiasmi helps account for the effects of Lecavalier's iconic, material performances, which circulated imagery and gathered meaning through performative exchange at micro- and mass-scale.

A considerable part of the power of Lecavalier's dance, then, resides in the kind of "crack in being" it opened up for viewers—that is, the viewership it generated and the attendant challenge it posed at a certain moment in time to received orders of value around bodies in dance and in everyday life. As an iconic figure, she laid image to significant political shifts unfolding in the city and beyond; her dance, perceived as brand new, was instead dense with history: sourcing modern dance practices and punk aesthetics and methodologies; contact improvisation and breakdancing; body language and sign language; queerness and ethnicity, including her own French-Canadian working-class family and choreographer Édouard Lock's migration history as a Moroccan Jew. For fans and colleagues alike, her dance opened fabulous fissures of possibility.

To invoke the saint and the icon here is not to participate in myth-making but rather to take seriously Lecavalier's star power while invoking a performance economy bound by devotional acts of viewing, making, and thinking. If a considerable part of the work of the dancer lies in reception and discourse, it's worth remembering that there is no icon or image without material act. On one hand, iconicity and imagery crafted into meanings through acts of spectatorship; on the other, action compressed and contained within the image—action developed through the rigors of training, the love and pleasure of being with the friends who danced with her, and in her generosity as a performer on stage. The anthropologist Clifford Gertz, following Shils, has located the quality of charisma in "the concentrated loci of serious acts." He writes,

---

[58] Mondzain, *Image, Icon, Economy*; and Mondzain, "Image, Subject, Power."

It is not, after all, standing outside the social order in some excited state of self-regard that makes a political leader numinous but a deep, intimate involvement – affirming or abhorring, defensive or destructive – in the master fictions by which that order lives.[59]

More recently, theater scholar Joe Roach digs further into the phenomena of charisma, in ways that extend my understanding of "serious acts." Moving past banal understandings of charisma as individual charm or pure talent, he situates the attraction to stars within the realms of technique and viewership. He writes,

> Theatrical performance is the simultaneous experience of mutually exclusive possibilities—truth and illusion, presence and absence, face and mask. Performers are none other than themselves doing a job in which they are always someone else, filling our field of vision with the flesh-and-blood matter of what can only be imagined to exist. With an intensity of focus beyond the reach of normal people, those with It can embody before our eyes these and other antinomies.[60]

Yet, whereas he reads the phenomenon of "It," or charisma, as public resource and projection grounded in the experience of vicarity and the viewer's own lack, I see a dialogue between devotional acts of viewership—simply understood as open engagements with the performer—and Lecavalier's "serious acts"—as a dedicated worker aiming her labor at dance, performance, and by 2010 choreography—through the frame of Mondzain's "crack." Which is to say, as a fabulous opening up of possibility that may go far to explain her iconic stature as a globally known performer, working with David Bowie, Frank Zappa, and Nam June Paik, her imagery beamed live around the world.

Her serious acts, bound to stage performance, street scenes, and brief forays into advertising and film, generated ricochet moves: imagery and interpretations that fueled the rise to iconicity. Part of the cultural work of the dancer, then, might be understood as conduit—saint-like, to the

---

[59] Clifford Geertz, "Centers, Kings and Charisma: Reflections on the Symbolics of Power." In *Local Knowledge: Further Essays in the Interpretative Anthropology* (New York: Basic Books, 2008), 122, 146.
[60] Joe R. Roach, "It." *Theatre Journal* 56, no. 4 (2000): 555–68; 559.

extent that they draw our gaze and explode received ideas in the culture. In the fragments that accompany this text lie the incomplete stories and unofficial histories that begin to suggest the power of Lecavalier's cultural labor, while returning us to the scene: a hand-made, pre-digital time, when face-to-face encounters mattered, in the theater and on the street (Figure 1.2).

Figure 1.2 Lecavalier, Parc Lafontaine, July 29, 1990. Photo: © Linda Dawn Hammond/IndyFoto.

ICON/STREET

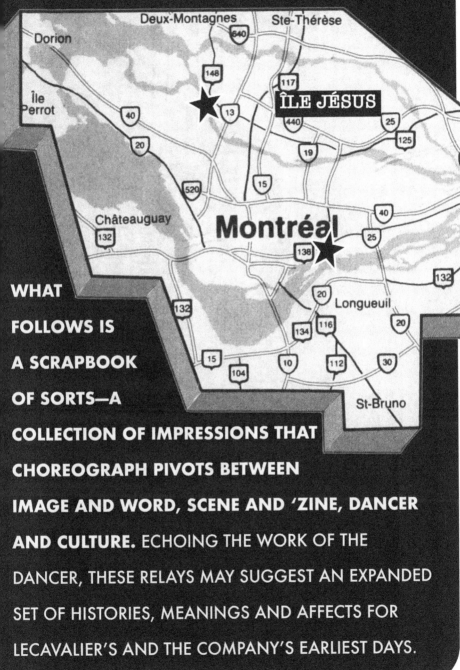

WHAT FOLLOWS IS A SCRAPBOOK OF SORTS—A COLLECTION OF IMPRESSIONS THAT CHOREOGRAPH PIVOTS BETWEEN IMAGE AND WORD, SCENE AND 'ZINE, DANCER AND CULTURE. ECHOING THE WORK OF THE DANCER, THESE RELAYS MAY SUGGEST AN EXPANDED SET OF HISTORIES, MEANINGS AND AFFECTS FOR LECAVALIER'S AND THE COMPANY'S EARLIEST DAYS.

1.3 Montréal island and Île Jésus, stars indicate Sainte-Dorothée and Le Plateau

SAINTE-DOROTHÉE

1.4 Early days with Groupe Nouvelle Aire.
Photo: Claude-Félix Blanchard

I used to hitchhike all the time. Into the city to take dance class. I lived in Sainte-Dorothée, which was different then. Now it's part of Laval, it's like a big suburb. But then it was a village. Sometimes it took many rides to get from home to the Plateau. I met a lot of people. All kinds. When they asked if I was a musician—because of the way I looked—I told them I was a contemporary dancer and they were always a bit disappointed, as if it was less interesting. "Contemporary dance" meant nothing to them. —LOUISE LECAVALIER (2024)

… I saw that most people got me wrong: long blonde hair, blue eyes, kind of reserved, this "little girl." The more you put gloves on to speak with me, the more I—oooh (shudders)—I don't get it at all. How can I act? People talk to you like you're an idiot. So I cut my hair, dyed it black. It helped a lot. And that was when I started with Édouard. —LL (2010)

I left *Les Grands* (Ballet) because I want to do something creative. And there was nothing, there was nothing in Montréal really, there was Pointépienu and they told me it would take six months before I could do anything. I said, you know, "I've been training for 17 years, I dance professionally for seven years, but I can't dance? I am a dancer!" People were still thinking so in a box … we wanted to try to do new things. —MIRYAM MOUTILLET (2020), founding dancer with Lock Danseurs/La La La Human Steps (1980–1983)

All of the established dance at that time was looking at us; they were impressed but, at the same time, because we didn't use codified language they were saying, "But it is not dance." They thought we were performance art, moving performance art, some kind of street dance, they didn't know what … We were outsiders, and we didn't wear tights and tutus. —LOUIS GUILLEMETTE (2014), founding dancer/Lock Danseurs/La La La Human Steps (1980–1983)

1235 SANGUINET

(CONVENTUM)

I had already started to work with contact improvisation in Québec City, before I came to Montréal. I'd been to San Francisco and worked with Mangrove and all those people. It was all based on somatic work, very personal. Groupe Nouvelle Aire had an event called Choréchanges, and we shared a night with other experimental choreographers. That's where I saw Édouard presenting that solo with Miryam—a 20-minute solo without music, and I was just blown away, and was like "Wow, what's that?" It was deconstructed ballet. After I presented, Édouard came to me and said "Oh, wow, I like the way you move, it really connects with the way I work ... would you like to try and work with me?" And I said, "Of course," but I didn't know which form it would take. And I was not at the level of Miryam, doing pure ballet. I was more into contemporary and multi-dimensional techniques, I'd followed different schools. But he worked with me one-on-one—and we developed my way of moving.
—LG (2014)

1.5 December 1981. Photo: Ron Diamond

We weren't punk, but it was au courant, it was the period. We weren't harsh, we weren't aggressive. We were people pushing boundaries. We didn't drink … or do drugs … we had no money. When you are in the action, you don't think about the action. We were doers, that's the way I see it; we were doers. We were not intellectualizing what was happening, and we were acting. —MM (2020)

> I really loved photography and graphic arts, I never studied that but back then I became the guy to ask to make your poster for your theater piece. Édouard saw my work through a friend and came over to talk about a poster. Then he saw this electric guitar, a beautiful Gibson SG, yellow, and asked, "Do you play?" Yeah, but I'm shy so I went in the other room and played it using a screwdriver like a bow. That's when he asked me to make music for the next show (*Oranges*).
> —MICHEL LEMIEUX (2020), founding performer with Lock Danseurs/La La La Human Steps (1980–1984)

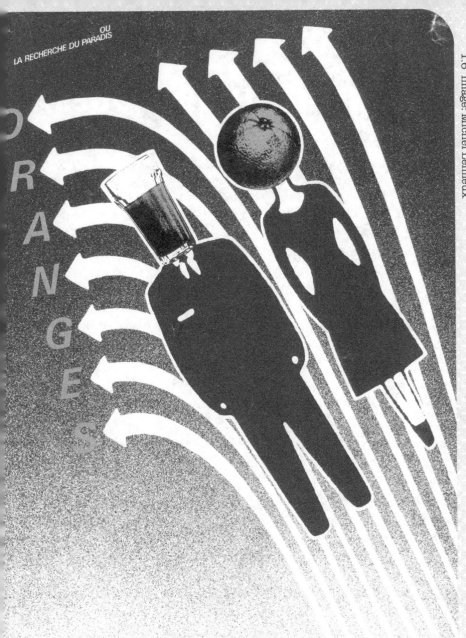

305–307
SAINTE-CATHERINE OUEST

(GALERIE VÉHICULE ART)

I was maybe twenty-one, twenty-two when I started with Édouard. Those early days were such a good time for the company … there was no big aura around us, just a buzz, and a lot of openness. I loved everything Édouard was doing. I tried to see everything, all the details, to not miss a beat and analyze it technically. I wasn't thinking "I'm going to copy this or that," or "I'm going to be a great dancer." I wanted to get close to what I saw. What I saw was complex, there was a lot of information in his way of moving, different than anything I'd seen. He had a beautiful mixture of things: he was interested in contemporary dance, ballet, in everything that was happening in New York, the downtown scene. He was fluid and liquid in his way of moving: skinny and loose, something Moroccan—something from there, something from New York, something from here. —LL (2012)

There was a lot of experimental work around Montréal at the time, there was a lot going on at Véhicule, it was a gallery on Sainte-Catherine's with artists like Monty Cantsin, Zilon, Marie Chouinard … We would work and work in the studio, but when it's finished, it's finished, and we would go to a museum or go see something other than dance … We were attracted by these forms of art, very much, but we didn't talk about it. We were into the contemporary way of processing ideas, instead of just picking up the ideas of others. **What we worked on were the gestures, the vocabulary, the movement.** That will always be the core and the source of the work. And the rest? The form it takes, the argument, it arrives at the end. —LG (2014)

What was happening for me wasn't exactly what was happening for the general public. For the general public, there was a kinesthetic excitement—it was contemporary dance that felt a little like a rock show. I was excited not just about the movement vocabulary, per se; for me, it wasn't more or less interesting than what I'd seen in contact improv, except for the speed element. But the concepts were exciting! **And there was that iconic moment when Louise lifted Marc up in her hands into the air—that women could do that.** —DENA DAVIDA, curator/artistic director, Tangente (2012)

1.7 Lecavalier with David Bowie, July 1, 1988. Photo: Anton Corbijn/Getty Images

3981–7
SAINT-LAURENT

(COOPER BUILDING)

I always wanted to rehearse more. I was never happy enough with how I was doing it—I thought, "it can be better." I just read this biography of Marilyn Monroe, how she always said, "I'm going to do another take—I can do it better." That's how I was in the studio—like, "Let's do it again." I could ask [the other dancers] 25 times, I could do it to the point of exhaustion. It was crazy. But it was not like anyone told us to do it, we did it because it was fun, and we didn't have to be home for dinner. —LL (2012)

> ... Oh, I loved that space. But it was cement, so it was hard. And I jumped from it a million times. We worked directly, no carpet. There were two big support columns. A bathtub painted pink with La La La written on it (I think I did that ...) And a futon hidden in the corner. It was not too charming, but we didn't care. It was perfect. —LL (2012/2024)

1.8 Photo: Étienne Tremblay-Tardif

I had been working part-time at a laundromat and going part-time to University. I was making minimum wage, and someone, a regular customer, came in and said that La la la apparently was looking a drummer, and specifically a female drummer. And I kind of laughed at it. And then I found out that the audition was really close to my apartment on St. Laurent. And I thought "Ah well, what harm could it be? ... I went to the interview and I wasn't asked to do anything really crazy challenging, and I remember leaving and thinking I got the job. I think it was more of a visual thing, what I looked like, what I projected, the energy ... I quit the laundromat and I had ten days to learn the show. It was the end of August, it was for the Edinburgh Festival. And we were going to play in front of 3000 people. —JACKIE GALLANT, musician/videographer, drummer with La La La (1991-1994)

Édouard wanted to work with specific people because it intrigued him, the way they move, and he wanted to catch that essence, and work with and see how he can transform, metamorphose this and push further. He was anti-specific style … With Édouard, we were always working one-on-one, everything was like old couture: everything is designed with and for the dancers. It was a very intimate work we did together. —LG (2014)

1.9 Photo: Jack Udashkin

I had a friend who had a studio in the Cooper Building, when everything was transferring over. The clothing industry was leaving the area, either disappearing or moving to Chabanel, and artists were taking over. Well, you were taking [sewing] needles out of the floor on a regular basis, and these were the environments artists were working in, Édouard included – he had a studio on the third floor, I think. He stayed there for years before moving to Rialto. —PHILIP SZPORER, journalist/teacher/filmmaker, Montréal (2014)

1.10 Photo: Allan Raym[...]

5723 AVENUE DU PARC

(Rialto Theatre)

It was a very small community … We met … after *Lily Marlene* (1980) and I just saw her on the street and said, "Do you want to do something?" And she said sure. And that was kind of it. I remember her not showing up for rehearsals a few times, and then me seeing her on the street and saying, "Hey what's going on?" And she said, "Ok, I'll show up." There were very tiny, little conversations, they had absolutely no weight to them … It was an incongruous bunch of people that made up the history of La La La, especially in the 1980s, where there were all sorts of influences. —ÉDOUARD LOCK (2022), Choreographer/Filmmaker, La La La Human Steps (1980–2015)

I was selling music back then, and I realized that the presenters buying music were also buying dance. If I had a contact, I could do two or three things at these [showcase] conferences every year … I was in Toronto and picked up the *Toronto Star*, Bill Littler had a review of a piece called *Oranges*. Now, he called it the best piece of dance or choreography that had been done in Toronto in the last 10 years. Now, I know Bill. He was a pretty tough cookie. So I called around, called the Canada Council to find out more—they said, "Good luck … " Good luck everything, finding them, getting money to support what you could describe as a rock-and-roll group … Basically, it took me six or seven numbers to track him [Lock] down in Montréal. And I found him and I went to see him. And we talked for the whole afternoon. Maybe there was this background, he's Jewish-Moroccan, I'm Greek … To cut it short, we agreed.— GEORGE SKALKOGIANNIS, Representation, Management, Producer, La La La Human Steps (1982–1992)

1.11 Last night of *Businessman* at the Rialto: Lock (left), Skalkogiannis (right). Photo: Jack Udashkin

3927 SAINT-DENIS (L'EXPRESS)

We spent long hours in the studio, and we didn't have much money. Afterwards, we'd go out to bars—not so much clubs—sometimes to hear music, more just for drinks and talking. We used to go to l'Express. The waiters would bring us bread and any bottles of unfinished wine. And other places too. I liked the characters, the tough girls, the bohemians, the late-night crowd, the Québécois... We were Québécois, but we were not so involved in the political scene. Our work was in the studio: it was just the beginning, and we were finding our language. —LL (2010)

For me, the most important thing is people, people first, and if you want people to work—and we were all super poor, we had no money, we were doing three jobs!—but it's normal, that's what dancers do. When I was there, I worked on grants, we got grants, that was a priority—let's make sure that people are paid for rehearsals so we can pay our rent and eat—because there's some that don't, but me I still eat. —MM (2020)

There was social life, yes ... but ... I couldn't believe how hard they worked. To me, that was the big thing. Just how much they gave during the show. People would get hit in the nose, and there was blood on their nice white shirts, and it was almost like a boxer—there was this kind of ... "Okay, I have this injury, and you just tape the arm back on and you go." —JG (2020)

I was about twenty, twenty-one at the time. I hadn't yet become a journalist, I was on the cusp of things, and I was taking classes. I remember the excitement of those times, and what was very different was the engagement of the community ... It was about watching art and dance that was in the process of making its mark, and it affected everybody. Everybody who was interested in dance, people taking classes, people interested in contemporary work. Groupe de la Place Royale had left the city, Groupe Nouvelle Aire had effectively finished its run, Les Grands [Ballets Canadiens] was catering to a different audience, les Ballets Jazz was doing its own thing and very successfully. So you had this swell of interesting people, many of them friends who had been with these companies but also came in with their own influences ... There was a kind of low-level activism: questions ranging from, "Why should we care about dance?" to the sense that what is happening with the arts and culture at that key moment in the eighties was happening in Montréal as a kind of mecca for convergence.
—PS (2014)

1.14 Photo: Robert Nadon/La Presse

318 SAINTE-CATHERINE (THE SPECTRUM)

I saw Nina Hagen at the Spectrum. And I wanted to play there. I thought "Let's make dance accessible to everyone, not just the dance world and these special places: theaters and opera houses…" When Édouard was at the studio, we worked in silence—he never choreographed to music. When we rehearsed, we danced to … well, I remember Prince, the Tom Tom Club, there were others … We used

that energy to push us and see if the movement worked at that level—it was like a checkpoint. The music was exciting, it communicated and it was popular: simple and complex. We didn't want to be these cool aesthetes that lived in a closed world, **we wanted to be with the people.** —LL (2012)

I was working as a projectionist at Cinema V. And it was so random, how I saw in the *Gazette* an article about these guys [playing at the Spectrum]: film, video, and weird dancing. I thought, OK—this is not your average show and so I took a chance on it ... And I was completely mesmerized by Louise and the rest of the band. And Louise was the most amazing. Because you looked at her and ... Well, first, there was that whole androgynous thing they had going: she had the mustache, and the crazy wild blonde dreads, and she's flying around and you literally don't know if she's a man or a woman. It was that eighties thing. Androgyny was everywhere, and we were all questioning sexuality. And with Louise you couldn't figure it out: there was something so attractive and also scary; it was back-and-forth. I remember literally feeling like I had to move out of the way because it felt like she was going to fly off the stage. It had that kind of impact. —**John O'Neil (2014)**, projectionist (1997-2003), La La La Human Steps

1.15 + 1.16 Photos: Linda Dawn Hammond

There was something very excessive about what we were doing. And, to a certain extent, the people in the company did not put a clear dividing line between what was going on onstage and what they were doing outside of stage ... they would literally step off the stage without touching the make-up, they just go and live their lives, like they were extending whatever they were doing on stage into the real world ... We would spend hours doing things that would be considered time-wasting ... for instance, for *Human Sex*, Zilon the artist would apply glue-gun patterns on her tights and corset every night, it took hours. Everything was process, it didn't begin with the start of the show. It was constant. —EL (2022)

As for the media, they really focused on the androgyny, the strong woman and subverting gender stereotypes in dance. I think for us, it was a non-issue ... It was extremely physical for everyone, myself included. It was really liberating to have that power and to do something that's so physically demanding every night ... —JG (2020)

3443 SAINT-DENIS (LES GATERIES)

I was just back from Berlin when I first saw them. I'd written a piece about squatters there – it was amazing. The scale! Maybe 200 houses, every house had forty to fifty people living in it! It was so organized, it was working so well. That was the first piece I published ... They were clean-cut, new wave. We were punks, hippies – they were more like dandies. I was working as a DJ at Foufounes [Électriques] ... They were aesthetes. We hated them. But they had our respect—they were out there, opening things up, going international ... I remember I had a friend who worked in this café, Les Gateries. She used to come in there all the time. And it was big! She was so strong. I didn't know much about dance, I didn't see much dance. But every one was like, "Have you seen her?" It was like seeing Isadora Duncan. Everyone was talking about her. She was burning ... burning hot. I remember seeing the company: the cod-ed-hand movements, very rapid. Even then, I knew it would get old, and it did very rapidly get old. But it was all her. She was a superstar. —Benoît Chaput, poet/publisher, *L'Oie de Cravan Press*, 2010

DANSE MUSICALE POST-MODERNE

BUSINESSMAN in the PROCESS of becoming an angel

Drophisme I'IMBAGO
Photo JACK UDASHKIN
Portrait de M. MOUTILLE

Le 20, 21 mai 21h00

La La (Lock/Danseurs) est une compagnie de danse qui poursuit, puis trois ans, une carrière fort remarquée au sein de la danse actuelle Amérique du Nord. Elle réussit par la marginalité, l'audace et la recher- e continue de sa gestuelle à s'imposer comme un phénomène artistique e premier plan.

MEMBRES
Lee Eisler (artiste invitée)
Louis Guillemette
Louise Lecavalier
Michel Lemieux
Edouard Lock
Miryam Moutillet

Direction artistique
Edouard Lock

Musique
Michel Lemieux

Paroles des chansons
M. Lemieux, E. Lock

Costumier et décorateur
Denis Larose

Conception visuelle
E. Lock

Direction de production, et eclairage
Alain Lortie

Son
Benoit Durocher

Assistante de production
Sylvie Baillargeon

Les membres de La La La ont contribué à divers niveaux artistiques et dans plusieurs secteurs administratifs de cette production.

CHANSONS
1. So I
2. Julie Muscle
3. Something, somewhere
4. Business Treasure
5. Venetia
6. IBM
7. Steamy cloud

NOUS REMERCIONS:
Le Conseil des Arts du Canada
Le Ministère des Affaires Culturelles
Tangente, Danse Actuelle

Représentation exclusive,
Direction d'artistes Skalkogiannis

I was in punk rock bands, that was my thing, I was known as Jackie the drummer. I'd played in so many punk bands, there were so many ... Bubble Gum Army, there was one called Just For Mom ... Yeah, I'd been doing that since the early 80s. And, you know, nobody was doing it, there weren't really interesting places to play, there was no media interest, there was nothing. Nobody was doing it ... the aspirations were ... We were just doing it because we liked punk rock and it was our version of it. There were lots of different variations of it, just an underground music scene.
—JG (2020)

1.17 + 1.18 Images: Courtesy Linda Dawn Hammond

There were so many influences coming from all over the world, but I'm thinking about the punk scene that was coming out of England in the late seventies – that affected the way people were thinking about performance and the radical nature of what performance was or could be. I think of Édouard more as an internationalist. He was affected by these elements, he was back and forth between New York. And don't forget that people like Louise were doing that, too. And people were listening. Nothing was being transmitted by computers, it was all live. And stuff was being sent through mail, on handbills, you were getting information from magazines, records obviously, concerts. It was a very different time.
—PS (2014)

I remember we were touring England … and we went to a wishing hill in Bath, a huge thing where if you managed to run from the bottom to the top, then your wish will come true. I couldn't make it. I ran, I stopped half away. Louise made it. She went from the bottom all the way to the top and I asked her, "What was your wish?" She said, "I wasn't thinking about a wish, I just wanted to run." That was it. That was Louise. —EL (2022)

She was very quiet, she was very … I would say … shy, when we met her, but I could have a feeling of how much was going on inside her. And I started training her, trying to explain the movements, where they could go and how you can twist them into another thing. She took that, and she worked extremely hard, like nonstop, nonstop … the thing that Louise did, she went farther. She took all of this material, she really put it in her body, she started taking risks with some movements, and she did that a lot with Louis Guillemette together … That was not my thing, maybe it was so far from my training, but Louise started developing that and it was extraordinary what she did.
—MM (2020)

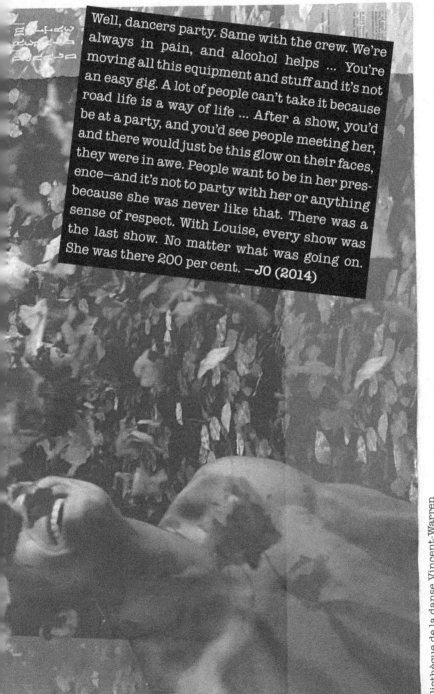

> Well, dancers party. Same with the crew. We're always in pain, and alcohol helps ... You're moving all this equipment and stuff and it's not an easy gig. A lot of people can't take it because road life is a way of life ... After a show, you'd be at a party, and you'd see people meeting her, and there would just be this glow on their faces, they were in awe. People want to be in her presence—and it's not to party with her or anything because she was never like that. There was a sense of respect. With Louise, every show was the last show. No matter what was going on. She was there 200 per cent. —JO (2014)

1.19 Photos: Édouard Lock. Poster: Courtesy Édouard Lock/

Bibliothèque de la danse Vincent-Warren

1.20 Photo: Wolfgang Kirchner

The amount of pressure on her shoulders was just insane. With *Infante*, there were no understudies. It was impossible for there to be an understudy for Louise, because all of the video and all of the film. It was her image in that show, her in armor, and her being attacked by dogs, or falling from the sky. So everything was on her shoulders. What I felt was that there was a lot of pressure, because it was such a big show and there seemed to be a lot of, the bigger the balloon, the bigger the pop if it failed. —JG (2020)

Our generation, we were really focused on doing our own work and making our own rules, so the only way to do that was to do our work here and abroad. Because just doing it here was not possible, there are not enough people, not enough spectators, so we were focusing on opening, and it happened to be a good moment for opening to the world … We all voted Yes for the referendum that didn't win but we were not really focusing on national issues … it was the beginning of *mondialization*.
   —ML (2020)

1.21 Photo: Linda Dawn Hammond

PARC LAFONTAINE

I would say, in the 80s, there was the first happening of the gay scene in Montréal, but it was really gay, it wasn't queer. There was nothing for lesbians, nothing for trans but it was still a beginning and I think probably we were influenced by that ... Probably. But we were looking at a lot of different things ... Of course, Laurie Anderson. And Klaus Nomi was a big influence for Édouard and Louise ... The sound became more industrial, really aggressive ... very aaarrgh. It developed progressively, this raw, punk rage. That's where we started liking different things and I was like, "Whoa! Are you really gonna go there? I'm not going to go there." —ML (2020)

I moved to Montréal in 1982 from British Columbia and the Yukon ... I had previously been involved with the Toronto punk scene back in the late 70s and on moving became part of the local Montréal punks. I originally moved to Lafontaine and Panet, as I wanted to live in a French-speaking area ... Somehow Édouard came to know of my photography, enough to invite me to photograph his show at the Spectrum in 1983 ... That was when I first saw Louise dance. The performance itself was excitingly physical—confrontational, quirky movements, amusing décor and original music. Louise was astounding—her presence immediately captivating and her athleticism broke all expectations of tradition male/female roles, which I personally appreciated ... in my world view, gender roles were meant to be disrupted, or better, discarded entirely. —**Linda Dawn Hammond, Photographer (2020)**

1.22 With street artist Zilon, post-Sex Garage benefit. Photo: Linda Dawn Hammond

I first saw them at a march ... There were the Sex Garage raids in Old Montréal in July, where the police raided this afterhours club and assaulted a number of people. And it was a huge galvanizing moment for the LGBT community. And that summer there was a big demonstration, a march that I took part in that ended up in Parc LaFontaine. There was a stage, and there were rumours that *La La La* were going to perform. I was just *really* curious because I had heard and seen little images, but back then you didn't have the media saturation that you do now ... And they performed for about three minutes. It turned out they did the opening, the fake opening of the show *Infante C'est Destroy*. **It's really short, but it's just this explosion...like a crazy duet with Louise and Donald.** And so they performed for literally less than five minutes and everyone was just stunned. You know? It was just this ... assault. —JG (2020)

2

Non Non Non

Material Labor and the Excess of the Virtuoso

I was not like Mary Poppins in any way. I was resisting this thing we have with women dancers: she comes from nowhere, she appears like Mary Poppins, she drops on the earth, untouched by things. So, no. I lived things hard and intensely and I'm from the earth, not from the sky.

—Louise Lecavalier[1]

It was always very much a dancer driven company. People assumed, 'Well, she's doing something extremely physical therefore she has to be forced into the idea. But no. As you can see now, with the way Louise is handling her career and the things that she does now are extremely physical, she's the one defining what she does. There's always been an attraction in her about excess, that's part of who she is and it dovetailed well in terms of my interests.

—Édouard Lock[2]

Non Non Non je ne suis pas Mary Poppins is the title of a short solo made and performed by Louise Lecavalier between 1981 and 1982. Danced on at least four different occasions, the work offers a snapshot of the pivotal moment when Lecavalier transforms in attitude and style from "ballet girl" to punk, woman to "cyborg," dancer to icon. Momentarily between

---

[1] Quoted in Raymond St-Jean, Dir. (2018) *Louise Lecavalier: Sur son cheval de feu*. 102 min. Ciné Qua Non Média. Filmoption International.
[2] Édouard Lock (2022).

projects with La La La Human Steps, the period represents a foray outside of the company structures that had raised her in dance, notably with Pointépiénu and Groupe Nouvelle Air (GNA). At the time, La La La's style was emergent; it had yet to realize its signature vocabulary and look. Revisiting *Non Non Non* through oral history accounts, journalistic descriptions from the period, and photographic documentation,[3] I argue that a careful reading allows for a deeper understanding of Lecavalier's material contribution to company aesthetic, repertoire and reputation. Part *cri de coeur*, part manifesto, *Non Non Non* offers a call to reject the disciplinary and gendered expectations placed on dancers as virtuosic instruments of choreographic vision; and reflects on the work of the dancer at a transitional moment between deindustrialization and financialization, when the nature of work itself as a generalized category appeared to be shifting.

Lecavalier was *principal* dancer with La La La Human Steps for nearly two decades. Yet the term only becomes a common descriptor in the 1990s, mid-way through her tenure, as the company grew larger, its structure more formalized, and its dancers more reliant on ballet as formative training. I read the term "principal" as a hindsight assessment of the centrality of Lecavalier to the company, while simultaneously marking the hierarchies of position that have structured so much dance historically. To think of hierarchy in dance is to invoke power in multiple directions: choreographer as director, author, and historic figure—often masculinized; and dancer as interpreter, instrument, and marginalized figure within dance history—often feminized. In her work on women in dance, Sally Banes traces the representations of women from the Romantic Ballet to postwar choreographies and finds the field "feminized" and its "texts" malleable and difficult to verify.[4]

---

[3] Whereas the limits of descriptive writing and photography to evidence the really real of history are well established, and acts of reading may always threaten to lead into interpretive games, the oral histories, written accounts, and photos for *Non Non Non* form an enticing set of clues around which to return to the work, not as truth but as a set of incomplete fragments that help us speculate on the work and its possible meanings.

[4] Sally Banes, *Dancing Women: Female Bodies Onstage* (New York: Routledge, 1998).

Lynn Matluck Brooks, in her study of early dance, describes the history of women in dance as "doubly invisible,"[5] twice confounded by gender bias and the "elusive" nature of dance as material. Such obstacles hover around the term "principal," as a marker of rank, a settling of relations between a singular performer and the company, and an invocation of the arduous categories of *value* within classical and theatrical forms of dance.

If Lecavalier would become central to the company's identity, the role of the choreographer within La La La was always clearly defined. By all accounts, Lock's unique vision, his unusually detailed and fluid gestural ability, his high charisma and radical ambitions had long clinched his leadership role as choreographer and author of work, both in his first company Lock Danseurs (1980–2) and in La La La Human Steps (1983–2015). Lecavalier, across many interviews, has celebrated Lock's invention and affirmed his vision:

> He worked with us all very particularly; he's never been the choreographer who just says improvise and then selects, he had the ideas. He made every single movement, on each person, for them. And we would react to the things he would suggest, elaborate. When he was not actually showing the movement—big jumps, for example, things he didn't do himself—we would try something and he would accept or reorient. He wasn't always in the studio, he didn't need to be … we'd rehearse alone to build the kinetics of the choreography.[6]

La La La co-founder and former Grands Ballets dancer Miryam Moutillet recalls: "We *loved* Édouard, I mean, we really loved him—we would have done anything for him."[7] Similarly, La La La musician and performer Michel Lemieux remembers, "I was an outsider with this group—I didn't know dance really and was surprised by how we worked in this hierarchical way. Édouard was the boss. And he was

---

[5] Lynn Matluck Brooks, *Women's Work: Making Dance in Europe Before 1800* (Madison, WI: University of Wisconsin Press, 2007), 3.
[6] Lecavalier (2012).
[7] Miryam Moutillet (2020).

a genius."⁸ These accounts—told to me by many others such that in tandem with looking at this work, I too fell in love—testify to Lock's creative leadership and primary role as choreographer.

Yet, at the company's inception, when Lecavalier made her solo, movement aesthetics developed through unmarked danced labor in ways that belied the orthodoxies of company structure and the familiar divisions of labor between choreographer and dancer and in movement structures such as the classical ballet's *pas de deux*. "We weren't really a company yet," Lecavalier recalls, "we were finding our language."⁹ The company's way of working was evolving but its material effort in the studio nonetheless anticipated the ideal of collaboration common amongst choreographers and dancers today. Over long hours in the studio, working in pairs and trios, the dancers elaborated Lock's movements and contributed new material or aesthetics: Moutillet, for instance, bringing gestural hand details akin to sign language to the company; Louis Guillemette, bringing the athleticism and weight sharing of contact improvisation; and Lemieux, a former theater student bringing an interdisciplinary approach to technology, sound, and music. Lecavalier joined in 1981, and at least initially it was unclear to her what she would contribute:

> When I first saw his work, I didn't think I could fit there ... It was the same people who were dancing with Groupe Nouvelle Air but in Édouard's work they were more spectacular, and more human. There was something really loose, the lines were loose. They walked onstage like ordinary people, they carried themselves in ordinary ways ... it was more quotidian; at the same time, they used what they needed. Édouard gave ... liberty in the technique. So that interested me.¹⁰

Lecavalier liked the work's complexity, array of materials, and its sense of necessity. But she was still very much searching, working with Daniel Lévéille and Paul-André Fortier among others. She had just left GNA, when Lock phoned to invite her to work on *Oranges: ou la recherche du*

---

[8] Michel Lemieux (2020).
[9] Lecavalier (2016).
[10] Ibid.

Figure 2.1 Flyer for *Non Non Non je ne suis pas Mary Poppins*. Photo: Jacques Perron. Image courtesy Louise Lecavalier/Fou Glorieux.

paradis (1981). At a pivotal moment for the company, between Lock Danseurs and the creation of the new company La La La, Lecavalier made *Non Non Non*; a short work, even a minor work to the extent that its viewership was limited and it has not entered the repertoire in any formal way. Nonetheless, it offers insight into the material contribution she made to the company's aesthetic, challenging long-held suspicions of critics about the limits of her agency under Lock's direction. More, it stands as a critical reflection on the work of the dancer; and, perhaps, anticipates shifts in the nature of work more broadly by century's end (Figure 2.1).

"They didn't know it was me": first-hand accounts

Somewhere between 1981 and 1982, Lecavalier made a 15-minute solo entitled, *Non Non Non je ne suis pas Mary Poppins*. The work was created during a period of study in New York, in between the productions of

Oranges (1981) and *Businessman in the Process of Becoming an Angel* (1983), at the urging of friend and company member Michel Lemieux who was putting together an evening of solo works with Miryam Moutillet and Louis Guillemette and invited her to join. It was a period of great turmoil for Lecavalier, unsure of her role within the company and in doubt about what she would do next. *Oranges* (1981), her first production as a dancer with Lock Danseurs, had been successful; critically beloved, with an extended run in Montréal and touring dates, she remained uncertain of her ability to perform the work and to fit into a company of stellar dancers. At the same time, the company was newly formed, the process was emergent and uneven—she wanted more rehearsal time, for herself and for the work.

Joining after what was a remarkably short induction into dance, beginning her training at 15, and working with Pointépiénu and GNA between 1977 and 1980, she wondered if she could keep up:

> I'm very hard on myself. I was thinking, "I'm the worst part of the show ... like, I hope I can disappear behind everyone else." I thought, "I'm not going to stay with this group for long—he's going to get rid of me soon" (laughing). Still ... "I'm so happy to be with them because they are fantastic and I love what they do—and I'm privileged to be here and I hope no one notices me ...." My feeling was, I'll never achieve that.[11]

Lecavalier's words mark the profound criticality that drove her to do more and try harder over a forty-year career in dance performance. It was a critique she would bring to bear on the material as much as on herself. Wary of praise, intensely uncomfortable with hype, her efforts, at times excessive by all accounts, would nonetheless serve as a galvanizing force within the company as they continued to refine their ideas.

In New York during a break from the *Oranges* production, and with a grant from the Canada Council to pursue further study in dance,[12] she

---

[11] Lecavalier (2011).
[12] From a press release for a tour of *Oranges*: many artist bios list funding awards from the Canada Council or Ministère des affaires culturelles du Québec. Tangente collection.

had the distance and the time to experiment outside these concerns; she remembers, "I think it was a good occasion for me to be free. Because I was so in admiration and awe of his [Édouard's] work at that time, it didn't let me be free." *Non Non Non* develops in this transitional space, temporarily away from her commitments to dance in Montréal, working where and when she could: in dance studios after class and in temporary digs, including the lofts of postmodern dancemaker Simone Forti and experimental performer Pooh Kaye. She first presented the solo in a combined program for twelve dancers at a studio showing in Manhattan;[13] and subsequently in Montréal, Vancouver, and Lennoxville, QC over 1982–3.[14]

What did Lecavalier do, and what did audiences see? *Non Non Non* was a structured improvisation, actively resistant to the elevated stature of "choreography," and leaning into performance art as a genre with its emphasis on visual image, theatricality, and politics, as well as ordinary and uncodified gestures alongside the vocabularies of modern and contemporary dance. In the dance, Lecavalier enters a darkened space, wearing sunglasses and carrying a backpack. She traces the walls, leaning on them, collapsing against them, and muttering to herself in an unscripted, stream-of-conscious way—as if lost. She turns the lights up, with a mimed expression of shock; she reacts as if the presence of the audience is unexpected. Then music starts; she remembers it was "something by [Astor] Piazzolla," and she dances briefly with high intensity, "throwing [her]self everywhere." At the very end, she throws the backpack on the floor and its contents—oranges, a notebook, glasses—spill out across the stage. She exits.

Lecavalier remembers that she worked on the movement for *Non Non Non* first—and that it felt "hard," that the process was stressful.

---

[13] Lecavalier (2016). As of date, no information about this event has turned up in my search of various archives.
[14] Montréal, QC: Véhicule Art (307 Ouest Rue Ste. Catherine); November 25–8 and December 16–19, 1982; alongside new work by Michel Lemieux (*L'Oeil rechargeable*) and Louis Guillemette (*Récolte du fou*). Performances happened as well as in New York; Vancouver; and at the University of Sherbrooke in July 1983.

The shadows of disciplinary training loomed large. With Lock, she had found a highly compelling creative partner and model choreographer, setting what she described as a very high standard for movement invention. At the same time, she held a generalized critique of the "step" as overly precious; she was resistant to choreography's privileged status. She remembers,

> I developed my own way of moving, throwing myself everywhere. And I thought, "Oh, at some point, I'm going to make some movement with my backpack, and then come in and go along the walls: collapse on the walls here and there, like this freaky person." That's how I was, in a way; I just exaggerated a little bit, to be more theatrical ... The main point was not to show some steps, it was to show a mental state, an emotional state.

Here, Lecavalier foregrounds expression and rejects the stature and stability of choreography as an historical form.

At the same time, she centers herself as the source of material, marking the danced image's overlap with her own identity and life experience at the time—at once committed to dance and quite critical of its orthodoxies; at once, working in dance and yet questioning her role there. She had left GNA in 1980, which had been the height of experimental dance in Québec and garnering considerable critical attention: "I saw what was happening ... It was becoming a regular company: less experimental, more judgmental ... the scope of the work was narrowing, and I left." Whereas GNA had been formative, with an open mix of artists and approaches to choreography, by 1980 its structure had become more routine, and Lecavalier felt it was becoming complacent. With *Non Non Non* she offers a portrait of the dancer starting anew, rejecting the comfort of the familiar and the priorities of established companies: her character acts solo and challenges the virtuosity expected of the dancer, literally climbing the walls and dropping the bag before walking offstage.

Recalled as tense, high-energy and *noiresque*, critical reaction was mostly positive. Dance writer Linde Howe-Beck, perhaps evidencing a pattern of low expectations for creative ideas from dancers, found *Non*

Non Non to be "surprising," "convincing," with Lecavalier described as a "lovely face," committed to giving the audience "pleasure."[15] Presenter/curator Dena Davida offered a more substantive assessment: "There was a long corridor, kind of murky, and I remember her sort of crawling along the walls rather than being in the center of the space. That was a strong image. And I felt she had something to say as a choreographer."[16] *Le Devoir* critic Suzanne Asselin gave the most detailed account, quoted here at length; Lecavalier, she writes,

> breaks the magical quality of the character Mary Poppins and makes us land on firm ground …. This punk anti-Poppins hits hard reality. She constantly stumbles against the walls (of reality perhaps), which become an extension of the floor. The sky doesn't exist. The raw light, the unbridled movement, the choppy rhythm, the precarious balances, the dynamic silhouette animated by a natural softness. She leaves, leaving only the contents of her purse. No dreams.[17]

These last two accounts, though brief, nonetheless confirm a vivid and critical image: the gendered figure in the spotlight, decentered; the verticality or uprightness and polish of dance, challenged; the capable façade of the iconic nanny/mother Mary Poppins, defaced. Working the registers of mimesis, theatricality, and exaggeration, *Non Non Non* appears to have prioritized expression over technique; dance over choreography; and critique over compliance, qualities that resonate deeply with La La La repertoire as it developed through the 1980s.

Equally, the objects chosen for the dance speak pointedly. The backpack recalls the day tripper or school kid, a less gendered artifact than, say, the handbag. The one who carries the backpack is prepared, competent; at the same time, the carrier has baggage, is weighted by history. But in throwing down the bag, its contents spill out and remain onstage after her exit. Does the gesture suggest a casting off of

---

[15] Linde Howe-Beck, "Lemieux Upstages Dancers." *Montreal Gazette*. November 27, 1982: D-6.
[16] Dena Davida (2014).
[17] Suzanne Asselin, "Solos entre la folie et la réel." *Le Devoir*. November 30, 1982: 6. [Translation by the author].

burdens, or a revelation of inner life? Is the rolling orange an assertion of independence from the company, a reference to *Oranges* as her sole engagement with Lock and the company to that point? Or is it a marker of the material and immaterial residues of performance—its remains and its excess? All of the above, and in dialogue with the notebook and sunglasses as equally symbolic objects, the gesture of objects falling out begs questions of authorship, understood as ownership of labor; and identity, as performative, emergent and spilling over.

Michel Lemieux remembers the piece vividly: "It was not dance, it was performance."

> You might have expected some overlap with what Édouard was doing but no. She was totally distinct .... It was really *brut*, really raw. It was the beginning of the Louise of today, very different than what she did in La La La.[18]

Lemieux and Lock had visited Lecavalier in New York when she was working on the piece and, while there, they made a short work entitled, "Dishes," possibly for the 10th Anniversary Benefit for the performance space, the Kitchen.[19] He remembered an evening at Pooh Kaye's loft in New York, where Kaye improvised an animal dance for half an hour from a new show she was working on; for a sustained period of time, Kaye moved around the contours of the space, totally focused, completely transformed in a way that "blew their minds." Michel thinks this might have been an influence: "It was clear that, with *Non Non Non*, Louise was improvising on the canvas."[20] For Lecavalier, the time in New York constituted an important breakthrough for her work with the company; she remembers, "I think Édouard could see what I could do and after that he let me loose in his work ... he trusted my intuitive, performative sense."

In genre and attitude, *Non Non Non* hovers somewhere between dance and performance, best situated alongside much of the solo

---

[18] Michel Lemieux (2020).
[19] June 14–15, 1981.
[20] Lemieux (2020).

performance emergent in the late 1970s and early 1980s, closely linked within Canada to the rise of artist-run centers and small performance spaces, including clubs;[21] and to harsh political and economic times that compelled a critical stance. Solo performance sought out uncodified, ordinary, or expressive gestures; blurred distinctions between dance and performance art; and included in Canada figures like Marie Chouinard, Robin Poitras, and Elizabeth Chitty; and, in the United States, Elizabeth Streb, and Pooh Kaye. With its crucially small-scale economy and compact, portable structures, solo performance provided a critical forum to foreground matters of identity and politics as written on the body. Notably, it prefigures the rise of independent choreographers and project-based work in response to shifts in funding and increased economic precarity to come by the end of the 1980s.[22]

The dance presented a counter-vision and critique of the idea of the dancer as analogous to Mary Poppins, the character from P. L. Travers' 1934 book by the same name and popularized in Lecavalier's time by the 1964 film from Disney.[23] If Disney's Poppins was eternally cheerful and unflappable in her position as Nanny, she was also *magic*—that is, and borrowing from anthropological accounts of how cultures come to see something as magic, her labor had *an effect that bore no relation to a cause that could be seen—its skill was hidden*.[24] Poppins' role as a nanny offered Lecavalier an iconic form of reproductive labor on which

---

[21] For more, see Diana Nemiroff, "A History of Artist-Run Spaces in Canada, with Particular Reference to Véhicule, A Space and the Western Front" (MA Thesis, Concordia University, 1985).

[22] Hetty Blades unpacks the increasing precarity of contemporary dancer to show "how the socioeconomic contexts of dance artists and ontology of dance are intrinsically linked and have drawn attention to the evolving shape of choreographic work and works." Hetty Blades, "Projects, Precarity and the Ontology of Dance Works." *Dance Research Journal* 51, no. 1 (2019): 66–78; 67.

[23] See P. L. Travers, *Mary Poppins* (New York: Clarion Books, 2006/1934). For scholarship on Poppins, see Ellen Dooling Draper and Jenny Koralek, Eds., *A Lively Oracle: A Centenary Celebration of P.L. Travers, Creator of Mary Poppins* (New York: Larson Publications, 1999); Jerry Griswold, "'Mary Poppins' Creator P.L. Travers Is Even More Fascinating than Her Fiction." *Washington Post*. December 14, 2018; Edwina Burness and Jerry Griswold, "The Art of Fiction LXXIII: PL Travers," *Paris Review* (1982): 210–29.

[24] See Marcel Mauss, *A General Theory of Magic* (New York, London: Routledge, 2001).

to ruminate; as a domestic worker, the nanny is associated with the gendered, invisible labor of childrearing. What's more, the domestic work of the nanny makes possible the public work of the bourgeois elite, in this case the family breadwinner and patriarch Mr. Banks. Echoing the way in which danced labor underwrites choreography yet typically has emained hidden in performance, Lecavalier's account of the magic nanny shows the work.

For dance scholar Ariel Osterweis, one of the mechanisms through which dance has typically concealed its labor is through the phenomenon of virtuosity; she writes, "virtuosity is characterized by nonchalance in the face of overachievement."[25] She links this kind of excellence in dance to excess or surpluses in movement and affect that challenge critical vocabularies and modes of reception.[26] Osterweis notes the critical discomfort generated by the virtuoso, alternately beloved or criticized as "too much," helping to account for early readings of Lecavalier's *oeuvre* and Lecavalier herself that have tended towards pathology in terms of seeing the work as violent, risky, or otherwise masochistic. Cooper Albright, for instance, sees in her dance a cultural anxiety wherein "hyper-fit bodies flash across the stage in a flare of immediacy that is always threatening to burn itself out."[27] The virtuoso cranks up affective response, and the dancing seems too hard, too fast, too much; the virtuoso is hard to assimilate, challenging descriptive powers and received ideas of how and what is valued.

Lecavalier's own recollection of the piece is particularly telling; she remembers that she was developing the image of *reacting* to the audience, unusual within the context of contemporary dance's pattern

---

[25] Ariel Osterweis, "Disavowing Virtuosity, Performing Aspiration: Choreographies of Anticlimax in the Work of Yve Laris Cohen, Narcissister, and John Jasperse." In *Futures of Dance Studies*, ed. Susan Manning, Janice Ross, and Rebecca Schneider (Madison, WI: University of Wisconsin Press, 2020), 431–44; 434.

[26] Ariel Osterweis, "The Muse of Virtuosity: Desmond Richardson, Race and Choreographic Falsetto." *Dance Research Journal* 45, no. 3 (December 2013): 53–74.

[27] Ann Cooper-Albright, *Choreographing Difference: The Body and Identity in Contemporary Dance* (Middletown, CT: Wesleyan University Press, 1997), 55. See too: Ann Cooper-Albright, *Engaging Bodies: The Politics and Poetics of Corporeality* (Middletown, CT: Wesleyan University Press, 2013).

of cool regard. Her crafted image of being lost onstage produced a strange confusion one evening for at least one audience member:

> On the second night, I came onstage and somebody thought I was really lost; they dragged me to sit in the audience. And I thought, "This is going to ruin the show, they didn't know it was me." When I started onstage, and they came up to me, I was thinking "Oh my god, somebody wants to do contact improvisation." I was—eeah!—moving with him and then I realized, "Whoa, he's sitting me down here [in the front row of seats]." I stood up again and went back on stage.[28]

The misread evidences the significant overlap between the performed character and Lecavalier herself as source materials for creative work, and finds the dancer literally grappling with the gendered dynamics of power rooted in notions of realism and the strictures of socially codified identity. In her work on feminist performance circa the 1980s, Lynda Hart notes the phenomenon wherein "the female body on stage appears to be the 'thing itself,' incapable of mimesis, afforded not only no distance between sign and referent but, indeed, taken for the referent."[29] Yet if sight allowed for the error, the agency of performance—"I stood up again ..."—offered a corrective. The tension between the real and the performed, the dance and its viewership, between virtuosity and the performed critique of virtuosity animated a work that matched the fury and agency of hyper-kinetics ("I flung myself all over") with a story that arced from tentative arrival to powerful exit: the throwing down of the bag, the refusal to carry more.

The critical appropriation of female heroes from across literature and history has been a common strategy within twentieth-century performance art; feminist performance scholar Rebecca Schneider sees such appropriations as "the manipulation of an interval for critical analysis toward the potentialities of an "otherwise."[30] That is, the

---

[28] Lecavalier (2016).
[29] Lynda Hart, "Introduction." In *Acting Out: Feminist Performances*, ed. Lynda Hart and Peggy Phelan (Ann Arbor, MI: University of Michigan Press, 1993), 1–12; 5.
[30] Rebecca Schneider, "In Our Hands: An Ethics of Gestural Response-Ability." *Performance Philosophy* 3, no. 1 (2017): 108–25; 110.

reference to the "then" of the character and the "now" of the performance creates distance, inviting audiences into a critical reflexivity. Lecavalier's Poppins evidences this temporal layering, which served as a shorthand and orienting referent: an invocation of the popular as a way to avoid having to tell a story in the work and, thus, foreground its gestural politics and expressive movement. Expectations of proximity between the dancer as subject and the character as representation remained in productive ambiguity, as *Non Non Non* showed viewers the requirement to virtuosity expected of both dancer and nanny. The effect was to cast out an excess of meaning to challenge received notions of the gendered performing body as idealized, productive, and controlled.

Or, as José Esteban Muñoz puts it, "sometimes misrecognition can be tactical."[31] For the misrecognition described above marks a resistance to Lecavalier's performance, returning us to cultural attitudes of the 1980s and the pervasive presence of patriarchal thinking today.[32] More, it underscores Lecavalier's solo as a mode of "disidentifying";[33] beyond its defiant title, and not only for the ways it troubles the image of Mary Poppins as magical "Other" in terms of gender and class, *Non Non Non* charts a nuanced path, *showing* a physical and emotional excess that challenged viewers to rethink virtuosic female labor within the valorizing economy of productivity and excellence as control. Thinking again of Muñoz's work, he writes, "Identification itself can … be manipulated and worked in ways that promise narratives of self that surpass the limits prescribed by the dominant culture."[34] To disidentify is to find a third path, a way more ambiguous way than simply to oppose. Lecavalier's Poppins is at once performing for the audience and reacting to the audience, at once skillful and critiquing skill, feminized (she wears a dress) yet breaking

---

[31] José Esteban Muñoz, "The White to Be Angry: Vaginal Davis's Terrorist Drag." *Social Text* 52/53, vol. 15, nos. 3 and 4 (1997): 80–103; 82.

[32] Especially after the fall of *Roe v Wade* in the United States in June 2022 and the rise of Right-wing, fundamentalist political projects internationally.

[33] See Muñoz: "Disidentification resists the interpolating call of ideology that fixes a subject within the state power apparatus. It is a reformatting of self within the social, a third term that resists the binary of identification and counter-identification." "The White to Be Angry," 83.

[34] Ibid., 82.

expectations associated with feminized dance performance: at once, too much and not enough.

Lecavalier's interest in Mary Poppins didn't take the form of prolonged study; her research was in the studio, and in her own lived experience, yet it nonetheless resonated with co-temporaneous feminist writings that sought to trouble the link between vision, representation, and identity.[35] The best of feminist performance marked "a critical effort to free the female body from its overdeterminations as a body saturated with sex, site of pleasure for (an)other, subjected and devoid of subjectivity."[36] Whereas Lecavalier's focus remained unwaveringly on the act of dancing and dancemaking rather than on explanations of the work's value, our conversation about *Non Non Non* nevertheless ended with the following assessment:

> There were people doing this, taking on "beauty" and making anti-aesthetics, I wasn't the first ... but it is always necessary, we're still learning this. And it's like feminism. *Rien est gagné*, it's not over. You have to keep going.[37]

"I became myself": photographic accounts

At some point that year, the photographer Jack Udashkin made a set of studio images of Lecavalier performing *Non Non Non* (Figure 2.2). Udashkin remembers that the images were not made explicitly for promotion; instead, making photos was just another part of what they did, how they worked, as a group of artists profoundly engaged with the visual image, its power to circulate and the critical information it could provide about bodies, movement, and the landscape of contemporary

---

[35] Peggy Phelan, *Unmarked: The Politics of Performance* (New York, London: Routledge, 1993).
[36] Hart, "Introduction," 5.
[37] Lecavalier (2016). In a 2024 read through of this chapter, she added: "Every single reassessment of your power or position as a woman has a big value."

Figure 2.2 A portion of the contact sheet for *Non Non Non je ne suis pas Mary Poppins* (c.1982). Photo: Jack Udashkin.

life.[38] Udashkin, a polymath producer and curator who was then working with Margie Gillis, was also a self-taught photographer and his ubiquitous presence within the Montréal performance scene as a producer, manager, friend, and fan meant he had the chance to shoot freely in back-stage, behind-the-scenes, and after-hours moments.[39] The images, then, were not goal oriented but rather part of a collective process, or creative scene as "cultural laboratory."[40] Making images within La La La's circle was a methodology for doing as much as for seeing. Understood as an incomplete set, the photos nonetheless provide a glimpse of Lecavalier's emergent identity and material clues about her dance.

What is immediately visible is her nascent physical transformation from ballet girl towards punk icon. In Udashkin's photos, Lecavalier has cut her hair, short at the sides, longish at the back: more mullet than punk, and newly dyed black, in what was a strategic effort to distance herself from the conventions of the ballerina and the expectations of docility associated with a young blond girl.[41] She has described these revisions of style and self-image as an explicit rejection of stereotypes in dance and for women; and she remembers,

> I became myself at some point. It was hard to become yourself in dance—the technique that I had learned was to be like everybody else, to hold on tip-toe and jump as high as everyone else. You had to be with the others. There were all these rules. Which was good to learn but you can get stuck.[42]

Also slipping into view is the appearance of the muscled dancer, the hard body that would become such a point of discussion around Lecavalier and La La La Human Steps—what I take to be a shorthand

---

[38] Jack Udashkin (2020).
[39] Lecavalier remembers Udashkin was just "around," a reflection of the intimacy of the scene and Udashkin's involvement in a variety of capacities within it. They were not shooting formally for promotional purposes, nor for any reason other than to make images. Udashkin had a love of dance and an ongoing practice in photography, including street photography and performance documentation. He does not recall the shoot.
[40] Will Straw (2002), "Scenes and Sensibilities." *Public*, no. 22/23 (2002): 245–57.
[41] Lecavalier (2016).
[42] Lecavalier (2012).

into the work's complexity. Visible musculature has long been antithetical to ballet culture; some muscles can be worked, others need to remain hidden. The presence of muscles has tended to be policed along gender lines across many forms of elite movement, sport, and body training. Tanya Bunsell, in her work on female bodybuilding, notes that "muscles have always been associated with men, as a signifier of masculinity, strength and power."[43] Whereas other performers of the time, notably body builder Lisa Lyon, immortalized in photographs by Robert Mapplethorpe, had laid waste to the notion that muscles are uniquely the terrain of the masculine, part of Lecavalier's legacy was to build and reveal her muscles, not as simple adornment nor as political provocation, but to power iconic moves like lifting her male partners in what remains a radical revision of the division of labor for dance.

In the 1980s and 1990s, writers were not so sure. By the late 1980s, the extremity of her musculature, in tandem with the speed and perceived violence in the La La La repertoire, appeared to many less as a sign of agency, more as an abject, dangerous, or yet another unrealistic goal of visual perfection. Writing contemporaneously with La La La's production *Infante, c'est destroy* (1991), Ann Cooper Albright challenges the ready association of musculature with power; and notes a tension between Lecavalier's muscles and a gendered use of weight and space that feels "coerced." She writes, "Her body tends to move as a series of disconnected parts ... Because she lets go of any spatial intention with her movement, her dancing can take on a brutal, almost masochistic quality."[44] Susan Leigh Foster, in her classic essay on the ballerina as phallus, written in part with Lecavalier in mind, expressed concern with the segmentation and isolation of body parts for the dancer through escalating and oppressive training protocols:

> The harder-edged bodies, the abstract geometries, the athleticism found in today's productions do not substantively alter the surround

---

[43] Tanya Bunsell, *Strong and Hard Women: An Ethnography of Female Bodybuilding* (New York: Routledge, 2013), 40.

[44] Cooper-Albright, *Choreographing Difference*, 49.

of cultural and aesthetic issues, inherited from the nineteenth century, that continue to define ballet today.⁴⁵

Scholarly literature, perhaps echoing the journalism that tended to second her work to the role of muse, questioned just how progressive Lecavalier's physicality and stage presence was; its strength and skill viewed as spectacle, too easily aligned with marketing and commodification.⁴⁶ Control, it seemed, had to be remote, in the hands of the choreographer, and the location of skill as elsewhere was codified through multiple descriptions of her as muse, machine, cyborg.

Lecavalier lived it differently. She remembers, "Everything in movement was interesting to me—I thought, I know so little and so I have to learn everything. I wasn't someone who went to the gym to work on this or that muscle…. I only worked to find the movement."⁴⁷

> At the beginning, I had bruises—because I had no muscles, I couldn't do the big jumps. But as I developed and learned and practiced the ways of doing it, the muscles appeared.

Lemieux remembered an extremity of training across the company in the early day; he recalled seeing bodybuilding magazines at Lock and Moutillet's apartment and felt this may have been part of company culture.⁴⁸ He remembered seeing Lecavalier walking around with weights on her forearms and legs, in everyday contexts, to build strength;⁴⁹ and he situated this within a range of body modification practices associated with the period. "She worked very hard and was *très exigeante*—very demanding of herself." Lecavalier too remembers

---

⁴⁵ Susan Leigh Foster, "The Ballerina's Phallic Pointe." In *Corporealities: Dancing Knowledge, Culture, Power*, ed. Susan Leigh Foster (London: Routledge, 1995), 1–26; 7–8.
⁴⁶ Ibid., 7.
⁴⁷ Lecavalier (2010).
⁴⁸ Michel Lemieux (2020).
⁴⁹ Lecavalier remembers this as a kind of misplaced understanding of how to develop strength as the company developed its vocabulary; she and others in the company attached small weights to their arms and legs for "maybe a week." "These were tiny little weights … it didn't work, and we didn't do it for long." Lecavalier (2024).

the intensity of those early days, admitting that in hindsight her drive could be misinterpreted.

Yet preparing the body for dance is part of the work of dancing; for her, that meant, at different times over different years, dance classes across multiple forms and a complementary training regime that included running (a favorite practice for building stamina), cycling, boxing, swimming, the elliptical machine, yoga, and PerfMax.[50] Her most formative work, however, was at the studio in rehearsal. She describes a materialist discovery of her body: it grew and developed durationally, through hours in the studio and an emergent sense of what was required to do the work. This is the manual labor of dance—at once necessary to its production, yet often unpaid and surplus to the limits of dance as a form of employment, unmarked, easily lost to history.

Labor transforms, and muscles index manual labor. Lecavalier's muscles modeled a substantially different kind of dancer. They powered new moves—spectacular lifts, athletic floor work, heightened speed—that challenged a stale division of labor within concert dance wherein male dancers jumped and lifted, and women appeared weightless or on display. Lecavalier belied expectations of dancers as sylphs and confounded illusions of weightless, suspended in air dancing. She raised questions for viewers about the very nature of the body they were seeing. As critics in the popular press wondered if she was a man or a woman, spectators described the excitement of witnessing powerful movement that shook up the gender binary as it existed at the time. Whereas developing one's body can always be read as "normalizing" to the extent it produces disciplined bodies and feelings of control and power, context is key here. Lecavalier's emergent strong body would go on to challenge visually and performatively the conventions of the ballerina and the modern dancer as understood in the 1980s; hard, athletic, lifting rather than lifted; and part of a

---

[50] PerfMax is a Montréal-based gym (1995–) that emphasizes training for effective kinesthetic and proprioceptive performance.

Figure 2.3 Lecavalier in *Non Non Non* (c.1982). Photo: Jack Udashkin.

close-knit ensemble, performing shared tasks rather than appearing as ballet's *etoile*. To cite queer scholar Paul Morrison, "a body that openly declares itself 'built,' not born, necessarily challenges the operations by which gender understood as the body's naturally given imperatives, come to organize the erotic field."[51] Yet Lecavalier's motivation remained on the side of dance research: to know more in the work, for the intensity of the questions she felt driven to ask as well as for the sheer pleasure of effort, the physical high of endorphins and the fun of working with friends.

If Udashkin's contact sheet evidences the dancer in the early phase of a physical transformation, it is equally suggestive of *Non Non Non*'s movement qualities, aesthetic and critique. His camera follows the action mainly through mid-shots, emphasizing the face, arms, and upper torso, in what I take as his reading of the work's most significant

---

[51] Paul Morrison, *The Explanation for Everything: Essays on Sexual Subjectivity* (New York: New York University Press, 2001), 115.

features—Lecavalier's profound attachment to expression, evidenced here in work with the bodily features most readily associated with identity and non-verbal forms of communication: the face, hands, and arms. If the history of Western theatrical dance has tended to fetishize the legs of the dancer, one could read the photographic focus here as a counterview emphasizing subjectivity. Of course, this recalls La La La's use of hand gestures and non-verbal language, already on view in *Oranges* (1981). Reading this account, Lecavalier noted that legs powered the work, too—notably in running and jumps that equally underwrote the work's momentum and hinted at the fully articulated athletics of La La La repertoire to come. In these frames, I see the horizon tilt: the dancer claiming space, arms and legs spread laterally, thrown out wide; head and torso skewed, leaning, reaching; the body muscled and angled differently, anticipating the achievements of La La La's *off-axis* technique as it would be fully articulated by *Human Sex* (1984) (Figure 2.3).

The "more" of virtuosic labor

Something further haunts me in these images, suggestive of the material conditions for working dancers circa the 1980s: the figure of the dancer with her back against a wall. The cinder block walls of the performance space, the makeshift costume, a sleeveless dress on loan from Miryam Moutillet. Lighting is improvised, her friend Jack takes the pictures, a friend hams it up offscreen compelling her smile. This is a DIY economy, makeshift and small scale. Fun to be sure. And yet: exhausting, at times dangerous, always contingent, and money too tight to mention.

At the time, Lecavalier lived hand-to-mouth, staying with friends, sleeping on sofas or else sharing spaces with several roommates; paid employment included occasional teaching and paid performance work. She received one grant to study in New York, at a time when state funding for individual artists and fledgling companies was abundant, fueled perhaps by national and provincial tensions and a focus on cultural programming as a critical tool in the assertion of a national culture.[52] She recalls, "At some point, there was some money—I think by *Human Sex* (1985), we were paid $350 a week. For a period of time. We'd work as long as possible, but sometimes the company would have no money, then we'd go on unemployment. And we'd still work, still rehearse."[53] Moutillet remembers that she and Lock prioritized grant writing through it all, on principle: "It might not last long, but we paid dancers." Company manager George Skalkogiannis remembers a more informal way of working; "When they needed money, they'd stop by the office; if there was money, I'd write a cheque."

To contemplate such material conditions today is to mark the turn to productivity as absolute logic, across a decade of "free" trade policy in North America from Reagan's "common market" speech of 1980 to the signing of the tri-lateral NAFTA (1994) agreement that would seal the fate of the city's working class. Prioritizing finance and investment rather than working people and jobs, the economic scenography pried open space for some, while crushing others; and foretold a shift to the so-called knowledge economy, wherein illusory notions of progress and individual merit continued to veil the losses of capitalism. In Montréal, manufacturing employment fell 70 percent between 1967 and 1988; and manual forms of labor like the construction industry in which Lecavalier's father worked receded from view and from value.

Clare Leigh La Berge, in her discussion of decommodified labor as "everyday unwaged yet formal and professional work," argues for "the aesthetic as a sphere of cultural production and consumption that offers a fleeting respite—even for a moment, even if contingent—from the capitalist imperative to buy and sell

---

[52] Between 1973 and 1983, Canada Council funding increased from 19 million to 60 million (*Canada Year Book* 1985, 469).
[53] Lecavalier (2020).

labour."⁵⁴ That optimism is certainly apparent in the early days of La La La, where good friends, cheap rent, and state funding helped underwrite the work of dance, and wage labor was to be avoided, for the way it stole time and added boredom. Yet such optimism would sit uncomfortably alongside the realities experienced by many concert dancers by the 1990s: at once, the devaluation of virtuosity, understood as politically suspect or as a commodity; and, simultaneously the expansion of hidden labor, evidenced in the field's drive towards increasing technical mastery, often the sole responsibility of the dancer as company support diminishes and the self-produced project model becomes the norm.⁵⁵

Lecavalier's short reflection on work appears at this moment of transition, as access to work and financial stability—never guaranteed, especially for cultural workers—wained. Within the structure of La La La, dance work fueled others kinds of labor that blurred the lines between the creative and other tasks. In the early days, for example, dancers engaged in tacit, informal activities that might be loosely understood as rehearsal direction and/or production management. At the center of the creative work in the studio, Lecavalier was also active in logistical planning, such that this existed at the time. Lecavalier remembers,

> There was a time when it felt too *n'importe quoi* schedule-wise; I thought it needed organization. And I hope I'm not wrong about this, but I think I was the one to start organizing it a bit. Before I started with the company, for sure other dancers did this too. And maybe this could have happened with other dancers in my time, but I was a good communicator.⁵⁶

---

[54] Claire Leigh La Berge, *Wages Against Artwork: Decommodified Labour and the Claims of Socially Engaged Art* (Durham, NC: Duke University Press, 2019), 11. See too Judith Hamera, who writes: "Ballet soloists ... beckon spectators with the phantasmic possibility of artisanal ownership of one's own labour, through efforts so exceptional and so sublime they transcend gravity." In Judith Hamera, "The Romance of Monsters: Theorizing the Virtuoso Body." *Theatre Topics* 10, no 2 (2000): 144–53.

[55] Hetty Blades, "Projects, Precarity and the Ontology of Dance Works." *Dance Research Journal* 51, no. 1 (2019): 66–78.

[56] Lecavalier (2020).

In the end, I had to get to work and understand it in my own way. Just working, working, working and finally to make schedules and have order and have reflection on this thing: why it's working, why it's not working …. It wasn't like I was a kind of authority, Édouard was the boss. With the dancers, we were equal. But I was like, "Let's go! Let's do it again, let's do it again." I could ask to do it twenty-five times, and I wouldn't even notice if people were angry. Maybe they would be like, "She's crazy." But, in the end, they trusted me, I guess, because we went further, and the movement evolved.[57]

George Skalkogiannis remembers checking in with Lecavalier first before booking tours to sort the company's availability; he recalls,

La La La could have happened without her, but not that fast and not that good. You can have an idea but someone has to make it a reality—and you need someone working at that level …. I used to fall asleep and wake up, she'd still be there rehearsing. And Louise took the leadership in the studio and on stage …. I mean, Édouard would disappear. But who was going to take care? He would come back with some interesting ideas that would take six months to get done, but the dancers worked on it steadily. I remember one show in Vancouver, it wasn't ready, it flopped the first night. But then it was revised, restructured and the next night we got a standing ovation. That was Louise.[58]

Across these different accounts, I underscore the combination of affective labor—the intellectual, collaborative, and socio-managerial tasks—*and* manual labor, with its arduous levels of physical work in the studio and preparatory training for readiness, that came together to make the work possible. Feminist philosopher Silvia Federici has described domestic labor as "the reproduction of the most important

---

[57] Lecavalier (2011).
[58] George Skalkogiannis (2020). Lecavalier remembers the Vancouver show differently and recalled an excellent response from audience and critics. "What was hard was that we rehearsed all day long so we were dead tired by the time we got to the theatre. When we set foot on stage … we came on like three monsters, exploding with all these kilowatts of energy, Marc, Claude and me. We thought, how can we keep going at this level?! The show is an hour and a half." Lecavalier (2024).

commodity capital has: the worker's capacity to work."⁵⁹ Within the ensemble of La La La, the combination of informal tasks and danced labor conjoined with material impact for the company, none more significant than its capacity to perform.

Ultimately, her identity becomes the signature for the company, from *Human Sex* (1984) onwards, featured in media and promotional material and written about widely in the international press. With her powerhouse moves and androgynous physicality and look,⁶⁰ Lecavalier will go on to become central to the image of the company as cultural vanguard. After *Businessman in the Process of Becoming an Angel* (1983), a number of members left the company, including Moutillet, Guillemette, and Lemieux. Lemieux remembers the aesthetic shifted thereafter,

> It was Louise, the energy of Louise ... The company became more punk, more risk, the sound more industrial. I think it came a lot from Louise, from the rebellion of Louise.

Whereas Lecavalier is today internationally recognized and indisputably a star, named Officer of the Order of Canada (2008) and Companion of the Ordre des arts et des lettres du Québec (2015), that status—and the notion of her as Principal—wasn't a given in 1981. She had only been dancing for six years; and was acutely aware of her lack of training. "Anyone was better than me," Lecavalier said, in what was perhaps then a fair assessment, mitigated by an unusual commitment to work. Skalkogiannis remembers that, whereas members of the downtown—the hairdressers, video artists, theater and production people, designers, and bar staff—were supportive and excited by the company, the established institutions were not so sure: "The Canada

---

[59] Silvia Federici, "Precarious Labor: A Feminist Viewpoint." *Variant* 37 (Spring/Summer 2010); 23–5; 24.
[60] It's worth noting the importance of context here; whereas today notions of flexible imagery might feed a neoliberal narrative, then the ambiguity of gender and sexuality contained in her image was part of its political power and represented a true challenge to the gender binary.

Council were worried about funding us—they didn't know if we were a dance company, or a rock band."[61] Recognition would come later, as a rear-view supplement that elides the time-based effort that shifts some combination of talent and interest towards developed technical skill and then again something more.

One way to understand Lecavalier's own virtuosity is through the notion of work ethic;[62] that is, her unusually strong work drive to dance that shaped the company's aesthetic in palpable ways. Across multiple accounts and recollections from colleagues and from Lecavalier, the commitment to practice and effort shone through. Lock remembered,

> She was absolutely focused on exploring dance, that really was her prime concern …. She put an inordinant amount of effort into everything …. For both of us, nothing else mattered.[63]

Guillemette recalled a drive that could border on pathology: "When rehearsal was done, it was done. We'd leave and go into the city and have drinks. She would keep going, she had to keep going." Lemieux recalled one afternoon at Véhicule Arts:

> It's like I said, she's a tank. So, move or die, that's it. She has to do something, and she's doing it. There's no hesitation. There's no fear, no sense of risk. She's a bit daredevil, you know—she was crazy even. And I saw Louise in rehearsals—wow! I'd be improvising, and Édouard and Louise would be saying, "Oh, this is good—keep that, do it again." And then I'd improvise, and they'd say, "Do it again." I saw Louise falling, taking a hit to her head, and collapsing … And we'd be like, maybe we have to call an ambulance …? No. She'd take a few minutes. And then she did it again.[64]

---

[61] George Skalkogiannis (2020).
[62] I am indebted to American curator Helen Molesworth's terrific account of postwar visual artists contemplating the nature of work. Helen Molesworth, "Work Ethic." In *Work Ethic*, ed. Helen Molesworth (Baltimore, MD: Baltimore Museum of Art, 2003), 25–52.
[63] Édouard Lock, "The Canadian Choreographer Édouard Lock Brings His Apocalyptic Vision Back to Britain." *The London Times*, Tuesday October 22, 1996, 26.
[64] Michel Lemieux (2020). Note that Jack Udashkin and George Skalkogiannis recall similar moments.

That drive is easily pathologized, perhaps more so today within the context of early twenty-first-century corporate domination, with its need for "high" performance; "performance measurements" and ubiquitous faith in "performance reviews" across many everyday work contexts. Performance Studies scholar Jon McKenzie notes the tension between this top-down pressure to perform and the potential of cultural performance as resistant and transgressive, affirming performance's potential to operate as a "normative force."[65] Yet Lecavalier's intensity is at least partly a function of the work of the dancer generally—that is, to develop capacity in skilled or specialized forms of movement, sustained training and effort are required. As Osterweis has pointed out, "virtuosity cannot be theorized in the absence of technique."[66] Lecavalier's technical precision is well known, and it has enabled an unusually rich depth of research and capacity in performance. The solo *Non Non Non* evidenced a crafted theatrical entrance and exit that bookended a danced hyperkinetics of the kind she would become known for. Less about deskilling or totally rejecting technique, with *Non Non Non* she used the creative tools available to her to call out virtuosity as a problematic.

Critiques of virtuosity, and reflections on danced labor, had happened before. From the union affiliations of modernist dance activists in New York in the 1930s to the task-based dances associated with Judson Dance Theater in the 1960s, work as subject and method for dance had happened before. Notably, choreographers had already shown the material effort of dance, as it is, *sans* representation—perhaps best typified in Yvonne Rainer's *Parts of Some Sextets* (1965) wherein dancers lug mattresses across the stage demonstrating the manual knack and arduous weight of doing so in cool, matter-of-fact terms. Or alternately, in *Trio A*, with its anti-heroic phrasing and inward

---

[65] Jon McKenzie, *Perform or Else: From Discipline to Performance* (London, New York: Taylor & Francis, 2001), 15.
[66] Osterweis, "Disavowing Virtuosity," 433.

expressions, Rainer marks the affective labor of dance performance in the disciplined refusal of the spectator's gaze.[67]

Non Non Non, by contrast, distills a fragmented, critical narrative of gendered labor, using theatrical, danced, and gestural forms to call attention to virtuosity as a problematic. Lecavalier's critique of virtuosity as at once narrowly prescribed and compelled in asymmetrical, gendered and classed ways situates itself within the high-contrast, gestural forms of 1980s performance art and dance-theater. Simply put, Lecavalier tells a story about labor through danced allusion to narrative and spectacular kinesthetics, at once performing virtuosically and critiquing virtuosity. The difference follows dance scholar Judith Hamera's distinction between dances that depict something *as* work, that is, in taking on representational and thematic elements of work; and the fact that dance *is* work, ever making use of laboring bodies that are "hyper-disciplined, hyper-labouring and hyper-visible."[68]

The two need not be exclusive, as Hamera notes, and certainly there was overlap within *Non Non Non* where three possible virtuosos appear at once: the Mary Poppins of the title, whose domestic labor enables the Banks' parents to manage family and business as upper-class elites; the freaky character being created on stage, who rejects the archetype of Mary Poppins and refuses the illusions of performed labor and gender; and Lecavalier herself, the mover/thinker/worker through whom the dance is performed. Across each, virtuosity as phenomenal skill and performed excess is offered up for consideration. Across each, the work of the dancer slips into view along two planks: dance as affective and cognitive labor, bound by convention, company practice, and audience gaze; and dance as manual labor, formed through ongoing effort in the

---

[67] Mark Franko reads this iconic work as "objectifying effort" and describes "task work" as dismantling the distinction between work and leisure. To my mind, the work cannot be read outside of its critique of gender in dance—and so, it is less about labor per se than about invoking gendered laboring bodies as a problematic. See Mark Franko, "Dance, the De-Materialization of Labor, and the Productivity of the Corporeal." In *Choreographing Discourses: A Mark Franko Reader* (London: Routledge, 2018), 203.

[68] Hamera, "The Romance of Monsters," 147.

studio and on stage, and by daily physical training required to produce skilled performance.

Paolo Virno, in his discussion of immaterial labor and the pianist Glenn Gould, observes that the virtuoso performs "*an activity which finds its own fulfillment (that is, its own purpose) in itself,* without objectifying itself into an end product, without settling into a 'finished product,' or into an object which would survive the performance."[69] Since this work, others have turned to the dance virtuoso particularly as "the figure par excellence of immaterial labor itself."[70] Federici, however, cautions against the hyperbole of immaterial labor, which simultaneously universalizes and hides again the working body as production machine.[71] Notions of immaterial labor have tended to emphasize the intangible, ephemeral aspects of performance—its irreproducibility, even as they have generated a misrecognition that allows for the continued separating out of manual and cognitive forms. The residuals of performance—that is, the bodies, histories, and practices produced by acts of dancing—continue to, in fact, perform beyond the proscenium event, as per Lecavalier's crafted body, "hyper" kinesthetics, material performance, and circulating imagery.

Hamera, who describes virtuosity as a dramatic encounter between performer and viewer, a relational economy collectively understood and sanctioned,[72] finds that virtuosity is nothing short of a "highly allegorical, nostalgic activation of imagined, idealized relationships between the body and work abandoned by the relentless motility of capital."[73] Her work helps account for the discursive excess around our understanding of the virtuoso—at once, generating excitement and anxiety around performed

---

[69] Paolo Virno, "On Virtuosity." In *A Grammar of the Multitude: For an Analysis of Contemporary Forms of Life* (New York, Los Angeles: Semiotext(e), 2004), 52–5; 52, original italics.
[70] Mark Franko and André Lepecki, Eds., "Editor's Note: Dance in the Museum." *Dance Research Journal* 46, no. 3 (2014): 1–4; 4.
[71] Federici, "Precarious Labour."
[72] Judith Hamera, "The Labors of Michael Jackson: Virtuosity, Deindustrialization and Dancing Work." *PMLA*, Special Topic: Work, 127, no. 4 (2012): 751–65; 753.
[73] Ibid., 752.

affective and manual labor—and offers a useful lens for understanding how Lecavalier's performances, initially seen as somehow outside of the contours of dance proper, come to be seen as dance virtuosity over the course of the 1980s. As industry waned and the intangible forms of work associated with the digital sphere grew in scale, and as the neoliberal state abandoned its role in individual life, it is unsurprising that some in concert dance sought to emphasize the pragmatics of the laboring body. Physical strength, high speed, and athleticism, beginning with La La La, I argue, and evidenced in Québec's *nouveau bouger*, the Flemish New Wave and European dance-theater of companies like DV8 Physical Theatre, dominated the dance-theater of the time.

Lecavalier's *Non Non Non*, at once pointing to the gendered nature of work and rejecting imperatives to productivity, anticipates these changes and offers a modest corrective to utopic views associated with the work of the artist and so-called immaterial labor. Returning to the solo years later, I see it as a portrait of dance labor's expanding contours—at once public and private, manual, affective and intellectual, technically skilled, and something more—and an argument against the romanticization of the virtuoso's material labor and the endless valorization of productivity, especially for women and marginalized peoples.[74]

Coda: in search of collective head

Returning to Udashkin's photographs of *Non Non Non*, I see in frame after frame the dancer's total absorption or surrender into the movement: eyes closed, head thrown back, arms reaching, pleasure (Figure 2.4). In multiple frames, the concentration of the dancer, eyes focused, alert to the moment, effort on view. In some frames, her gaze is direct, fully conscious, and fully in control. And elsewhere: I see

---

[74] Dan Irving cautions against the use of "work ethic" as a sanitizing, redemptive label. Dan Irving, "Normalized Transgression: Legitimizing the Transexual Body as Productive." In *The Transgender Studies Reader 2R*, ed. Sandy Stone and Aren Aizura (New York: Routledge, 2013), 15–29.

Figure 2.4 Lecavalier in *Non Non Non* (*c*.1982). Photo: Jack Udashkin.

mimetic performance, theatricality, feigned poses, and then Lecavalier's wink and smile to someone behind the photographer, outside the frame (Figure 2.5).

Here, the photographs ask us to consider the space and personnel off-screen and beyond the frame. Dance scholars Sherril Dodds and Colleen Hooper, in their discussion of "facial choreography" in dance on film, describe the "choreographic interface" as the intertextual meeting point between faces being filmed and/or faces on and off screen.[75] While their work invites deeper attention to the micro-gestural vocabulary of the face and the context of the photographic shoot, my interest is to simply note the dynamic spatial context—with multiple artists active in the space, gesturing to the larger scene as assemblage around a practice[76]—and the sense of aliveness and agency in Lecavalier's gaze, corporeal attitude, and the community of artists with which she worked.

---

[75] Sherril Dodds and Colleen Hooper, "Faces, Close-Ups and Choreography: A Deleuzian Critique of So You Think You Can Dance." *The International Journal of Screendance* 4 (2014): 93–113.

[76] Will Straw, "Some Things a Scene Might Be: Postface." *Cultural Studies* 29, no. 3 (2014): 476–85.

Figure 2.5 Lecavalier in *Non Non Non* (c. 1982). Photo: Jack Udashkin.

Figure 2.6 Working together: La La La Human Steps in *Human Sex* (1985). Photo: © Linda Dawn Hammond/IndyFoto.

By agency, I aim to affirm the dancer's authority in the production of dance, following Carrie Noland's description of embodied agency as "that ambiguous phenomenon in which culture both asserts and loses its grip on individual subjects."[77] Agency is kinesthetic, she writes, noting that "all gestures are performative, insofar as they bring into being, through repetition, a body fabricated specifically to accommodate their execution."[78] More, her brief accounting of "distributed agency" as a set of relations between individuals and objects begins to complicate centralized notions of agential control, evoking the notion of subjectivity as a collective process[79] and investing clear agency in Lecavalier's material transformation and interpretive development of the repertoire (Figure 2.6).

For, as Virno notes, the virtuoso "*requires the presence of others*"[80]— the virtuoso's most political aspect, wherein witnesses are necessary since—in his account—the activities of the virtuosic artist generate no end product. Whereas I have argued for the material impact of Lecavalier's work, his emphasis on a relation of doer and viewer is critical to any account of *Non Non Non* and to the foundational years of La La La. As La La La began work on a new project, *Businessman in the Process of Becoming an Angel* (1983), practices of co-creation and "devised theater" weren't yet part of the vocabulary, nor were they standard practice. Yet the terms nonetheless capture the exchange that fueled La La La's invention in the early years. Skalkogiannis was unequivocal that Lock and Lecavalier worked as a team: "You can't separate them: one animal, two heads." Louis Guillemette remembered the intimacy of the La La La process:

> We worked very closely together, everything was designed with and for the [specific] dancers—it was very intimate the work we did …

---

[77] Carrie Noland, *Agency and Embodiment: Performing Gestures/Producing Culture* (Cambridge, MA: Harvard University Press, 2009), 3.
[78] Ibid., 17.
[79] See Rosi Braidotti, "Introduction," *Embodiment and Sexual Difference in Contemporary Feminist Theory*. 2nd edn (New York: Columbia University Press, 2011), 3–20.
[80] Virno, *A Grammar*, 52.

> Édouard was too much into creation, he would transform, change, add all the time. He had a way of working ... like editing. At a certain point, we forced him to create an order ... I mean, we have to present something.

Dena Davida, herself trained in contact improvisation, found in the work "a combination of those four personalities:"

> Louise, Louis, Miryam, Marc—those four people coming from four different aesthetic points of view .... And Édouard coming from cinema. So his aesthetic always seemed like an amalgam of those people. Because my impression was, from conversations with him and interviews he did which I read, was that since he wasn't dance-trained per se himself, that he counted very much on contributions from his dancer/collaborators.

Such accounts foreground an emergent emphasis on collaboration, a phenomenon associated with shifts in work in the late twentieth century compelled by a shifting economic landscape and the rise of the technosphere. Noyale Colin and Stefanie Sachsenmaier, in their work on collaborative performance, describe "the new status of the director/choreographer as facilitator" and mark this shift in authority as a key characteristic of new work in the early 2000s.[81] Their research identifies the double-edged nature of collaboration in dance: at once, an expansion of practice and a recognition that challenges the stability of the choreographer; and, equally, a neoliberal phenomenon that swaps out formal paid work for more ad hoc, temporary, and self-produced configurations and the pressure to perform as a team.[82]

For her part, Lecavalier has consistently centered Lock's creative leadership and movement invention, even while noting the individual

---

[81] Noyale Colin and Stefanie Sachsenmaier, *Collaboration in Performance Practice: Premises, Workings and Failures* (London: Routledge, 2016). See too Boyan Manchev, "The Collaborative Turn in Contemporary Dance: Performance Capitalism and the Emancipation of Artistic Production." In *Dance: A Catalogue*, ed. Noémie Solomon (New York: Les presses du réel. New York Series, 2015), 189–208.

[82] See Blades, "Projects, Precarity and the Ontology of Dance Works" and Bojana Cvejić and Ana Vujanović, Eds., "Exhausting Immaterial Labour." *Exhausting Immaterial Labour in Performance—The Journal for the Performing Arts* 17 (2010): 4–5.

contributions of her colleagues. What, then, might the term "contribution" suggest here vis-à-vis collaboration? Perhaps a return to understandings of what Fred Moten discusses as, following Lygia Clark, "collective head"—real assembly, "the gathering of things in the flesh ... where the performed devotion of calling and responding in an arrangement refuses every enclosure of its resources."[83] His thinking, utopic to be sure, is nonetheless suggestive of a type of artistic labor bound by distributed agency, whereby the promise of collaboration as collective practice and mutual recognition returns, emphasizing the political potential of assembly as agency rather than the more sinister visions of neoliberalism as entrenched modality. Returning to Noland, she describes the phenomenon of distributed agency as a set of kinesthetic relays between different kinds of actors.[84] And whereas the degree of effort and kinds of feelings associated with such relay no doubt may move in any direction, Lecavalier's solo and her subsequent practice in the company offer a different view.

Whereas *Non Non Non* evidences Lecavalier's emergent identity and a political critique of gendered danced labor, in these final frames from the Udashkin images, one might discern a vision of work unfolding at the intersection of a creative community. After *Non Non Non*, Lecavalier let go of choreography and returned fully to the company. "I said, no, never again—it was too stressful."[85] Collective work was more fun, allowing for sustained research in a fluid shifting context. It would be thirty years before she choreographed again, with *So Blue* (2012), a work Lemieux and others immediately connected to the earlier solo for its idiosyncratic gestural vocabulary and high energy. Following their visit to New York, the group returned to Montréal and refocused on

[83] Fred Moten, "Collective Head." *Women and Performance: A Journal of Feminist Theory* 26, no. 2 (2016): 162–71; 163.
[84] Noland, *Agency and Embodiment*. See also Enfield and Kockelman, who describe agency as a phenomenon bound by flexibility and accountability, a situation where "multiple people act as one, sharing or sharing out the elements of agency." See N. J. Enfield and Paul Kockelman, Eds., *Distributed Agency* (Oxford: Oxford University Press, 2017).
[85] Lecavalier (2012).

Businessman in the Process of Becoming an Angel (1983), an exuberant, poetic portrait of artists in the crosshairs of a changing world.

Businessman, though, would be the last collaboration with all four founding members: Louise Guillemette, Miryam Moutillet, and Michel Lemieux departed soon after to tour their own work. By 1990, the company had jumped to international stardom—touring constantly, and slowly turning to ballet as its primary idiom. Starting with *Infante, c'est destroy* (1990), as the company grew larger, Lecavalier felt increasingly distanced from the creative work, and the eccentric collection of ideas and characters in the company faded. Gender roles became more entrenched, the female dancers got naked, the men wore suits. By the time Lecavalier retired from the company in 1999, "work" had formalized and become confined to rehearsal hours and touring. The intimacy and ad hoc pleasures of the early years had faded. Lecavalier moved on.

3

Punk Neo-Expressionism in the Early La La La Repertoire

I never wanted to talk before rehearsal. I didn't want to arrive at the studio and say more than, "Allo, Allo" to everyone. And I didn't what to be hopping everywhere, trying out with different choreographers, trying to be part of everything, smooth, smooth with everyone. I needed to be apart, somehow ... I want to be fresh in the studio with the impressions I get from living. The dance world is not what I want to talk about on stage. I want to talk about my impressions of the planet, who I am, what I lived, how I survive on this planet. What I encounter in the street, what's going on in my mind.[1]

—Louise Lecavalier

When we were first finding our vocabulary—the off-axis, the turns and falls—I thought, "Okay somewhere in another part of the world, somebody is doing the same thing." It felt like it must have been bigger than us, like it was in the air.[2]

—LL

The scene at the Montréal Spectrum was raucous. Nina Hagen, the iconic punk performer from East Germany, was performing, and the sense of transgression—to spit the forbidden and speak what can't be said—was part of the draw. A critic for *Pop Rock* had earlier praised Hagen's musical persona as an exploration of character, veering

---

[1] Louise Lecavalier (2024).
[2] Lecavalier (2020).

"between mythology and mythomania."³ The *Montreal Gazette* noted that "a mob of individualists turned up at the Spectrum to hear the unbelievable Nina Hagen," in an article that focused on the crowd's fashion—fishnet stockings, yellow tutus, leather jackets, dog collars, and Doc Martens, rather than the performance itself.⁴ Just one moment, perhaps, in a lively scene that included local punk and New Wave acts like the Asexuals, Rational Youth, and Men Without Hats; art-house pranksters like neoist Istvan Kantor/Monty Cantsin; and international artists like Kraftwerk, Devo, and the Boomtown Rats. Yet, for Louise Lecavalier, watching in the audience that night, Hagen's concert stood out for its acute vision of female performance, for its punk expressivity and for its profound audience connection, beyond anything she had seen in dance. Soon after, La La La would bring its "dance-musical" *Human Sex* (1985) to the Spectrum, in an embrace of the popular music context uncommon for concert dance at the time. "It was a bit my idea, with Michel [Lemieux]," Lecavalier recalls. "We were saying, 'let's open things up, let's make dance for everybody.'"⁵

Lecavalier's recollection of this event threads several ideas for consideration in this chapter: on the one hand, it points to the importance of assembling a distinctive audience for the company, particularly significant within nationalist politics in the province; and, on the other hand, it underlines the substantive impact of the minor, the lesser known and often feminized sources of creative innovation that have shaped the break-out innovations associated with Lecavalier, Lock, and the company La La La Human Steps. The Hagen scene, I argue, points to a cultural relay between modernist Europe and Québec that can enliven current understandings of Lecavalier's work as well as complicate narratives of dance history and national identity as these have been made in Québec. As critical accounts tended to situate Lecavalier in mythic terms, she herself zeroed in on the power of female

---

³ Ferdinand Durepos Jr., "Die frau von Berlin: Nina Hagen." *Pop Rock* 10, no. 2 (February 21, 1981): 15.
⁴ Barbara Katz, *Montreal Gazette*. February 7, 1984, D8.
⁵ Lecavalier (2010).

performance in relation to the collective. In what follows, I draw a line between Lecavalier's interpretation of an emergent punk dance-theater during the 1980s and the aesthetic legacies associated with European expressionist dance, gathered under the rubric *Ausdruckstanz*, that circulated in early twentieth-century and postwar Montréal, well before the cultural shifts associated with the province's post-1950s Quiet Revolution. Both Lecavalier's and La La La's iteration of a punk dance-theater and earlier forms of expressionist dance developed intensely affective, highly personalized dances that, at their outset, choreographed new relations between movement, meaning, and the collective body.

Sociologist Simon Frith, finally, reminds us that popular music is, above all, a social event: "Its cultural purpose is to put together an audience, to construct a sense of 'us' (and them)."[6] Frith's argument points to the power of popular forms like punk to create new practices and narratives of identity and belonging. This chapter situates Lecavalier's explosive dancing and La La La's emergent dance theater within a revised collective project—part of an opening up of elite cultural forms to alternative and subcultural audiences. More, it marks the role of the dancer as producer of aesthetic, intellectual, and informational exchange; and complicates nationalist narratives of Québec dance history that have prioritized the new and the original over significant historical presence. In what follows, I make four moves: first, I read two key early works, *Oranges: ou la recherche du paradis* (1981) and *Businessman in the Process of Becoming an Angel* (1983) to describe the La La La aesthetic as performed by Lecavalier; and reflect on this aesthetic as punk neo-expressionism within the context of its time. Next, I offer historical sketches of mid-twentieth-century expressionist performance, teaching, and dancing that I argue have shaped the aesthetic and the Montréal scene more broadly. Finally, I return to Lecavalier and the work of the dancer as a "knowledge transformer"—that is, as an interpreter and disseminator of historical traces within an explosive, emergent dance-theater.

---

[6] Simon Frith, *Music for Pleasure: Essays in the Sociology of Pop* (New York: Routledge, 1988), 156.

Oranges, Businessman: reading the early repertoire

Before 1985 and the international acclaim that came with *Human Sex* (1985), the company made two works that are significant to understanding the nature of their developing aesthetic: *Oranges: ou la recherche du paradis* (1981) and *Businessman in the Process of Becoming an Angel* (1983). *Oranges*, the second work of the La La La repertoire after *Lily Marlene in the Jungle* (1980) and the first in which Lecavalier performed, fuses dance, graffiti, and live rock music in an absurdist assemblage of cultural materials from the day. About an hour in length, the documentary recording of the work unfolds as montage in what is a faithful accounting of its live structure—a series of scenes set against enormous paper backdrops that are written on, torn down, replaced, then torn down again, recalling the presence of the city as scene and scenic backdrop for their activities; and anticipating the prominence of screens in later company productions with their emphasis on multimedia and cinematic elements. The company members are foundational: Louise Lecavalier, Miryam Moutillet, Louis Guillemette, Michel Lemieux, and Édouard Lock, dressed sharply in black dress pants, white dress shirts, with collars and rolled short sleeves and bare feet. They pick up spray cans, tracing bodies on the wall or writing phrases that seem at once banal and evocative: "Oh, Baby!," an eye-roll at the scripts of seduction; or *"la memoire purifiée,"* a dark nod at attempts to control cultural memory. Dancers drop in and out, hang back and watch the action, snack on an orange, or smell roses. In one scene, Lock and Moutillet balance on a column of glass milk bottles, advancing slowly as Lecavalier extends the line, moving bottles from rear to front, ahead of the dancers. It's an absurd task—without utility or purpose, save for its simultaneous evocations of play, precarity, and collective focus. In another scene, nascent versions of the iconic barrel roll appear, notably in Guillemette's more upright, loose body—a softer, lyrical version—and in Lecavalier's more acrobatic variation—that is, stronger, rounder, more propulsive from ground to air and at higher speed (Figures 3.1 and 3.2).

Punk Neo-Expressionism 117

Figure 3.1 Miryam Moutillet and Louise Lecavalier in *Oranges*, December 1981. Photo: Ron Diamond.

Figure 3.2 Miryam Moutillet and Michel Lemieux in *Oranges*, December 1981. Photo: Ron Diamond.

The writer Guy Patenaude, in an uncited account taken from a press kit, describes the work as follows:

> It's a funny piece and a microcosm of the city, a soft city with soft walls, subject to paramount human will. Running through paper walls lacerates the wall, not the runner as layers and levels of paper are torn or folded, each with a colour. Greens with reds, orange with blue, to create a riot of colour in the theatre in much the same way as neon signs flash and duel in the city night. A cartoon and a comic vision. In the midst of all that, love affairs—stylised and elegant and amusing—dot the landscape of the piece. The serpent in Paradise. The performers are hot house plants. They are oranges. *Oranges in Paradise*.[7]

It's dance theater leaning into performance art, a motley assemblage of movement techniques, modern and contemporary, but including gestures to the ballet that would dominate the company after Lecavalier's retirement. The iconic sensibility of the company is clearly in view. Yet these are still ordinary bodies at work: softer, less muscled, more fluid; and these are dream-like scenes, non sequiturs reflective of an early 1980s punk and new wave aesthetic noted in films like *Diva* (1981) that played with coincidence and chance, surface and style, and the street as a kind of bricolage machine. The semiotics of signed language are there too: as two fingers make a V that frames the eye—part mask, part camera lens; or else frame the face and tap the heart. Patenaude describes these as "hand dances," and notes an attention to articulating the body's "extremities": arms, hands, fingers. Between visual image and text and dance and gesture that seem to point to expressivity itself, *Oranges* is a saturated landscape where signs proliferate but meaning remains unfixed.

Two years later, the company's identity crystallizes in *Businessman in the Process of Becoming an Angel* (1983), described on its flyer as a "danse musicale post-moderne." A filmed version for a performance at Dance Theater Workshop in New York in 1984 shows the revised make-up of the

---

[7] Press kit for *Oranges*, November 14–15, 1981. *Musée d'art contemporain*; La La La Folders, Tangente Danse archive, Montréal.

company: Lecavalier, Marc Béland, Claude Godin, Jacqueline Lemieux, Frédérik Bédard, and Édouard Lock. Its aesthetic is fully formed, with a greatly heightened sense of theatricality, interdisciplinarity, and athleticism; and a clearly articulated punk intention in its soundscape (Lemieux's raucous, dialogic electric guitar) and costuming (torn, paint-splattered spandex and sneakers). Once again, montage structures the dance as a series of scenes, with much applause in between and musical interludes featuring drums, synthesizer, and vocalist. At times, the movement actively invokes thresholds of communication: an early duet, for instance, uses hand and arm gestures almost exclusively, signing dialogue through vernacular gestures that bring to my mind street fights and kid games, right hooks and pat-a-cake. Throughout, spoken word switches easily between French and English: "We're all the same, just men and women"; or "Qu'est qu'en tu fais? La La La ...." The work invokes language and movement codes, flattening or inflating them, making them absurd (Figure a 3.3 and 3.4).

At times, the movement is big in shape and scale: airborne spins and rolls, power jumps and floor dives, unusual lifts and feats of

Figure 3.3 Photo shoot for *Businessman*. Photo: Jack Udashkin.

Figure 3.4 Louise holds Édouard. Photo: Jack Udashkin.

strength, intense speed that challenges sight and memory. Sometimes, the commitment is palpable; we watch them work, tracking the effort through gathering speed, momentum, and weight bearing. Then just as quickly: are they marking the movement? Or simply tired, or sloppy, and fuck you if you don't get it. Quickly, the affect of the performers shifts from work-like concentration to boredom, sheer pleasure to postmodern deadpan. There's a recurring dog character named Max, and dog cut-out structures for dancers to balance on, a cartoonish wink at the dog-eat-dog brutality of the cultural and economic landscape circa 1983.

A short Radio Canada news clip by Québec journalist Paul Toutant captures the spirit of the work, as well as the company's drive to connect with new audiences: Édouard and Michel perch above a storefront along rue Ste-Catherine, singing into microphones to the crowd below; on the street, Louise, Miryam Moutillet, Louis Guillemette, and Lee Eisler are seen stopping rush-hour traffic for fifteen minutes to dance excerpts from the material. On camera, Lock describes the "businessman" of the title as the hero and sex symbol of the 1980s because they are the "survivors"; he is smiling and serious as he makes the claim that, at this particular cultural moment, "survival is sexy." Company manager George Skalkogiannis remembers the title as an explicit critique of neoliberalism: "They had great radar for what was happening, and that was when you had [American President Ronald] Reagan and [Canadian Prime Minister Brian] Mulroney saying, 'Let business solve the problems.'"[8] Shifting registers between the pointed and the oblique, the work remained enigmatic, generating ambiguities and a need for audiences to connect different elements and be "in-the-know."

Both *Oranges* and *Businessman* suggest a strong expressionist tendency, wherein making dance relevant was a key motivation: to make images that related to their lives, that their friends could recognize, that ordinary people would come and see. Audience connection was central to La La La, who played initially in small theaters like the Eskabel, where it had a sold-out three-week run in 1980; and music venues like the Spectrum, the Rialto and Foufounes Électriques, garnering an audience that was not comprised of specialized dance fans. "I wanted to bring people to the theater," Lecavalier said, "to have something to say that was urgent, relevant, that our friends could relate to."[9] Dance producer Dena Davida remembered how unique the expanded audience for dance became; there was visible excitement, and "you saw for the first time

---

[8] George Skalkogiannis (2022).
[9] Lecavalier (2016/2024).

the black leather club crowd walking into the opera house."[10] Critic Max Wyman wrote that the dance drew crowds and "not just the dance crowd, and not just the young, but a wide spectrum of individuals—punks, rockers, people who had never looked at dance before but were drawn by its embodiment of the anarchic expression of its age."[11] Commentators such as these mark the legibility and impact of their aesthetic—a critical approach that felt urgently needed within its social-political moment. Returning to Lecavalier's thinking, the goal was relevance—to have something to say that could cut through the dead weight of established tastes and the limits of class as these shifted during the early 1980s.

As La La La gained increasing attention through the 1980s, contemporary observers would nonetheless refer backwards, explicitly linking the aesthetic to expressionist dance without engaging too deeply with what that might imply. For instance, the dance historian Iro Tembeck was perhaps first to understand Lock's early work with Groupe Nouvelle Air as "a forerunner of the neo-expressionist dance theater so popular with Montréal choreographers in the years that followed."[12] Tembeck links the term neo-expressionist to content—Lock's use of symbolism and depiction of an "inner voyage" in works like *Temps volé* (1976) and *Remous* (1977)—and in so doing beckons that range of artistic production from painting to theater and cinema that sought during the early part of the twentieth century to express the powerful, unstated registers of daily life.[13] Yet though her scholarship is critical in pointing to the traces of *Ausdruckstanz* history in Montréal, she nevertheless argues that it faded from relevance and its "direct link was never explored nor exploited in order to nurture growth."[14]

---

[10] Dena Davida (2012).

[11] Max Wyman, "Edouard Lock: Showman or Shaman?" Presentation, Royal Society of Canada, Ottawa, November 19, 2004. https://maxwyman.com/2016/08/02/edouard-lock-showman-or-shaman/

[12] Iro Valaskakis Tembeck, "Dancing in Montreal: Seeds for a Choreographic History." *Studies in Dance History* 2 (1994): 90.

[13] See John Willett, *Art and Politics in the Weimar Period: The New Sobriety 1917–1933* (New York: Pantheon Books, 1978).

[14] Iro Valaskakis Tembeck, "Politics and Dance in Montreal, 1940s to 1980s: The Imaginary Maginot Line between Anglophone and Francophone Dancers." In *Canada Dance: Visions and Stories*, ed. Selma Landen Odom and Mary Jane Warner (Toronto: Dance Collections Danse, 2004), 271–86; 277.

There is a longer history of expressionist dance in the city, associated with a wave of immigration from Central and Eastern Europe in the early part of the twentieth century and the arrival of dancers who carried with them a range of artistic traditions; and prepared the ground for the innovations of La La La and the *nouveau bouger* (New Dance) mode of dance-theater that arrived in the 1980s. From Mary Wigman's performances at His Majesty's Theatre on Guy Street in the 1930s to the arrival of dance teachers and performers directly trained by Wigman or otherwise bearing related traditions, dance forms that prioritized expression and uncodified or otherwise resistant forms of dance movement circulated across the city. If one dominant narrative has tended to foreground the achievements of the *Refus Global* (1948) generation,[15] recognizing the important work of dancer/choreographers Françoise Sullivan, Jeanne Renaud, and Françoise Riopelle, that history has bolstered the idea of Québec as cultural innovator and unified society while enabling a certain distance from Europe as colonial force and tainted political zone. A foundational figure like Renaud, for example, who established *Le Groupe de la place royale* in 1966, has cautioned against singular origins for modern dance in the province. She points to Elsie Salomons, who studied with Kurt Jooss and Rudolph von Laban in England during the late 1930s and opened a dance school from 1956 to 1976; for Renaud, Salomons' teaching was critical to the development of dance in Québec.[16] Salomons' emphasis on "creative dance"—that is, improvisation and exploration in and outside the limits of formal technique—served as a critical counterpoint to much of dance training in the city at the time.[17]

---

[15] The "Refus Global" (Total Refusal), a manifesto published in Montréal in 1948, stands as a radical departure within the history of arts and culture in Québec; led by visual artist Paul-Émile Borduas, with sixteen signatories including the dancer/choreographers Françoise Sullivan and Françoise Riopelle, the work explored surrealism and automatism, and rejected academic styles. See Ray Ellenwood, Ed., *Refus Global: The Manifesto of the Montréal Automatists* (Holstein, ONT: Exile Editions, 2010).

[16] Jeanne Renaud, with Denis Marleau, "La Danse moderne au Québec; autour d'un témoinage de Jeanne Renaud." *Jeu: cahier de revue de théâtre* 32, no. 3 (1984): 43–8; 44.

[17] Thanks to Linda Rabin, founder of *L'École de danse contemporain de Montréal* (1981–), a former student of Salomons, and a former teacher of Lecavalier at GNA; she shared recollections of Salomons' class with me over coffee in Montréal in 2023.

These earlier histories allow us, in the words of dance scholar Susan Manning, to "discern an alternate history of modern dance, as artists and educators move between the frames of myriad nation states."[18] More, they allow us to understand the work of the dancer as a critical link in what Kate Elswit has described as a "micropolitics of exchange,"[19] where the contextual shifts and migrations of dancers over time leave significant traces, survivals, and resurgences that challenge the "contours" of conventional historical narratives with their patterns of major/minor, insider/outsider.

Parsing the La La La signature

Four key elements are on view in *Oranges* and *Businessmen* that I argue constitute the La La La signature circa the first decade and dilate the expressive registers of the dance. These are: *off-axis*, speed, non-verbal language, and montage. One of Lecavalier's most significant contributions lay in the development of *off-axis*, the company shorthand for the high-energy athleticism that became its defining element. *Off-axis*, with its off-kilter barrel rolls, uncodified leaps and stage dives, sought to reorient the vertical axis of the body. It played with normative senses of direction, line, speed, and flow, the later alternately bound and unbounded; and moved between powered-up launches into the jump and surrender to the ground or a partner. It was literally sensational—that is, highly affective in its heady relation to normative orientations of uprightness, speed, and flight. More, its volatile energy and blurred shapes contrasted the gestural details, physical breaks, and theatrical moments that featured direct audience address, spoken word, or simple, absurdist actions.

---

[18] Susan Manning, "Dance History." In *The Bloomsbury Companion to Dance Studies*, ed. Sherril Dodds (London, New York, Oxford, New Delhi, Sydney: Bloomsbury Academic, 2019), 303–26; 314.

[19] Kate Elswit, "The Micropolitics of Exchange: Exile and Otherness After Nation." *The Oxford Handbook of Dance and Politics* (New York: Oxford University Press, 2017), 417–38; 419.

Moutillet remembers, "The jumps, the turns, the level of risk and how you catch yourself to the floor …? That was Louise …. And I'd give that to Louis too."[20] Whereas Lock directed, worked on the movement individually—like "couture"[21]—and brought visual ideas to the group, Louis Guillemette brought weight sharing, unusual partnering, and the elements of play routed in his training in contact improvisation that then was shared with company members through studio practice. Yet it was Lecavalier, with her outsized commitment to exploring possibilities and her dedication to building strength, who took *off-axis* farthest. She remembers working for hours, by herself; with Claude Godin and Marc Béland; and with the full company, to hone the material: "We wanted to make big, fat steps … to be huge and take up as much space as possible."[22]

The *off-axis* vocabulary required a high degree of skill and effort to perform and was not without practical and thematic risks. Whereas some critics speculated on the work's symbolic violence, others worried about the costs to the dancers' bodies. Lecavalier has mostly downplayed injury, seeing the limits of the body primarily as a challenge to manage; but noted that as the company moved towards ballet in the 1990s, things became more difficult:

> With *Infante*, the work started to go in two physical directions: Édouard tried to incorporate ballet lines and bigger extensions of the legs; and, at the same time, he wanted to go more hardcore and go farther with the *off-axis* and the partnering challenges. These things didn't go well together in my body. To have the speed, the huge extension and the power at the same time …? It was a weird combination, a conflict between strength and looseness, and my body hadn't yet adapted to it. Because I jumped all the time, my thighs were bigger, I had almost ten more pounds of muscle than now—I needed to be strong to keep power in the attack of the movements on stage for more than an hour-long show … Plus the hours of rehearsal prior. It made my body pretty tight.

---

[20] Miryam Moutillet (2020).
[21] Louis Guillemette (2014).
[22] Lecavalier (1997).

> With *Infante*, I started to take ballet classes every day, thinking I needed them to better my technique ... it was a contradiction. So, in the end, I got injured.[23]

Lecavalier's colleagues noted a near-mania like drive to develop the technique and rehearse and perform the work; in multiple interviews, they too saw the potential danger of the material as well as her drive to develop and perform it. Yet Lecavalier, who agrees that in the early days her work ethic could go too far, also points to the difference between performing extremity and being in the thralls of it:

> There's a danger in the work because it's hard to do, that's all. It's not like the movement is dangerous itself; it's to stay with it, to have the strength and stamina to keep going and still perform the complexity ... It's so complex, so intricate. I work on the technique a lot. And I hit the floor but softly ... 99.9% of the time, it works. I know it so well that the risk is next to zero .... If the hit is hard, it means something isn't working technically.[24]

Dance historian Sherril Dodds, in her discussion of punk social dance, makes a similar distinction between real and simulated violence, identifying extreme forms of movement as performed demonstrations of physical commitment, personal investment, and authenticity:

> Whether it is in the obsessive interest in the music, the extreme physicality of the dancing or a radical stylization of the body in terms of dress and image, the individual articulates an affiliation with selected subcultural values that suggests a strategy for personal empowerment was literally sensational—that is, highly affective in its heady relation to normative orientations of uprightness and air, speed and flight.[25]

Whereas much of the literature around popular and subculture forms pits claims to agency against victimhood—in ways that echo with speculation on Lecavalier's agency in the dance—Dodds emphasizes

---

[23] Lecavalier (2016).
[24] Lecavalier (2011).
[25] Sherril Dodds, *Dancing on the Canon: Embodiments of Value in Popular Dance* (Basingstoke, UK: Palgrave Macmillan, 2011), 164.

the *possibility* for agency in the transgression of social norms associated with extreme or excessive aesthetics; and links the performance of extremity to expression and belonging (Figure 3.5).

A second defining feature of the repertoire, and closely entwined with *off-axis*, is speed, perhaps among the most noted elements of La La La's aesthetic, requiring tremendous technical skill and commitment from the performers to achieve the intended challenge to perception.

Figure 3.5 Developing *off-axis*, Claude Godin and Louise Lecavalier. Photo: Jack Udashkin.

Speed took work: beyond the ongoing maintenance of a performing body able to do the work, it pressured the extraordinary timing of the *off-axis* movement, a phenomenon noted by American dance critic Marcia Siegel who perceived Lecavalier's leadership in cueing movement, very much in dialogue with partners in the work.[26] Lock has described his affinity for intense speed consistently over many years in the following terms:

> I don't understand it. If you have a body moving very quickly the understanding of its shape, maleness, femaleness, beauty, ugliness, youth, age ... These elements are more related to judgment than to observation. When we make the observing process more difficult, one of the first things we lose is judgement.[27]
>
> Painters have said to me that you can't be abstract in dance—that you're stuck in a realistic art form with empirical shapes that you can't change. But I think while looking at a dancer who is moving very quickly, as mine do, the audience at some point loses perception. They will not understand the shape anymore ... In this way, on some level, I am creating an abstraction of perception ... and start[ing] to see it as a flux—something that is changing and non-linear, with a structure that is abstract. I want to create a series of shapes that fight against the stability we crave.[28]

Speed affords the body, and the dance, a kind of abstraction, working to expand the field of expression and challenge notions of the performing body as "real" and vision as truth. Here, what you see is not what you get. Yet, it is at the same time not *not* what you get. Speed trades here in a boundary effect: capitalizing on the performing body's ability to allude and elude in tandem with the material body's ability to act.

Lecavalier, for her part, has across many interviews emphasized the distinction between what it *feels* like to dance versus what it *looks* like;

---

[26] Marcia B. Siegel, "Dance Analysis—Lock's Duo." Unpublished Notes from a Presentation at the Department of Performance Studies, New York University (New York: October 4, 1990).

[27] Lock in Szporer, *Hour*, January 18–24, 1996.

[28] Lock in Daryl Jung, *Now*, October, 1992.

she has always hated the expectations of visual compliance, whether in matching her appearance to her attitude; her technical skill to her value as a dancer. She remembers, "When I first started dancing, the upside was how I felt in dance. The downside was being looked at ... I didn't want to be judged on my look or analysed on aspects of my body."[29] Speed tended to challenge received ideas about the body as a stable configuration of gender, race, and class.[30] As a kinesthetic value, high speed was performative: it created the adrenalin rush associated with doing and watching the defying of ordinary modes of comportment. And it was expressive: its driving momentum was viral, thrilling, pushing back at softness, politeness even, its perceived extremity conveying a sense that the normative was breaking apart.

Two further elements on view in *Oranges* and *Businessman* evidence key elements for the company going forward. Its use of *gestures*, akin to non-verbal or body language, with distant echoes of American Sign Language, manifested in smaller, detailed movements for arms, hands, fingers, and face. Dancer Miryam Moutillet was central to the building of this vocabulary; Moutillet herself remembers,

> We were flying to Ottawa, to le Conseil des Arts du Canada; we were trying to get funding and we had nothing prepared to show them other than what we could create on the way. The first time we started using gestures and things like that was sitting in the plane because there was no space, no room to move, and so I created a routine on the plane with Édouard. And that's what we presented and that's what got us the money.[31]

Moutillet felt that in isolating small movements, the dance could function "as a camera," drawing in the eye and providing an important contrast to the bigger, full body acrobatics on view; the desired effect was one of "intimacy." Uncommon within dance contexts at the time,

---

[29] Lecavalier (2020).
[30] See Stephen Low, "The Speed of Queer: La La La Human Steps and Queer Perceptions of the Body." *Theatre Research in Canada* 37, no. 1 (2016): 62–78.
[31] Miryam Moutillet (2020).

the gestures offered a different communicative code, opening access to non-specialized, popular audiences unfamiliar with the formal lexicons of dance and reaching for new kinds of legibility. At the same time, this element resonated with anxieties about language rights as a dominant narrative within Québec at the time, with the passing of Bill 101 (1977) that had set new rules for the use of French within public life (Figure 3.6).

Finally, *montage* refers to Lock's practice of editing as primary choreographic tool; that is, his attention to the reordering of visual materials and movement imagery in time and space, made tangible through the structuring of scenes, movement loops, and his use of film, video, and screens in performance. The borrowing from film language feels right, given Lock's training as a film student at Concordia University in the late 1970s; and given the close attention he brought to scenographic, cinematic, and photographic elements in the repertoire. Founding company member Louis Guillemette remembered,

> He was too much into creation, he always had things to transform, change, add all the time. And when the piece is like that you start

Figure 3.6 Signing work: Claude Godin and Louise Lecavalier. Photo: Jack Udashkin.

to present it but it's always moving; he was always pushing, cutting, keeping it alive. He had a way of working like editing. It's never been a continuing process in terms of arriving at a final piece, never.[32]

Montage, perhaps, followed the relentless pace of Lock's mind, and its effect was to undermine expectations for narrative coherence and challenge stabilities of logic, movement, and visuality. La La La's montage dovetailed with its widespread use as a choreographic method in the dance theater emerging on Québec and European stages in the 1980s, notably in works by Pina Bausch, Jan Fabre, and others. Yet, equally, it emerged simultaneously with the rise of music TV, as revised governance around network TV came to pass and expanded forms of mass media became available. MTV's Robert Pittman described his understanding of how music videos function: "People don't watch these clips to find out what's going to happen. They watch to feel a certain way."[33] Within these contexts, montage foregrounded imagery *sans* context, delivering an affective wallop and expanded readings for the work.

Taken together, these elements produced a real and felt radicality to the aesthetic—real, to the extent that it required and showed a high degree of skill and effort and presented distinctive material imagery for dance; and felt, to the extent it *looked* extreme and rendered the facticity of the body illusory. Lecavalier would assert that their aesthetic "isn't violent but [celebrates] something extreme within us."[34] Lock has said that work grew more extreme as a way to physicalize the extremity of the intellectual process, of interiority itself.[35] The dance historian Iro Tembeck related their work to the emergence of punk and new wave movements, to popular and mass forms, and the threat of Americanism with its "fast food, video clips, and breakdancing."[36] In the next section, I read their work as punk neo-expressionism, a reaction to the cultural

[32] Louis Guillemette (2014).
[33] Frith, *Music for Pleasure*, xx.
[34] Catherine Bush, "Sex and Violence and Rock 'n' Roll," *Montreal Eye*, October 29, 1992.
[35] Édouard Lock, "Adrienne Clarkson Presents" (1991–2).
[36] Tembeck, "Dancing in Montreal," 92, 121.

stasis that belied the extreme socio-political shifts of the 1980s and ricocheting between local histories and an emergent globalism. With punk in circulation from the mid-1970s on as a portable[37] sound, style, and scene, it was equally a way to construct new kinds of identities and ways of belonging; a tool for critical expression; and a framework through which to understand the company's extremities of act and affect.

Punk neo-expressionism

Cultural Studies scholar Simon Critchley, himself a former punk, has written that the primary message of the phenomenon is that, "You can do this, anyone can do this."[38] No special training required. It was a message marked in the early company's eclecticism and its rejection of academic styles in favor of a closer relation to its audience. Lock had dropped out of film school, and Lemieux had left the National Theatre School. And Lecavalier's formal training in dance had begun at 15, with her academic focus on medical science and biology at Bois de Boulogne, one of many newly formed junior colleges that aimed to bring wider access to higher education for French-Canadians.

If punk offered an immediate model of DIY methodology, it was also a stance to be taken, with ready-made critique to push back against authority: the fixed, the dumb, the boring, and the exclusionary. Within concert dance, that meant ballet, whose prominence had risen internationally during the 1970s in a so-called "ballet boom" fueled by events like the Baryshnikov defection in Toronto (1974) and films like

---

[37] Diedrich Diederichsen, "From Anti-Social Liberal Punk to Intersectional AIDs Activism: Sub-Culture and Politics in Eighties Europe." In *The Long 1980s: Constellations of Art, Politics and Identities*, ed. Nick Aikens, Teresa Grandas, Nav Haq, Beatriz Herráez, and Nataša Petrešin-Bachelez (Valiz, Amsterdam: L'Internationale, 2018), 31.

[38] Simon Critchley, "Rummaging in the Ashes: An Interview with Simon Critchley." *Punk Is Dead: Modernity Killed Every Night*, ed. Richard Cabut and Andrew Gallix (Winchester, UK; Washington, DC: Zero Books, 2017), 39.

The Turning Point (1977). In Montréal, that meant both rejecting the aesthetics and values of a dominant company like Les Grands Ballets Canadiens, from which Moutillet departed in 1980; as well as the rising prominence of new companies like Groupe Nouvelle Aire. Lecavalier remembers:

> When I left Groupe Nouvelle Aire, the main people who had attracted me to the company had already left: Paul Lapointe, Paul-André Fortier, Ginette Laurin, Édouard [Lock] … It was more top-down, more directed … like, suddenly, there was a more limited vision. I knew I didn't want it. I was more going into punk. I was not a rocker really but I was like a little punk girl, you know, with my hair dyed black and my pale face. I didn't look for a style, I was trying to get away from the "rules" of what dance is and what a dancer is supposed to be.[39]

Lock has said:

> I think there was a time when I was wanting to make dance louder, for lack of a better word, not more violent, but louder and to make a more extreme aesthetic statement at some point, like it happened in music.[40]

For founding dancer Miryam Moutillet, there was little time to reflect on what was happening; they were busy making work, rather than making the scene: "We weren't punk, but it was *au courant*, it was the period. We weren't harsh, we weren't aggressive. We were people pushing boundaries."[41]

The early movement repertoire was augmented through sound and vision. Shows emphasized live musical performance—rock, noise, industrial—with interactions between dancers and musicians and loose disciplinary compliance. Lecavalier's taste drove the company further towards the industrial, in company collaborations with Einstürzende Neubauten, for example. The sound often combined techno-pop, electric guitars, and driving percussion, featuring musicians Lemieux,

---

[39] Lecavalier (2011).
[40] D. Kelly, *Globe and Mail*, November 25, 1995.
[41] Miryam Moutillet (2020).

Rober Racine, and Jackie Gallant as core members of the company: costuming followed everyday and club aesthetics; they wore men's wear and black tulle, ripped or splattered spandex tights, and gender-mixing make-up. Elements of décor tended towards the everyday, the utilitarian, or the spectacular—TV sets and drum kits; graffiti as urban image and expressive movement; or else film and video, projected at epic scale and always produced by Lock himself. Punk photographer and activist Linda Dawn Hammond, at once a key participant and creator of one of the premiere records of the alternative cultural–political scene in Montréal across the 1980s, situates the term punk with overt political dissent and activism that were not at the center of La La La's activities. Hammond notes,

> It's true that Édouard had spiky black hair, and was a uniquely dressed individual, androgynous in appearance and alternative in his own right, but he wasn't an active member of the punk scene *per se*, which was a street movement. He moved in his own social circles and was not part of the *Foufounes Electriques* milieu, or any of the anti-capitalist or anti-war demos I attended and documented.[42]

Yet one of the profound pleasures circa the early 1980s was the certainty of the porous nature of scenes and the sense that artistic identity could be constructed, that fixed positions could be remade. To return to Critchley's view, punk allowed its makers "to push back against the pressure of reality with the force of imagination."[43]

Lecavalier has emphasized the company's efforts to find movement that was their own, that was authentic to their experience. An aspect of their work that she admired was that the company never "pretended"; she recalls,

> We never sat together and said, "Aw … let's make a piece about this thing or that thing" …. We worked on finding our vocabulary …. And if we fell down, exhausted, it was because we were.[44]

---

[42] Linda Dawn Hammond (2020).
[43] Critchley, "Rummaging in the Ashes," in *Punk Is Dead*, 30.
[44] Lecavalier (2016).

The demands of the physicality—the *off-axis* and the speed—insisted on a kind of honesty through the sheer effort of doing it. Yet small moments and actorly details—tough looks, cheeky smiles, deadpan speech, ordinary gestures—lent a critical distance that refuted any sense of the dance as unmediated or pure. The company cut variations of techniques—ballet, modern, gestural, quotidian, and more—with poses, at times, feigning battles or confrontations; at others, ending tender exchanges with direct address to the audience and mocking smiles. Whereas vintage rock imagined itself as working-class heroes with a grass-roots authenticity, Critchley reminds us that punk plugged in to glam rock's critique of the real as only another façade; he notes, "punk was about an experience of truth, of felt, heard truth that was made possible through inauthenticity, mediation and fakery."[45] The early repertoire bridged desires for authentic expression, made palpable in the stunning effort and affective qualities of the performance; with a critique of the artificiality at the heart of socio-cultural patterns, evidenced in the performance attitude, thematics, and gestural detail.[46]

The tension fueled questions about the status of the dance as expression. One critic praised their feat-like virtuosity, writing that it had succeeded in breaking "modern dance's stranglehold on fist-to-brow significance."[47] Another found "something witty in the almost mindlessly repeated permutations of jumps and falls and high-speed spins ... but what is it saying?"[48] As if big movement was merely stunt movement, outside interpretation, movement as pure fact. As if a barrel move—think pirouette, unleashed from vertical law—could convey little through its altered

---

[45] Critchley, "Rummaging in the Ashes," in *Punk Is Dead*, 36.
[46] When Lecavalier read this, we discussed the company's play with artifice—notably, in their direct addresses to the audience, which were often teasing or ironic; or, for example, in the fake opener for *Infante*, when a brief blast of music and dance occurred while the audience was still in the lobby, creating a rush to seating before it stopped and the show began proper. At the same time, she felt it important to emphasize the material realness of their performance: "I touched incredible things by pushing the body so far, even then. Something really real was there, and at moments I could totally get into a zone, a great zone—beyond judgment, beyond desire, just floating over the effort." Lecavalier (2024).
[47] Susan Mertens, *Vancouver Sun*, January 17, 1984.
[48] Ramsey Burt, "New Dance in Canada: Report from Le Festival international de nouvelle danse à Montréal." *New Dance* No. 35 (London: January 1986): 14–17.

relation to gravity and force. Here, critics move Lecavalier's athleticism and *off-axis* language to the fore, aligning the work perhaps with punk's claim to the nihilism as per something like The Sex Pistols' "No Feelings" (1977).

Baudrillard's notion of hyperreality comes to mind, wherein 1980s postmodern culture appears as an excess of signification and technology, and the subject "becomes a pure screen, a pure absorption and re-absorption surface of the influent networks."[49] Baudrillard, in his discussion of an America contemporaneous with La La La's emergent repertoire, remarks that "speed creates pure objects."

> It is itself a pure object, since it cancels out the ground and territorial reference-points ... speed is the triumph of effect over cause, the triumph of instantaneity over time as depth, the triumph of the surface and pure objectality over the profundity of desire.

Commenting on the mediatized landscape, Baudrillard sees only reduction and flattening in the proliferation of signs in the "desert of the real." La La La's complex aesthetic is easily read as a function of this landscape, and certainly international critics like Anna Kisselgoff and others remark on the element of sensation and repetition rather than coherent meaning. This was rock and roll, little else, "mainly about production effects."[50]

Perhaps the work may be best understood as a kind of "punk intensification",[51] a neo-expressionism understood as different and whose use of athleticism, speed, non-verbal gestures, and montage at once invoked meaning and authenticity—and their opposites. La La La activated a critical tension between live performance as really real (material dancing, bound to training and effort and experienced as live, authentic, and immediate) and layers of mediation through sound, image, and, occasionally, language in the form of direct speech to the audience or written word appearing on screens. Producing high-energy, rock-and-roll dance, the company undid the old hierarchies of value, placing fragment over whole, scene over narrative, mediation

---

[49] Jean Baudrillard, *America* (London, New York: Verso, 1988), 27.
[50] Anna Kisslegoff, "Mixed Media for Rock Music Lovers." *The New York Times*, October 2, 1991, C21.
[51] Diederichsen, "From Anti-Social Liberal Punk to Intersectional AIDs Activism," 31.

over pure dance to produce an affective "intensification."[52] Yet, whereas punk served as a "portable" circulating mode of critique, bound to the key affective states of the time, another set of artistic legacies, produced in earlier dangerous times, had already made available expressive resources and revised tastes for new kinds of dance.[53]

Expressionist tendencies

First, three short sketches from early to mid-twentieth-century Montréal:

German dance innovator Mary Wigman performs in Montréal in February and November of 1931. Huge crowds swarm His Majesty's Theatre on Guy Street. The *Montreal Gazette* exclaims, "Not in years has there been an artist who has created such a disturbance in the theatrical life of Montréal, or for that matter in any of the cities of America, which she has visited."[54] The French daily *La Patrie* is more critical, seeing "le triomphe de la culture physique" over the culture of dance; the critic bemoans "la loudeur," "les gestes carrés," and an apparent attempt "to make people forget that she was a woman.'"[55] As recounted by dance historian Marie Beaulieu, a polarized response ranges from ecstatic approval to dismay, seeing the work alternately as an assault on beauty and an important innovation in "la musique visuelle." *An urgent and critical modernism has entered the culture.*

[52] Ibid., 30.
[53] Ibid., 36.
[54] Thomas Archer, *Montreal Gazette*, February 23, 1931, 6.
[55] Eric Beaudry, *La Patrie*, February 23, 1931. Cited in Marie Beaulieu, "Accueillir la modernité avec Mary Wigman." In *Chroniques des arts de la scene à Montréal durant l'entre-deux-guerres: danse, théâtre, musique*, ed. Marie-Thérèse Lefebvre (Québec, QC: Septentrion/Cahiers des Amériques, 206), 112–33; 118–19.

In the mid-1940s, Québec dancer, choreographer, and visual artist Françoise Sullivan arrives in New York to study modern dance. At the Franziska Boas studio, she encounters distillations of *Ausdruckstanz*, through Boas who had studied with Wigman and Holm; and in workshops with Holm's assistant Mary Anthony. Sullivan is part of a cohort of Québec dancers in the city—including Jeanne Renaud and Francoise Riopelle, who are also studying with, among others, Holm and Anthony. Returning to Montréal, Sullivan and her friends will sign the surrealist manifesto, "Refus Global" (1948), with its transformative, poetic rage directed at a repressive Québec society. Together, they will be foundational for modern dance in the province. Renaud and Riopelle together found *l'École de danse modern* in 1958, establishing a critical infrastructure in the city; and Sullivan's *Danse dans la neige* (1948), an outdoor work made for documentation by camera, will become a benchmark of early performance art. Sullivan's own manifesto, "La danse et l'espoir" (1948), describes dance as a *"spontaneous expression of intense emotion."*[56]

That same year, another Montréal-based dancer/choreographer performs with her company at the first ever Canadian Ballet Festival in Winnipeg (1948). Ruth Abramovitsch Sorel—Polish and Jewish—is a stellar performer in Wigman's company (1923–8), who then tours and teaches in Poland before Nazi politics make life impossible. She escapes to Québec, by way of Brazil, in 1944. Sorel immediately founds the Ruth Sorel Dance

---

[56] Françoise Sullivan, "Danse et l'espoir" (Dance and Hope). In *Refus Global: The Manifesto of the Montréal Automatists*, ed. Ray Ellenwood (Holstein, ONT: Exile Editions, 2009/1948), n.p.

Group as well as schools in Westmount, Shawinigan, and Trois-Rivières. A brief glimpse of her dance at the festival is revealing: the clip is short, seconds only, but the sense of theatricality, charged emotion, and grounded movement is vivid.[57] In a description resonant with La La La's early style, historian Iro Tembeck describes "her doing Wigman-type spinning and using hand and arm gestures."[58] Returning to Poland in 1955, her work recedes from view locally as new priorities to support a national arts culture emerge. Yet her ideas continue to circulate via her students Yoné Kvietys (1924–2011) and Birouté Nagys (1920–), who together found the Montréal Modern Dance Company in 1952. Later, critics will credit her dance *La Gaspésienne* (1949) as *the first to embody a Québec thematic and identity.*

I offer these historical fragments as traces of expressionist dance circulating in Montréal, yet taken up by Québec culture and historians in asymmetrical ways. Such fragments belie formative tellings of the province's history that would draw a stark line between *la grand noirceur*—the repressive early twentieth century, wherein the ultra-Right premiere Maurice Duplessis presided over a largely rural culture and a dominant Catholic Church prohibited dancing; and the Quiet Revolution—wherein after 1960 a forward-thinking premiere Jean Lesage modernized the province through policy reform in economics, education, and the secular. A key narrative within concert dance is that no single modern technique took hold, save for the experimental context of the Groupe Nouvelle Aire (GNA) in the late 1970s. By this account, La La La arrives *deus ex machina*, its bold vision having little to no predecessors beyond the culture of exploration initiated by GNA—wherein both Lecavalier

---

[57] Roger Blais, Dir., *Ballet Festival*. 11 min. National Film Board, 1949. https://www.nfb.ca/film/ballet_festival_en/

[58] Iro Tembeck, "Flexible Identifies and the Necessity of Adaptability: The Case of Ruth Abramovitsch Sorel." Manuscript and notes for *Canadian Dance Studies Quarterly* 5, no. 1, (November 2004). Bibliothèque de la danse Vincent-Warren.

and Lock came up in the late 1970s. Whereas the GNA demonstrated an explicit interest in finding a distinctively local, Québecois style, its founder educator/choreographer Martine Époque trained at the Dalcroze Institute in Geneva, importing historical techniques and approaches into the company, and by the time of Lecavalier's involvement (1977–9) had shifted its focus towards greater "theatricality and emotion."[59]

To draw a line between Lecavalier's dancing as punk neo-expressionism and earlier forms of expressionism on view in Montréal is to underscore the seriousness of her dance study—"I tried to watch everything"—as well as her commitment to finding articulate form via the distillation and adaptation of the culture she moved in and through. At the same time, it marks a heterogeneity within Québec cultural production that recognizes the dance aesthetics shared and circulated by European, displaced and/or Jewish women dancing in Montréal, whose legacies may remain less visible due to inequities of experience and historiography.

Dance scholar Kate Elswit has cautioned against the use of the term *Ausdruckstanz* outside careful contextualization, noting it can never account for the diversity of practice found in Germany during the Weimar period; she reminds us of "what *Ausdrucken* stood for: the act of conveying, which demands that choreographers investigate their use of the body for expressive purposes."[60] Dance, of course, has long fostered a discourse claiming directness or immediacy of transferred emotion between dancer and viewer; Christina Thurner, for instance, in her study of the eighteenth-century ballet reformers in Germany who sought to

---

[59] Dalcroze and eurythmics comprise a parallel tradition to consider here. With its aim of developing advanced musical expressivity, a typical lesson, according to the scholar Selma Odom, went as follows: "rather than learning a dance technique or imitating the teacher's demonstration, [students] devise their own ways to step rhythmic patterns, sculpt phrases and create compositions." In the late 1970s, in addition to its influence at GNA, companies like Pointépiénu, where Lecavalier first began her professional training, offered eurythmics classes as part of their main curriculum. See Selma Odom, "Delsartean Traces in Dalcroze Eurhythmics." *Mime Journal* 23 (2005): 137–51. For more on GNA, see Michelle France Cloutier, "Groupe Nouvelle Aire." In *L'Encyclopédie Canadienne*, 2013. https://www.thecanadianencyclopedia.ca/fr/article/groupe-nouvelle-aire-le; and Martine Epoque, *Groupe Nouvelle Aire en mémoires 1968/82* (Québec: Presses de l'université du Québec, 2011).

[60] Kate Elswit, *Watching Weimar Dance* (Oxford, New York: Oxford University Press, 2014), xxiv.

replace technical virtuosity with "expressive signs of sensibility,"[61] shows how the very role of European theatrical dance evolved to rehearse emotion through an expressive exchange with the audience.

Yet the specific histories of circulation, adaptation, and repression associated with *Ausdruckstanz* offer a useful lens through which to see heterogeneity in the foundations of Québec dance. Susan Manning links the term to "a loose alliance of dancers who worked outside pre-existent institutions and created their own networks around studios and concert performances," intent on transforming through pedagogy and performance understandings of the body and German culture itself.[62] She traces a trajectory that finds the form first supported through student patronage, then via stage performance and the state during the late 1930s, marginalized during and after the Second World War and returning as an influence in the *Tanztheater* of the 1970s and 1980s. That trajectory helps account for its veiled status within Montréal, wherein dancers circulating between cultures have been less visible, especially as new cultural policies and the founding of the Canada Council for the Arts mid-century aimed at supporting the production of a national culture. Where noted, scholars have tended to see the presence of expressionist dancing as lost or dissipating.[63] Instead, myriad examples exist of robust teaching and performance practices in the city between 1940 and 1970. Among them: German ex-patriot Elizabeth Leese, who performed with Wigman-alumni Trudi Schoop and studied with Kurt Jooss, before arriving in Montréal in 1944 and opening a school (1945–60) that trained many young dancers in the city. Montréal-native Elsie Salomons, named earlier by Jeanne Renaud as a critical force in production of a modern dance in the province, studied with Laban

---

[61] Christina Thurner, "Affect, Discourse and Dance Before 1900." In *New German Dance Studies*, ed. Susan Manning and Lucia Ruprecht (Urbana, IL: University of Illinois Press, 2012), 17–30; 21.

[62] Susan Manning, *Ecstasy and the Demon: The Dances of Mary Wigman* (Minneapolis, MN: University of Minnesota Press, 2006), 7.

[63] See the following key essays engaging with Sorel: Noémie Solomon, "Imperceptible Virtuosities: Experimental Genealogies for a Contemporary Dance Field in Québec." McGill University Department of English Speakers Series, April 2024, 2014; and Tembeck, "Flexible Identifies and the Necessity of Adaptability."

and Jooss in London during the late 1930s, as well as with Dalcrozian Rosalie Chladek, before returning to establish dance training at McGill University (1956–76). Collectively, these figures brought new approaches to dancing previously unavailable within the culture.

Dance scholar Noémie Solomon, discussing Ruth Abramovitsch Sorel in particular, has gone far to suggest an experimental genealogy for Québec dance, pointing to "a history made of ruptures and discontinuities."[64] I focus, instead, on continuities and throughlines, masked via the politics of displacement, gender, or othering experienced by dancers from away and/or outside the linguistic and religious framework of French Catholicism. Contemporaneous with the high-stakes critique launched by the *Refus Global* generation, a critical mass of expressionist dancing in the city did its work more quietly, not through overt critique but via strategies of integration: performing, teaching, and setting up schools. If these distinctive strategies suggest binary subject positions—insider/outsider, citizen/displaced, belonging/alienated—Elswit's "micropolitics of exchange" makes way for slippage between such status, as some of the *Refus* artists were forced to leave Québec for New York and Paris after the publication of their manifesto; and some of the expressionist dancers returned home to Europe after the war's end.

My aim here is to highlight the productive contributions, rather than individual stories of loss; and to emphasize alignments between dance modernism and the *nouveau bouger*, rather than to reassert divides. In Lecavalier's depth of movement exploration and commitment to revised codifications; in her athleticism and speed; her revised presentation of gender, embodiment, and style; her choreographies of the face—a mocking grimace or challenging stare, I see the contorted expressions of *Ausdruckstanz* and proto-punks like Valeska Gert. In La La La's drive to transform dance and its audiences, remaking a collective body bound to high expressivity, a variation of Wigman's dream reappears. What is at stake in not seeing this legacy? While Manning's research shows how such narratives serve "to elide the German influence on American

---

[64] Solomon, "Imperceptible Virtuosities," 11.

dance and thus bolster claims of its Americanness,"[65] a similar kind of forgetting unfolded in the Québec context. Both in spite of and perhaps because of the requirement to remember its history—*je me souviens*—a more singular narrative of nation has dominated the formation of Québec, one which pivots around the French surrender to the English in 1759 during the Battle of Québec and the French-Canadian understanding of themselves as a colonized people. The drive to assert and "protect" French language rights and culture in Québec has had the effect of enshrouding the rights and histories of "others," especially those of immigrants. Whereas recent studies of Québec history note diverse ways of thinking about identity post-1980s, the question of xenophobism remains arch today—a backlash to the productive stretch of Lecavalier's early work and the internationalism of the 1980s—in the rear-garde actions of the right-wing Legault government.[66]

Montréal was and is an international port city, as profoundly shaped by migrations and ethnicities as by any singular or uncritical nationalism. But the circulation of ideas and aesthetics is never square; instead, they are carried, interpreted, and altered through kinesthetics informed by contextual and individualized practices.[67] Thinking through labor scholars Natasha Iskander's and Nichola Lowe's research on how tacit forms of knowledge shift in migration, the dancer in transit may serve as a game-changing force of cultural innovation and solidarity; less about straight translation of techniques from elsewhere, more about adaptations, the expressionist dancers of mid-century Québec may be seen as "knowledge transformers," who shifted their methods and revised their techniques to function in new environments. Less about purity, more about innovation, their work would go on to inflect dance

---

[65] Following Manning in Tressa Randall, "Hanya Holm and an American *Tanzgemeinschaft*." *New German Dance Studies*, ed. Susan Manning and Lucia Ruprecht (Champaign, IL: University of Illinois Press, 2012): 79–98, 79.
[66] See, for example, Behiels and Hayday, "Quebec Identity Politics in Transition," 694–703; and Daniel Latouche, "Quebec in the Emerging North American Configuration," 703–29. In *Contemporary Quebec*.
[67] See Noland on kinesthetic agency. Carrie Noland, *Agency and Embodiment: Performing Gestures/Producing Culture* (Cambridge, MA and London: Harvard University Press, 2009).

in Québec more broadly; and La La La Human Steps specifically. If punk offered an immediate and highly stylized transgressive mode of expression, the larger history of expressionism in the city suggests another powerful presence, wherein legacies of feminist performance knowledge at once create technical vocabularies and audience capacity to see and exceed theatrical and socio-cultural limits.

1980s: the return of the repressed

By the mid-1980s, Lecavalier and La La La were touring internationally, their *off-axis* athleticism marked by the knee-pads and sneakers they wore; their dance-theater altered via speed, horizontality, revised divisions of labor, the turn to non-verbal language, and more. Film scholar Allison Whitney, in her discussion of *Ausdrucktanz*'s effect on German film, describes a shared preoccupation for "dark themes, angular mise-en-scène, crude make-up and hyperbolic acting."[68] Her words are strangely resonant with La La La's aesthetic—think *Human Sex* (1985), with its intense, fragmented depiction of love, sex, and gender. Think Lecavalier, with her pencil-drawn mustache and ironic mimetic gestures punctuating radical action. Think, finally, of the company's revised vision of a material physicality: extreme shifts between air and ground, extreme gestures and its assembly of bodies in action, both onstage and off. That Lecavalier's iteration of this neo-expressionism would circle back to Europe, to influence companies like DV8 Physical Theater, Wim Vandekeybus and others associated with European dance theatre, the Flemish New Wave and so-called "Eurocrash" movements, underscores the significance of the dancer's cultural work.[69]

---

[68] Alison Whitney, "Etched with Emulsion: Weimar Dance and Body Culture in Expressionist Cinema." *Seminar: A Journal of Germanic Studies* 46, no. 3 (2010): 240–54; 240.
[69] Maeve Gradinger, "Dances of Disillusion." In *Ballett International/Tanz Aktuell* (October, 1995): 24–8.

Some dance critics situated Lecavalier and La La La within the larger aesthetic of *nouveau bouger*, emphasizing a felt rupture with the past and a sense of originality or "newness." This sense of "new," while capturing the feelings of excitement generated by the work, nonetheless often elided historical precedent. Dance historian Sally Banes offers one exception; Banes describes a shift in the 1980s towards movement's expressive registers, wherein the seemingly cool and "analytic" nature of the American postmodern dance she historicized is contrasted with a pressure to connect and communicate through a variety of choreographic tools. In an essay for the 1985 *Festival international de nouvelle danse*, she describes the return to content as the "return of the repressed," a reference to Freud's ideas about the history of consciousness wherein "what is forgotten is not extinguished but only repressed." She writes,

> Beyond narrative meaning, the new dance strives to express other features that the analytic dancers tried to purge from their work, such as character, mood, emotion, situation.[70]

Banes attributes this return as at once a reaction to postmodern dance and the ballet boom, as well as a response to "the temper of our times."[71]

The temper of the times was *extreme*. Within Québec, the body as an expressive tool was especially pressured, wherein passion for nationhood veered between political violence at the outset of the 1970s[72] and the election of a pro-sovereignty government in 1976 that sought legal frameworks to support the flourishing of an independent French state. In the context of the ratification of Bill 101, which set strict rules

---

[70] Sally Banes, *Souvenir Program, Festival international de nouvelle dance* (Montréal, Québec: Parachute Editions, 1985), 56.
[71] Banes, *Souvenir Program*, 52.
[72] Between 1962 and 1970, the *Front de libération du Québec* (FLQ) sought an independent state through increasingly violent means, culminating with the kidnapping and murder of Québec cabinet minister Pierre Laporte in October 1970. See Clément in Behiels and Hayday, *Contemporary Quebec*, for a reading of state response and human rights abuses under the imposed War Measures Act; see Sean Mills' *The Empire Within* for a history of adjacent, non-violent political activism, focused around decolonial and feminist projects.

for the exclusive use of French within public life, the dancing body's ability to perform covert, unspoken yet culturally available meanings may help account for the turn towards expressionism in the dance theater of 1980s Québec; and, indeed, to the popularity of La La La, which developed within a punk subculture and assembled audiences outside the contours of an arts establishment. To invoke expressionism within the Québec context is to tap into a widespread cultural anxiety, rooted in the legacy of colonization, around access to and rights of access to language: French, English, Indigenous languages, and more. Here, the return of the repressed circa 1980s, post-Bill 101, and amid a waning independence movement, assumes different weight, wherein La La La's heightened expressivity allowed the company—and its fans— to skirt linguistic tensions and capitalize on dance's ability to move between the signifiers.

Lecavalier's singular performance, then, may be understood in two adjacent ways: both as a felt lightning bolt, eliding the established confines of dance and nation to perform expansive views internationally; and as a collective endeavor of a different order, produced slowly over time through the unscripted, unspoken legacies of feminized dance teaching and transmission—the body-to-body learning and viewing in studios and on stages that include both the interpreters of *Ausdruckstanz* and the *Refus Global*. As the company's work became increasingly popular, it offered revised ideas about how dance performed and what it might say; and it produced a unique vision of the collective body, understood as a fist to the face of elite class formations and as dense with layers of history read as punk, yet infused with earlier modes of expressivity. To trace this relation is to underscore the unmarked role of the dancer as keeper and producer of aesthetic, intellectual, and informational exchange across the twentieth century.

4

Hybrid Body, International Cyborg

Rehearsals Against Purity

It is ... necessary to imagine a world of composite elements, without the notion of purity.

—Jennifer Gonzáles

By the late twentieth century, our time, a mythic time, we are all chimeras, theorized and fabricated hybrids of machine and organism; in short, we are cyborgs.

—Donna Haraway

With increasing fame, an innovative movement aesthetic and a visual style borrowed from the punk and post-punk scenes of New York, Berlin, London, and Montréal, La La La Human Steps signified a new internationalism for Québecers—both in terms of recognition and mobility. By 1988, and alongside fellow Québecers like Cirque du Soleil, director Robert Lepage and pop performer Céline Dion, the company was well-established and touring extensively. Lecavalier, too, was by then internationally renowned, singled out for the power and athleticism of her performance, as well as for its apparent androgyny which at once reconfigured the look and labor of the dancer and challenged audiences to keep up with identity understood as mutable, contextual, perceptual. What mechanisms drove this stardom, and how did dance prove so permeable across cultural contexts? Mid-way through 1988, and the *New Demons* tour, Lecavalier and company joined David Bowie for a benefit at the International Centre for the Arts (ICA) in London; and soon after Nam June Paik's satellite broadcasting event *Wrap Around the*

World (1988), which beamed images of their dance to twenty countries and 120 million people globally in advance of the opening of the 1988 Olympics in Seoul one week later.

A grainy YouTube video offers one account of their contribution. We see Lecavalier dancing with Bowie and Marc Béland in a performance of "Look Back in Anger," while Paik's signature effects moderately color the live representation. The movement is a familiar phrase from the repertoire: Lecavalier's duet with Marc Béland perhaps first seen in *Human Sex* (1985). Lecavalier and Béland perform the iconic big moves, while Bowie takes on the more pedestrian and gestural elements, as well as playing guitar and singing. For the YouTube edit, and collapsing the larger arc of Paik's satellite broadcast and subsequent video piece, a young Al Franken appears to frame their contribution with a familiar narrative for dance and culture—that is, dance as a confirmation of humanity's best values. In the YouTube edit, Franken introduces their segment as a news announcer encountering an alien interlocutor, Dr. Mobius, who has come to Earth to combat the human race's "virulent nationalism, ceaseless brutality and wonton disrespect for the needs of [its] own planet."[1] He then points to the dance as an argument for not destroying the earth, evidence of the human capability to "transcend artificial boundaries," underscoring Paik's vision of a global community forged through the technological collapse of time and space. Anticipating the speed and connectivity of the internet, and following on over a decade of experiments by Paik on the potential of live and canned broadcasting, this snippet of *Wrap Around* offers an idealistic vision of dance as evidence of shared language and humanity; TV as a public tool for connecting audiences across the globe through art; and, indeed, an idealistic vision of globalism as a mechanism for transcending borders and fueling cross-cultural understanding.

The clip is a useful snapshot of a company at the height of its powers and encircled by an emergent globalism—wherein humanist ideals of

---

[1] Nam June Paik, *Wrap Around the World* (1988). 47 min, color, sound. Electronic Arts Intermix. See too: (1988) "Wrap Around The World" excerpt with Al Franken performing the role of Dr. Mobius; www.youtube.com/watch?v=9Vb63Blefpk.

freedom and access still held currency alongside market determinations. In Lecavalier's home city of Montréal, the sense of cultural transition was palpable, as the economic and political landscape shifted post-1976. As the Anglophone population began to decline, French-language immigration increased considerably under the control of the provincial government; and the cultural make-up of the city began to diversify. Noting the shift in demographics that followed the Second World War, one scholar described the 1980s as "the time of the three solitudes,"[2] a reference to ethnic minorities as a cluster challenging understandings of Québec as uniquely French and English. At the same time, the zeal for fiscal restraint and privatization pushed power away from the intellectuals that had long shaped Québec politics and towards business elites and new economic partners. American president and Hollywood B-movie actor Ronald Reagan led the moment, followed by Thatcher in England; Mulroney in Canada, and Robert Bourassa, then premier of Québec, in what was seen to be at odds with the province's longtime, cultural understanding of government in the service of the people and bound by the "social contract."[3] Whereas the 1960s and 1970s had rung in a strong middle class, tight economic times and the conservative policies of the 1980s would pressure resources and access, alongside categories of identity and understandings of class, gender, and race.

Writing contemporaneously with the shifts that so transformed the 1980s, post-colonial studies scholar Homi K. Bhabha noted, "We find ourselves in the moment of transit where time and space cross to produce complex figures of difference and identity, past and present, inside and outside, inclusion and exclusion."[4] Reflecting on that moment, and in dialogue with repertoire and critical writing from the period, this essay takes up presentations of hybridity within the company, which I argue are most evident in Lecavalier's performance; particularly, its citation of whiteness, Blackness, and a spectrum of identity positions suggested

[2] Susan Ireland and Patrice J. Proulx, Eds., *Textualizing the Immigrant Experience in Contemporary Québec* (Westport, CT, London: Praeger, 2004).
[3] John Dickinson and Brian Young, *A Short History of Québec*, 4th Edition (Montréal: McGill-Queens Press, 2008).
[4] Homi K. Bhabha, *The Location of Culture* (London, New York: Routledge, 2004/1994), 1.

in between. Whereas much has been made of the play of gender in the work—its intersection with feminism and with queering the gender binary—less has been said about its ethnicity, particularly significant at a moment of expanding cultural transit. My aim is to think through the resistant nature of the work, which challenged visions of the body as matched to a stable, legible identity; and, more broadly today, offers an alternative view to easy understandings of *Québecité* as uniquely rooted in French language and culture, instead following Erin Hurley's research on the "changing sensibility of Québécois nation-ness, in the second half of the twentieth century."[5]

Whereas Lecavalier and La La La came to coincide with a national image of Québec as culturally unique, boldly innovative, and internationally recognized,[6] the company's invocation of hybrid bodies offers a compelling argument for revised understandings of the repertoire and the period. How, for instance, did Lecavalier's identity as a white working-class Québecer intersect with her androgyny in performance? What are we to make of her famous hairstyle involving dreadlocks, and what other traces of Black and/or diasporic performance might reside in the work? In what follows, I think through several key works from Lecavalier's stage and media performances of the late 1980s and early 1990s to understand more about her role as a beacon of bodily difference at a moment of global transition; Lecavalier's dancing and visual look, finally, reflected a deep unease with essentialized understandings of the body and rigid categories of identity in ways that local and international audiences connected to and that were central to its pleasure and power at the time.

Global grooves, gender hybridities

Wrap Around the World was a 90-minute live satellite event, presented in September 1988, a week before the Seoul Olympics opened and

---

[5] Erin Hurley, *National Performance: Representing Québec from Expo 67 to Celine Dion* (Toronto: University of Toronto Press, 2010), 10.
[6] Hurley, *National Performance*, 23.

conceived as a counterpoint to the competitive nationalism on view in the sporting event. The event featured live and canned performances by multiple artists, athletes, and folkloric groups, including "Trans-Atlantic Duet," a live tele-duet between dancer/choreographer Merce Cunningham in New York and composer Ryuichi Sakamoto in Tokyo. Staged across multiple time zones and in multiple cities, Paik's *Wrap Around* blended live performance with real-time image processing, documentary footage, brief interviews, and orienting sketches reflecting on world ecology and envisioning unity. Paik's recollection of his satellite arts series of events marks the idealism at its core:

> If we could assemble a weekly television festival comprised of music and dance from every nation and disseminate it freely via the proposed video common market to the world, its effects on education and entertainment would be phenomenal. Peace can be as exciting as a John Wayne war movie. The tired slogan of "world peace" will again became fresh and marketable.[7]

Wrap Around, with its collage imagery and channel-surf editing, places popular, folkloric, and avant-garde arts in relation, pointing to shared themes across national identities. In a proposal for the event, Paik writes that the occasion of the Olympics allows for collaboration "overcoming this century-old enmity or skepticism among different peoples."[8]

Yet Lecavalier's own memory of the event points to the arduous nature of geographic crossings and the ways in which the promise of global community might encounter obstacles, especially where different contexts and approaches produce different needs. For Lecavalier, the chance to work with Nam June Paik on the project came mid-way through the *New Demons* tour; it was exciting but not easy. She remembers,

> We had been on tour with *New Demons* for a long time, maybe 120 shows over two years, just tonnes of gigs and gigs and gigs. I was

---

[7] Paik, in *Nam June Paik*, ed. Sook-Kyung Lee and Susanne Rennert (London: Tate Publishing, 2010), 33.

[8] Paik, in *We Are Open Circuits: Writings by Nam June Paik*, ed. John G. Hanhardt, Gregory Zinman, and Edith Decker-Phillips (Cambridge, MA: MIT Press, 2019), 236.

> already a bit tired and I was injured at that time, badly injured to the knee, and Édouard was veering slowly towards ballet ... it was a different way of training and moving. And we were doing a show with David [Bowie] at the ICA [Institute of Contemporary Art] in London. So lots of gigs, and it's a stress too, really physically demanding. If the project had been boring, maybe I'd say no, let's do it later. But it was David, and I said yes.[9]

Lecavalier recalls the event happened with short notice. There was little time to prepare, and she had very little contact with Paik. The team flew in to New York the day before the event: Bowie, Lock, Béland, and herself. Friends came down from Montréal to see them, bringing new white costumes that had been requested to support the recorded event and its visual manipulation via Paik's techniques. But there was little time for dialogue. They had one day to rehearse, in a small studio designed for media production rather than dance; the space was extremely tight and didn't allow for big movement. Most striking for her was the sense of limitation:

> It was 9 am in the morning, maybe earlier ... I was jetlagged, there was no time for warm-up or to rehearse and set up the space for dance. The production team did it live in one-shot, and there was no space to move ... The whole situation was kind of numbing. And so many people see that video online now ... but for me I can see I'm not dancing well.[10]

The promise of a "global groove," with artists and audiences moving together, was tempered by the physical reality of travel, injury, and the limited scale of the space. Just as the video marks the tension between clear representation and Paik's creative manipulations of color, rhythm, lag, and glitch, Lecavalier's recollection of lived experience shows a gap between Paik's aspiration to collapse geographies and cross cultures and what happens for individuals on the ground.

---

[9] Lecavalier (2020).
[10] Lecavalier (2020).

Bhabha more recently has lamented that hybridity has become a kind of celebratory brand rather than critical tool; he writes, "Hybridity, in our global moment, has become a ubiquitous form of cultural universalism, the proper name of a homogenizing pluralism."[11] His critique points to culture as global schmear, packaged as flavor and authenticity and sold through aggressive marketing techniques and a flattening of the discourse. While today, the twenty-first-century global landscape appears to proliferate inequities of mobility and access, it wasn't always that way. Circa 1990, for Bhabha, and generations of readers since, hybridity began as a conceptual tool that fostered an "agency and affiliation not easily 'named' in the accredited architectures of political power."[12] Hybridity at once acknowledged histories of geopolitical movement, rejected identity as essentialist or fixed, and danced strategically at the border between state-crafted narratives and lived, collective experiences of identity. Its critique and potential emerged in and through its liminality. For Bhabha, "The hybrid voice— she, he it they us—can only accrue authority by questioning its *a priori* security, its first-person privilege, both grammatical and geopolitical."[13]

At that moment, Lecavalier raised critical doubt in the fixity of identity, and *Wrap Around* offers a quick snapshot of her dance as a push-back against hegemonic understandings of the gendered body and against the limits of vision as a mode of knowing. The short clip rehearses the by then familiar gestures associated with La La La Human Steps: the air-born barrel rolls, or *off-axis*; the coded movements for hands and arms that lean into non-verbal communication; the physicality, floorwork, and mimetic characterizations, for example, in tossing her male partner Béland to the ground and striding over to engage or confront Bowie. Whereas the work is flattened out, strangely undynamic on video and the constraints of the space alongside her restraint with her injury are visible—she shuddered to recall the

---

[11] Bhabha, in *Debating Cultural Hybridity: Multicultural Identities and the Politics of Anti-Racism*, ed. Pnina Werbner and Tariq Modood (London: Zed Books, 2015), xi.
[12] Ibid., xi.
[13] Ibid., xiii.

moment as she described it—her revision of the role of the *prima ballerina* is clear. In terms of corporeality, she is muscled, angular, strong. In terms of movement, she is athletic, working ground and air, gesturally uncodified by modern or ballet, and always performing at high speed—a core strategy instigated by choreographer Lock and realized by Lecavalier for confounding perceptions of the body. Above all, and rocking the status quo of gendered division of labor, she physically lifts Béland and Bowie; and, within the narrative structure, seems to play with one, then the other, as if for her own pleasure—sexual and otherwise. As questions about the work's implied violence, or sense of risk, gathered around the La La La repertoire, at least part of that perception of danger lay in a diffused anxiety about the revised status of the female dancer.

Through these mechanisms and by these actions, Lecavalier broke with the familiar ideology of the feminized dancer and the romanticized role of the principal by performing along a spectrum of cultural understandings of the feminine and masculine. Part of this was conscious and came from her own keen awareness of the limits placed on the female dancer in practice and through representation. In one interview, she said,

> All these precious or ridiculous images—I want to fight against that. With so many dances, women are presented in a limited way; they seem all wrong, like flipping out over romance or helpless, like falling apart over anything …. That's not how women are.[14]

Lecavalier has said that she never saw herself in the "shape of a girl," nor could she think about her mind as "specifically feminine."[15] "Of course, I am a woman but it wasn't for someone else to say how or what I should be." Before entering the dance world at 15, she felt quite limitless in terms of what she would do. She attributes this in part to the strength of her mother—an independent-minded teacher who worked full-time and approached child-rearing with a rigor and expectation

---

[14] Lecavalier (2016).
[15] Ibid.

of self-reliance—and to her childhood, growing up with three younger brothers with whom she played and rough-housed. A primary source of movement inspiration lay too in her father, a laborer who worked in construction and whose wiry, strong body and efficiency of gesture served as a key model.

Later, working alongside company member Louis Guillemette proved decisive; "we were just friends, playing around in the studio—if he lifted me, well ... why not give him a lift too?" The degree of play and effort, sourced through the weight-sharing technique of contact improv, would forever revise the gendered division of labor in dance. At the same time, as the action of the dance and its required musculature challenged essentialized notions of a gendered body more broadly, Lecavalier's strong body resonated within the Québec context and a French-Canadian history of working-class pride, while challenging more provincial conventions of women as homemakers.

Critics and viewers repeatedly saw risk in the work, for the dancers and for the viewers too; for example, one critic noting the "dangerous physicality,"[16] another describing the sense that Lecavalier was coming directly at us, "making an audience duck for cover."[17] The revised imagery and energy of their dance—crafted in Lecavalier's own body, in company vocabulary or in the narratives of the repertoire—was at once part of the company's early threat and excitement. Presenting differently was a factor in the work's ability to draw audiences from popular scenes outside of theater dance; more, it helped the work circulate internationally as modes of physical theater and visual spectacle took center stage, and third wave feminism and queer activism called for expanded understandings of gender. Younger audiences thirsted for real stories told in movement, stories that spoke to current experience and issues. Before terms like gender-fluidity and queerness became available in the lexicon, her presence onstage was androgynous in what was a striking expansion of the gender binary

---

[16] Kathryn Greenaway, "La La La dancer undaunted …." *Montreal Gazette,* March 7, 1990.
[17] Christopher Bowen, "Bodily Charmed." *The Scotsman,* October 22, 1996.

for concert dance; and, more, one that was felt within everyday life. Virtuosic, uncodified, ambiguous, and highly charismatic, her dance facilitated a kind of *gender reach*: movement outside fixed categories that felt hugely generative and that aligned closely with her and Lock's view of bodies "in the process of becoming."

Looking back now, after the 2008 financial crisis or amid the post-truth world of the internet, the idealism of Paik's *Wrap Around*, as mass event and cross-cultural collage, can feel naïve. But it's critical to remember the kind of alliances and ontologies made possible by the discourse of optimism and achievements that drove political activism in the 1960s and 1970s during the period when Paik cut his teeth and as new media technologies developed. During the 1980s, as an emergent globalism seemed to offer limitless access to border crossings and international markets, powerful and efficacious forms of collective political activism appeared at their zenith: the dismantling of the Berlin Wall (1990); the end of apartheid in South Africa (1991); and ACT-UP's fight for better health care and to end the AIDS epidemic (1987–2012). The success of movements such as these tended to affirm the potential of cross-cultural solidarity and coalition politics. In his work on Afrofuturism, technology, and race, Louis Chude-Sokei has identified a tradition of creolization—that is, the phenomenon of cultural blending—that, in addition to acknowledging the racism and trauma of history, "distinguishes itself by an equal commitment to the possible."[18] Amid this framework and against this cultural context, Lecavalier's performed ambiguity signified real possibility to audiences and to the discipline.

Appropriations/circulations

Questions about gender, and the attendant anxiety about extreme risk, tended to monopolize response to La La La and Lecavalier, yet

---

[18] Louis Chude-Sokei, *The Sound of Culture: Diaspora and Black Technopoetics* (Middleton, CT: Wesleyan University Press, 2015), 205.

the overlay between gender and race has largely gone unnoticed. One avenue for considering how the company telescoped the phenomenon of in-between identities might lie with Lecavalier's appropriation of dreadlocks, the iconic Africanist hairstyle and a potent symbol of Caribbean culture and power, which she wore briefly during the *Infante, c'est destroy* (1991) period. Though critics, audiences, and academics alike referred to Lecavalier's locks repeatedly—the dreadlocks recurring and defining as a descriptor in the popular press and imaginary—no critical attention was paid to them at the time. Taken as style, it was as if their meaning was self-evident: often code for wildness, otherness, or to cite Kevin Frank's scholarship, *dread*.[19] Here I read the dreadlocks as a marker of Black aesthetics in the work and interpret Lecavalier's appropriation, not as theft, but as part of challenge to notions of authenticity and purity (*"pure laine"*)[20] that continued to infect nationalist discourse in post-Second World War Québec.

I start as an ardent fan of Lecavalier's work *and* a profound skeptic about what it might mean for a white woman to wear dreadlocks. Around the same time period, particularly in the United States and popular culture, the term "wig-er" slips in and out of popular use as a term for "white youth said to be or claiming to be imitating African-Americans today."[21] I first imagined the term to be related to the idea of the wig, for its costume aspect suggesting fakery or inauthenticity, only later understanding its rhymed relation to the n-word—a function of my own whiteness and how it occludes knowledge.[22] Whereas Roediger historicizes the phenomenon as a form of racial cross-over, with the

---

[19] Kevin Frank, "Whether Beast or Human: The Cultural Legacies of Dread, Locks and Dystopia." *Small Axe* 11, no. 2 (June 2007): 46–62.

[20] The expression refers to direct descendants from the earliest French settlers in the province; the phrase is associated with a xenophobic nationalism and holds a pejorative sense.

[21] David R. Roediger, "In Conclusion: Elvis, Wiggers, and Crossing Over to Nonwhiteness." In *Colored White: Transcending the Racial Past* (Berkeley, Los Angeles: University of California Press, 2002), 212–40.

[22] I am indebted to recent work by Nicholas Mirzoeff, with its critical perspective that, "white sight does not see everything there is to see but projects a white reality." In Mirzoeff, *White Sight: Visual Politics and Practices of Whiteness* (Cambridge, MA: MIT Press, 2003), ix.

practice shifting uneasily between mimicry and critique, writers like Brent Staples and Greg Tate dismiss such attempts as naïve at best. In the words of the comic Paul Mooney, playing the character Junebug in the film *Bamboozled*, "White folks want to be Black folks, everyone wants to be Black…. I hope they start hanging n——again, we're going see who's Black."[23] With an eye to the lived experience of Blackness, and resonating with the scholarly traditions of feminist, queer, and Black studies, Mooney's joke gets at the dumb ease of white racial crossings, where the option to return to privilege always remains.

A parallel discourse here, unfolding with heightened urgency during the 1980s, particularly in Canada, focuses on the strategic use of appropriation since colonial times as a way to take and benefit from the lands, resources, and cultural artifacts of colonized peoples. In this tradition, appropriation flows in one direction—the powerful taking things from the less powerful. Problematized in contexts with an asymmetry of power, appropriation is only another form of cultural theft. Writing in 1993, in response to the proverbial flattening of discourse around an ethics of borrowing that tends to favor those in power, the artist/filmmaker Richard Fung explains, "The critique of cultural appropriation is … first and foremost a strategy to redress historically established inequities by raising questions about who controls and benefits from cultural resources."[24] Fung's thinking challenges us towards nuance and the need to privilege context in debates around the politics of appropriation.

Returning to Lecavalier's dreadlocks, I argue that rather than constituting an attempt at racial cross-over or a malignant act of theft, the style invoked specific forms of cultural hybridity and, for viewers in Québec and internationally, served as a marker of less legible ethnic histories and aesthetics embedded in the work. Here the process might recall what Chude-Sokei describes as the "syntheses, transformation,

---

[23] Paul Mooney, *Bamboozled* (2000). Spike Lee, Dir. USA. 2h 15min.
[24] Richard Fung, "Working Through Appropriation." *FUSE* Magazine V.XVI, no. 5+6 (Summer 1993): 16–24.

destruction and affirmation at the heart of creolization."[25] Historian Sean Mills has shown how the French-Canadian sense of itself as a colonized people fueled a strong identification with post-colonial peoples and discourses that resulted in productive acts of solidarity with Black communities in Montréal. His research has complicated the French-English narrative of culture that has tended to dominate the discourse in Québec. Whereas Lecavalier and Lock were not political artists, they were nonetheless politicized: Louise, as a working-class French-Canadian coming up during the late 1960s and 1970s as English interests that had once dominated provincial economics and cultural policy began to fade under the project of independence; and Édouard, as a Moroccan Jew, arriving in 1957 in the city, when Jews could still not attend the free public school system. In this context, and twisted up with their work in challenging gender and disciplinary boundaries in dance, the dreadlocks may read as a productive incursion against notions of *pure laine* Québec identity.

Press accounts establish the iconicity of Lecavalier's hair as early as 1984, describing it as a "mop of white-blond hair."[26] Through the 1980s, journalists repeatedly identify the performer by her "punk blonde hair,"[27] "the trademark mane of unruly blond hair,"[28] its "white" or "platinum" color. References to her dreadlocks come later, mentioned in passing, again without remark and in identificatory ways, as in "her famous dreadlocks";[29] or else assigned over-the-top descriptions, as in "her hair bleached brutally into a white, desiccated tangle."[30] The references to "ses tresses rasta"[31] are ubiquitous, foregrounding attention to her personal style, as well as the hairstyle and its attendant exoticization. Published photographs equally rehearse the association

---

[25] Chude-Sokei, *The Sound of Culture*, 190.
[26] Deborah Jowitt, "Honk If You Love Dogs." *The Village Voice*, October 9, 1984.
[27] Amanda Smith, "La La La Human Steps." *Dance Magazine*, March 1986, 97.
[28] Greenaway, "La La La dancer undaunted …."
[29] Liz Warwick, "Wild Thing." *Montreal Gazette*, October 2, 1995, E3.
[30] Nadine Meisner, "Superwoman." *The Sunday Times*, October 20, 1996, 2.
[31] Radio-Canada, "Louise Lecavalier: Libérée par la dance, adulée par Edouard Lock." March 29, 2016. https://ici.radio-canada.ca/ohdio/premiere/emissions/les-grands-entretiens/segments/entrevue/11632/louise-lecavalier-danse-franco-nuovo

between the dancer and the dreadlocks—for example, a 1994 image of Lecavalier air-bound wherein her hair constitutes a halo of light at the center of the image is captioned "Wiltern wildness,"[32] pairing the name of the historic Los Angeles theater with the company's well-established reputation for seemingly high-risk, wild movement. Dreadlocks, it seems, convey the performer and the company's difference, associated with a pleasure in extreme gesture: "terrifying flights," "high risk" barrel turns, or otherwise "violent" moves.[33]

Kevin Frank has identified how the Medusa story, associated with betrayal, rape, and death, has structured reception in popular Hollywood film franchises like *Predator* and *Pirates of the Caribbean*, conveying "dread and Otherness through the hairstyle associated with Rastafarians,"[34] rather than the empowerment and anti-racist messages.[35] Here, dreadlocks constitute "a deadly threat to supposedly utopian America or out-of-the-way societies." Yet dreads equally invoke advanced techniques and technologies. Louis Chude-Sokei has shown how historical forms of technology—automatons, robots, and other anthropomorphic forms—repeatedly referenced Black life as a threshold between the human and the non-human. He points to a colonial imaginary that conflated machines and the future with Blackness, long before Caribbean-infused sounds and styles, dub and dreadlocks permeated the aesthetic of cyberpunk film and literature.

In the case of Lecavalier, response hovers between fear and longing, fascination and forgetting, with the style rapidly noted then cast from view. What patterns of recognition and erasure, desire and hate might be operative here? On the one hand, hair may seem reductive as a point of focus—certainly, my own gaze here risks repeating modes

---

[32] Randy Leffingwell, "La La La Human Steps Brings Extravaganza to Wiltern." *Los Angeles Times*, March 26, 1994, F8.

[33] Reception of this order is equally seen in response to the queerness of the work, wherein queerness lives in the work in a variety of ways: for example, in the redistribution of gender-based labor (for example, Louise holds up Marc, rather than the other way around); or else, in the transformation of her body through effort, labor and intention, of which I've written in Chapter 2 of this work. See too Low (2016).

[34] Frank, "Whether Beast or Human," 46.

[35] Ibid., 47.

of fetishization. On the other, Lecavalier's wearing of the style may constitute a visible marker of histories and hybridities that animate the work, yet have been erased by the work of whiteness.

Louise recalls first wearing the style with *Infante, c'est destroy* (1992), a break-out work for the company in terms of international touring and success; and arguably one of the repertoire most closely associated with the dancer. *Infante* casts Lecavalier as a warrior, a powerful character and image of strength she intentionally sought to bring to the work.[36] With its transcendent, religious themes and imagery, *Infante* imagines Lecavalier as a Joan-of-Arc figure, alternately in control, and destroyed, yet always at the center—in serial pairings, trios and solos, and giant film projections, wherein she remains prime agent and actor. With *Infante* becoming an identifying "signature" work for the company, the wearing of dreadlocks become identifying for Lecavalier as a performer around this time, though in fact she would soon stop wearing the locks. Though speculation about violence in the work seem the primary pivot of reception, spirituality and empowerment are certainly another option, begging the question of how to reconcile high energy and a professional technique that renders the movement "safe"; and its devotional, ecstatic aspects that gestured to Catholic spirituality.

Lecavalier remembers the style developed initially as a function of bleaching her hair, and with an aim to render her work as a performer more fully visible:

> I thought, 'I'll make white, white hair and all you will see is the face, what I'm saying with my face. After that, they [media] talked about the dreads—but mainly that started because of the bleached air, it was so dry and I would be dancing these long hours, spinning and spinning—it started to mat, and I didn't undo it.[37]

What is striking to me in her account is at once the sense of difficulty she experienced in terms of being seen and understood as artist; and

---

[36] Lecavalier (2016).
[37] Lecavalier (2012, 2016).

the consistency of a materialist understanding of her aesthetic, wherein the look always came from making movement. Time and again in interviews, her profound discomfort with interest in appearances is palpable; she consistently has articulated frustration with the visual limits of identity, especially for dancers who incarnate a collapse between object and subject, dance and dancer. Coming up in the ballet and modern dance worlds of 1970s Montréal, she felt that teachers, choreographers, and audiences could get stuck on the look of a dancer; and noted how compliance to expectations and aesthetics were expected and enforced. Over time, she developed multiple looks as a strategy to counter limits and create opportunities—that is, transforming her appearance in order to survive and to be seen on- and off-stage, in a play with identity at once highly intentional, enabled by white privilege, yet deeply critical of consolidations of authority.[38]

Whereas Kobena Mercer and other scholars have noted the meticulous cultivation that is required to produce a Black hairstyle such as this,[39] Lecavalier resists ownership here. Rather than seeing this as a pivot away from agency, her words mark a profound ambivalence around matters of style and an anxiety around the gaze as ever gendered, raced act. To linger over questions of visual style, from her perspective, could only shift the attention away from the central project of making movement. It's worth noting here the phenomenology of dreads in performance: for while the Medusa character threatens to steal movement, turning those who gaze to stone, the dreads on stage are all about movement. On stage, her hair assumed a larger, animate quality: airborne, reaching out, radiating into space and full of life. Set in motion through an intentional body, activated particularly via repertoire of neck and head, the dreads claim space and expand the body, following its action, yet with a slight delay and a distinctive weighted quality. Here, dreadlocks extend her reach and challenge the limits of the individual body onstage.

---

[38] Lecavalier (2009, 2012, 2016).
[39] Kobena Mercer, "Black Hair/Style Politics." *New Formations* 1, no. 3 (Winter 1987): 33–54.

At the same time, the bleached-white locks tend to do funny things under theatrical lighting in terms of how her face appears on stage. For instance, in one filmed version,[40] her face recedes from view entirely in darkness, and her dreads in-and-as light assume the expressivity typically associated with the face. Elsewhere, full lighting makes her hair recede from view, all we see are the details of her facial expression. What remains is a sense of tension between revelation and masking; between sight and coverage, pointing to perception itself as partial and limited.

Kobena Mercer has described how cultural acts such as the cultivation of particular hairstyles were "stylistically cultivated and politically constructed in a particular historical moment as part of a strategic contestation of white dominance and the cultural power of whiteness."[41] Mercer identifies the emergence of dreads in England and elsewhere during the 1970s as a symbol of Black pride and authority, following the radical discourse of Rastafari culture and the cultural and political insurgence of reggae into the mainstream. More, in tracking the style's ricochet from situated meaning to its dissemination and commodification, he writes that the "back and forth indicates an underlying dynamic of struggle as different discourses compete for the same signs."[42]

What discourses compete for meaning in Lecavalier's wearing of dreads? More recently, as time passes and dancer and company receive multiple honors in the name of nation and state,[43] La La La is folded squarely into a narrative of *Québécité* and cultural distinctiveness.

---

[40] Société Radio-Canada *Infante, c'est destroy*. DVD. Collection: Bibliothèque de la danse Vincent-Warren, Montréal, 1994.
[41] Mercer, "Black Hair/Style Politics," 40.
[42] Ibid., 52.
[43] Lecavalier was named Companion of *l'Ordre des arts et lettres de Québec*; and Édouard Lock has received *Prix de Québec* (2002) and Knight in *l'Ordre des arts et lettres de Québec* (2001). Both are officers in the Order of Canada. *Québécité* may be understood as a mode of feeling Québecois; it is "a project/process of (re)construction of Québec that develops in reaction (read: in opposition) to the project/process of the country's Canadianization." Jocelyn Létourneau in Erin Hurley, the latter cited here especially for the formative work she does in folding a range of labor forms by women into the history of Québecois performance. In Hurley, *National Performance*.

Following Stuart Hall's work on "narratives of nation," in which he notes how national cultures take up forms of representation to gather and affirm unified images of themselves, these awards attest to the place of these artists within the national cultures of Québec, smoothing the work into coherent themes of innovation, achievement, and, primarily, international recognition that resemble the province's aspirations for statehood while all the while undermining the other productive ambiguities.

It is worth remembering that as beloved as their early work was, its meaning and their stature occupied a much more equivocal position in the early days. Was it dance, or something else? Was it theater, punk rock, or some kind of "street fight"? Was Louise a muse, or an instigator? A "man" or a "woman"? Or something else entirely: "cyborg," "demon," "animal," angel"? Early press accounts record a preoccupation with Lecavalier, configured repeatedly as a non-human, in ways that were gendered and racialized. Equally, the company aesthetic was understood as threatening, with both Lock and Lecavalier on record defending the work against claims of risk and violence. What audiences saw were high-speed moves; high-energy leaps and lifts inspired by contact improv, acrobatics, and breakdancing; communicative registers, including hand gestures recalling sign language, mime, and voguing; and a remarkable interdisciplinarity, blending dance, theater, film, and popular music. At the same time, they saw distinctive new bodies whose movement sought to challenge perception, and by extension, legibilities and classifications. At once, the aesthetic looked like nothing—and it looked like everything.

Here, I turn momentarily to scholarship on whiteness, not to consolidate pernicious racial binaries, but to mark the cultural pattern of practices and dispositions that attempt to exploit and exclude Black life.[44] As David Austin and others have noted, during this period, the

---

[44] David R. Roediger, *The Wages of Whiteness: Race and the Making of the American Working Class* (London, New York: Verso, 1999), 13. See too Cheryl Harris, "Whiteness as Property." *Harvard Law Review* 106, no. 8 (June 1993): 1714. She documents the movement of "whiteness from color to race to status to property as a progression historically rooted in white supremacy and economic hegemony over Black and Native American peoples."

political struggles of Africa and its diaspora "served as a metaphor for Québec identity,"⁴⁵ foregrounding white Québecers and eliding a history of slavery and racism in the province. Whiteness as a conceptual and political framework has relied on theft and erasure, whiteness lays claim, takes over. Yet in the story of La La La and Lecavalier, whiteness may help account for the too-easy absorption of the company into a national narrative within Québec that could not fully address the ambiguity of identity at play in Lecavalier's dance, in the repertoire, and within Québec society itself. Historian David Roediger, following Du Bois, sees whiteness as a time-based performative practice of differentiation and othering.⁴⁶ Which is to say, whitening takes work and it is the work of the social collective. First-draft reception in the popular press, and subsequent historiography, accelerated that effort, in seeing Lecavalier as muse or victim; and Lock as creative genius, appearing as if *ex machina*, sans origins.

Blurred identities in the repertoire

To take seriously Lecavalier's wearing of dreadlocks, used to describe her long after she stopped wearing them, is to read for hybrid identities and diasporic traces in La La La Human Steps. It is, in the words of Brenda Dixon Gottschild, to begin "digging the Africanist presence" embedded in the work. Gottschild places Africanist aesthetics at the very center of much American modern dance innovation and points to an "invisibilizing" process in hegemonic cultural and historical accounts of that history.⁴⁷ She writes,

> Although we do not and cannot reduce the intertextuality of the African-American/European equation to a laundry list of sources and

---

⁴⁵ David Austin, "Narratives of Power: Historical Mythologies in Contemporary Québec and Canada." *Race and Class*. Institute of Race Relations: 52, no. 1 (2010): 19–32.
⁴⁶ See Roediger, "The Wages of Whiteness," 6, 13.
⁴⁷ Brenda Dixon Gottschild, *Digging the Africanist Presence in American Performance and Other Contexts* (Westport, CT and London: Greenwood Press, 1996), 78.

influences, we desperately need to cut through the convoluted web of racism that denies acknowledgement of the Africanist part of the whole.[48]

In the decades that followed its publication, Gottschild's work set the bar for the discussion and acknowledgment of appropriation and theft in dance. Yet equally significant is the way her framework challenges historians to think in more nuanced ways about productive points of contact and influences that confound ongoing and pernicious ideas of purity in culture.

As a group of dancers working in shared ways well before collaboration functioned as a kind of neoliberal requirement, La La La emerged as a mélange of experience and approach. Yet central to this story is a profound love story between Lecavalier and Lock, a charismatic figure and company leader, in the short term, as a couple in the early years of the company; and, in the long term, as a creative duo with a relentless passion and inquiry into dancing and the body. Lecavalier brought a strong sense of rebellion and a working-class ethic and background to the work; raised in what was then the rural Ste-Dorothée by working-class parents, her identity as a French-Canadian uninterested in the hierarchies of historical Québec society ran deep. Her only post-secondary study was at CEGEP Bois-du-Boulogne, where she focused on the medical sciences and biology and danced after class in para-scholarly activities, all of which emphasized materialist, factual approaches to the body. For his part, Lock brought an omnivorous gaze to his work, rooted in a variety of interests—literature, cinema, and belatedly dance, which he first encountered at university in an elective class at Concordia with the choreographer Nora Hemingway. His heritage as a Jewish Moroccan immigrant, arriving from Casablanca in 1957, may have equally shaped his aesthetic, yet this has largely gone unexamined. Lecavalier remembers loving his way of moving: "something loose, soft, something Arabic." But more, she has always recognized his critical insight and expressive powers; she recalls,

[48] Ibid., 3.

Édouard was never this ordinary guy, he was not like anyone else. What I saw in him was ... something delicate, fragile, intelligent, poetic. I felt that we were outside the milieux somehow, outside the milieux of contemporary dance, the funding game, the social politics ... With Édouard—he's brilliant: his writing, his thinking, what he has to say about dance. It was an intelligence I was looking for—and if I had to do it all over, I would start with him again.[49]

I pause over this relationship to emphasize the collaborative, entwined nature of their invention; and to mark the heterogeneity of experience that bound the company together and infused their foundational processes.

Following the work of historian Iro Tembeck, a pattern of distinctive dance emerged in Québec in the 1980s, primarily associated with the experimentation of the Université de Québec à Montréal-based Groupe Nouvelle Aire. Yet, La La La equally aligns with a European dance history, bound by expressionist values and aesthetics likely distilled from traditions of *Ausdruckstanz* and *Tanztheater* taught in Montréal by a range of Eastern European immigrants in the mid-twentieth century. Among the company's defining contributions, consider the following: the minute gestural detail, especially emphasizing hands, fingers, facial expression, which index modes of communication and can be read as a refusal of postmodernist cool. The emphasis on hands to trace, convey, and sign meaning, referencing sign language, mime, and voguing, fall neatly in line with diasporic refutations of art as confounding or mysterious, somehow outside communal use.[50]

Or else think of how body orientations redraw space in resistant, unexpected ways as in the *off-axis* work which countered ballet's axis. If critics occasionally sited breakdancing as a reference point for the work, so too did company members. Founding company member

---

[49] Lecavalier (2016/2024).
[50] See Lillian Allen in Clive Robertson, "Lillian Allan: Holding the Past, Touching the Present, Shining Out to the Future." In *Caught in the Act: An Anthology of Performance Art by Canadian Women*, ed. Tanya Mars and Johanna Householder (Toronto: YYZ books, 2004), 103–4.

Louis Guillemette, for instance, has described the importance of seeing breakdancing in New York in 1981. He, Myriam Moutillet, and Lecavalier had traveled to the city on a state grant for ongoing training in dance, which involved taking classes in a wide range of styles, at Broadway Dance Centre and elsewhere; but equally visits to the Nuyorican Poets Café. He remembered the importance of breakdance as inspiration for the language they were developing with Lock:

> We saw all different stuff ... but what we brought back to the company was breakdance. The street dance, for sure, all of that floor work and way of interacting. Pushing, pulling, slapping each other ... more of that attitude.[51]

Guillemette took time in the interview to mark the importance of breakdancing as its own form, something they learned from but respected as a cultural form not for anyone's taking. He recalled company members' determination to find their own voice—to "unform form, to transform form." At the same time, he confirmed the importance of b-boys for reimagining energy, attitude, and performer roles—which is all the more striking given Guillemette's work in contact improv, often seen as a defining source of the company's aesthetic.

In early works like *Businessman in the Process of Becoming an Angel* or *Human Sex*, the dancers pace, confront, stare down, and in other ways seem to "battle" each other or the viewer. And while the use of floorwork as surface and springboard recalls contact improv as well, moments of full-body contact seem to mark particular breakdance moves like the worm. Lock would later describe the big air-born moves in his technique as "*off-axis*," a critique of ballet, a refutation of straightness—and a kind of resistant horizontality contrasting ballet's verticality. Equally of significance might be the form's cultural situatedness—the importance of neighborhood and street, Montréal as the larger stage—and the value of non-matrixed performance, that is,

---

[51] Louis Guillemette (2014).

letting go of character and playing oneself. Like the jazz musicians who so influenced New York's downtown performance scene in the 1960s, the b-boys offered a model of performance where the performer and on-stage character were one and the same.

Lecavalier has said that with La La La there was never any pretending—"we were who we were onstage." And she, too, has referenced forms of Black dance as a source of inspiration. She remembers,

> I saw breakdancing in the '80s, it was just starting. It wasn't an influence exactly—I knew that it was not the same as what we were doing, and that I couldn't do what they were doing. But they felt close in the way that they were in the street, and I was not far from the street. They were raw, they didn't claim to go—like with a ballet dancer, there's always this escalation about where you go. In the street, there is nowhere to go. It's just here. So there was a link in that way. There was something visceral in what they were making: their life was not easy, it was their only place to move, it was in the street and they used what they had to express who they were. In that way, I felt close to them. … what we were making, it was essential, it was urgent.[52]

If her formative training lay in ballet and modern, she has supplemented that over the years with steady physical training including yoga, boxing, swimming, as well as samplings of different styles including jazz and African dance, which taken together consolidated ideas about ground, weight, and energy.

Such energy dovetails with the heightened speed that has remained striking throughout Lock's choreography to challenge viewer perception and the solidity of form. He has been remarkably consistent in theorizing his movement aesthetic as a way to complicate seeing—what I take to be a challenge to the violence of sight, the visual limits of identity. He recalls,

> The only thing I can do is sufficiently disorient the perception of the audience so that, for a while, they're intensely awake and stop thinking

[52] Lecavalier (2016).

and start seeing the detail. We're in essence creating an uncertainty about what the body actually is.⁵³

Dance scholar Stephen Low has argued for this use of speed as a queering of gender binary, and indeed bodily identity itself.⁵⁴ But might this be read equally as part of a Moroccan Jewish aesthetic?⁵⁵

Aomar Boum has written about the phenomenon of the plastic eye, a Moroccan concept that brings together seeing *and* the intentional ignoring what is being shown for reasons of political expediency or survival. Noting that "Moroccans are socialized to express their grievances through 'ayn mika, "the plastic eye," one of Boum's informants says that "'Ayn/mika started probably as a phrase used for things that, though glittery, are unimportant and so should be ignored."⁵⁶ Analyzing the representation of Jewish culture within national museums of Morocco, Boum writes,

> I argue that the representational complexity of Jews and the Moroccan state's attitude toward ... museums are best understood through the concept of the plastic eye, which combines not only the faculty of vision (the "eye"/'ayn), but also the intentional act of ignoring what is exhibited (the "plastic"/mika), thus allowing Jewish history to be simultaneously foregrounded and back-grounded when it is politically expedient.⁵⁷

Here, for instance, in the context of Arab–Israeli tensions, Jewish artifacts may be shown but not labeled. Within a diasporic context, the meaning of that flexible eye shifts; while not discounting that a need or desire to blend may have been operative within 1980s Montréal, I simply want to point to the parallel between Lock's movement blur

---

⁵³ Lock, in Daryl Jung. *Now.* October 1992.
⁵⁴ Low, "The Speed of Queer."
⁵⁵ See too Hannah Kostrin's (2022) study of Jewish-Arabic hand gestures in the work of Yemenite-Israeli American choreographer Margalit Oved and her son Barak Marshall; she in part traces these to Buddhist and Hindu mudhras that migrated to the Arabic world in the twelfth century. https://www.youtube.com/watch?v=BcyynARycUc
⁵⁶ Aomar Boum, "The Plastic Eye: The Politics of Representation in Moroccan Museums." *Ethnos* 75, no. 1 (2010, March): 49–77; 53.
⁵⁷ Ibid., 54.

and blurring as both critique and strategy for survival, what Fred Moten has described as "blackness as the enactment of a blur"[58] (Figure 4.1).

Such thinking offers a preliminary account of how Black and Jewish aesthetics and thinking may have contributed to the development of La La La's *oeuvre* and been read on and through Lecavalier's performance. To be clear: this work as I read it makes no claim to be part of what dancer/choreographer d. Sabela Grimes refers to as the "Black movement continuum,"[59] a phrase I take to hold all predominantly African Diasporic forms rooted in the culture through history and practice. Yet the work challenges gross ideals of purity to the extent that Black, Jewish, and diasporic movement values live among the sources distilled and elaborated in the work. These, I argue, help account for the work's radicality, its ability to connect with audiences, and its broader cultural impact. Within a context of changing demographics in

Figure 4.1 Blurring the body. Photo: © Linda Dawn Hammond/IndyFoto.

[58] Fred Moten, Lahey Lecture: "And: A Reply to Daniel Tiffany's Cheap Signaling." Writers Read/Department of English, Concordia University, Montréal. September 29, 2017.
[59] d. Sabela Grimes, Presentation at Focus on Dance Research. Concordia University, Montréal. November 10, 2017.

Montréal, as notions of nationhood shifted post-1976 and the 1980–95 No referendums, the vision of hybridity proposed onstage by Lecavalier and Lock served as an important cultural opening for those interpreting company identity and repertoire.

Performing the cyborg

How are we to think, in the end, about the dance as channeling an urgent cultural hybridity, and where lie Lecavalier's own commitments here? In rehearsal and performance, she remained focused on her life as an artist, known for her work ethic, commitment, and generosity. Onstage, her partner-work, costuming, and astonishing musculature joined forces with repertoire thematics to rock received notions about the stability of gender and what constituted the feminine and masculine in dance. In the pleasurable confusion felt between the performed and the real, viewers speculated openly about Lecavalier's gender, while readings associated with race and ethnicity slipped into more coded terrain. Amid preoccupations with the high risk or "wildness" associated with La La La's dance, the rhetoric of threat produced by the press at once entwined and sublimated the mixing of race, ethnicity, and gender. Increasingly, the press associated her with the figure of the cyborg—visioned as a hybrid of machine and human and popularized in films like *Blade Runner* (1982).[60]

Response to Lecavalier often borrowed from the techno-vernacular and science-fiction narratives. One critic wrote, "Now that I have met Louise Lecavalier, I know at last that she is neither a man, nor some implacable bionic freak."[61] Others saw invisible technologies at work in the dance; for example, Tembeck noted that "the bodies seemed disjointed, at times floppy, at others charged with such nervousness

---

[60] Lyndsey Winship, "Cyberpunk Dervish: Louise Lecavalier on *So Blue*, Her First Work as a Choreographer." *Evening Standard*, July 1, 2014.
[61] Meisner, "Superwoman."

that it looked as though an electric current had gone through them."[62] *Village Voice* critic Deborah Jowitt described the dancing as "without volition—as if their bodies were being jerked into the air and dropped on the floor by invisible forces."[63] Something about the dancer and the dance appeared to cross the limits of received categories of embodiment, but what? Her costuming—her penciled-on mustache!—her muscularity, her virtuosity, the speed of motion and the ricochet between styles and codes dancing ...? The sense of Lecavalier, circa the 1980s, as futurity itself.

Such descriptions intersected neatly with feminist readings of the day that sought in the hybrid figure of the cyborg a model of progressive politics. To revisit feminist science scholar Donna Haraway's much-cited 1985 text:

> By the late twentieth century, our time, a mythic time, we are all chimeras, theorized and fabricated hybrids of machine and organism; in short, we are cyborgs. The cyborg is our ontology; it gives us our politics. The cyborg is a condensed image of both imagination and material reality, the two joined centres structuring any possibility of historical transformation .... This chapter is an argument for *pleasure* in the confusion of boundaries and for *responsibility* in their construction.[64]

Considerable literature has been produced since on the topic, charting an ambivalent path between the threat and promise of the cyborg to escape the confounding limits of a material body and as a post-human entity. Scholars have noted the cyborg's ambivalent political stature, which at once appears to challenge binaries yet can reinforce notions of purity of an imagined pre-hybrid state. More recently, Krista Lynes and Katerina Symes have described the cyborg as a *mode* of feminist

---

[62] Iro Valaskakis Tembeck, "La La La Human Steps," *Banff Letters* (Banff, AB: Banff Centre for the Arts, 1986): 58–60.
[63] Deborah Jowitt, "Honk if You Love Dogs." *The Village Voice*, October 9, 1984.
[64] Donna J. Haraway, "A Manifesto for Cyborgs: Science, Technology and Socialist Feminism in the Late Twentieth Century." In *Simians, Cyborgs and Women: The Reinvention of Nature* (New York: Routledge, 1991/1985), 149–82; 150.

theorizing; that is, as a way to take "pleasure in the confusion of boundaries, the capacity of figures to express imaginative possibilities that may unfix the contingent mechanisms of sex/gender."[65] As a way of theorizing, it may equally be understood as a way of gathering, under the sign of collective politics organized through shared concerns rather than fixed identities.[66]

The political potential of the cyborg, as with that of hybridity, insists on leaning into the borderline between essentialized entities. Here, I offer another story to help think further about the political life of Lecavalier's dancing. In 1995, Lecavalier appeared in Katherine Bigelow's *Strange Days*—her only feature-film appearance—in the minor role of bodyguard, cyborg Cyndi "Vita" Minh. That year, with international recognition in hand, having toured with Bowie and Frank Zappa, and having appeared in ads for Absolut Vodka and l.a. Eyeworks, opportunity for Lecavalier appeared to be limitless. Between shows, and recovering from a hip injury, she signed on for a small part in the film, a science-fiction parable about power, mediation, and the failure to see (Figures 4.2 and 4.3).

Strange Days is set in a dystopic future—that is, clearly not the present in terms of date and available technology and yet very much like the present, wherein whiteness takes the form of corruption and police brutality. Unfolding in Los Angeles over two days around New Year's 1999, the film follows former policeman, Lenny Nero, who has fallen from grace and become involved in the trafficking of high-intensity, highly addictive virtual-reality technology known as SQUID. In anguish over the loss of a girlfriend, ensnared by the VR-media himself, Lenny uncovers two hideous crimes caught on tape: the first, a rape of a young woman working as a prostitute; the second, the police shooting of Jericho One, a prophetic rap musician and cultural hero. The plot unfolds as Lenny discovers the two crimes are linked and must

---

[65] Krista Genevieve Lynes and Katerina Symes, "Cyborgs and Virtual Bodies." In *The Oxford Handbook of Feminist Theory*, ed. Lisa Disch and Mary Hawkesworth (New York: Oxford University Press, 2016), 122–42; 140.
[66] Ibid., "Cyborgs and Virtual Bodies," 124; and Haraway (1991).

Hybrid Body, International Cyborg 175

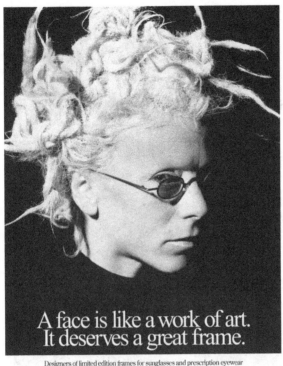

Figure 4.2 Photo: Greg Gorman for l.a. Eyeworks.

choose between personal or political commitments: to save his ex, or to turn in the tape to the authorities.

Or, better yet, this description: the film follows Mace, played by Angela Bassett, as powerhouse limousine driver and bodyguard, single mother, and friend to troubled former-cop Lenny. Set in an apocalyptic future marred by corruption, addiction, and violence, Mace drives Lenny around town on the last night of the year, the city a kaleidoscope of projections, moving images, and screens, in a bid to keep him safe and convince him to do the right thing. All action pivots around Mace—she holds the moral center—but will the film in the end be about Lenny or

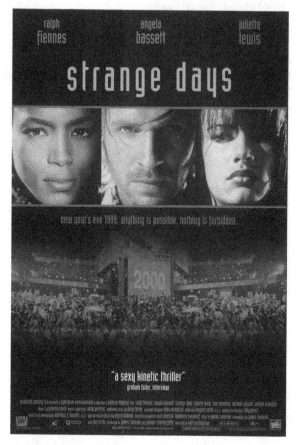

Figure 4.3 Poster for *Strange Days*. © 1995 20th Century Studios Inc. All rights reserved.

Mace? Will Mace exist to perform narrative labor, or will agency and pleasure and the real be really possible?

I pause over Bassett's character, since Lecavalier's functions narratively as opponent and conceptually as a minor echo. Both are bodyguards, both are cyborg-like, both wear extensions—braids or dreads: their bodies are expanded, their muscles are pumped, and they are associated with machines via weaponry and cars. Their bodies are crafted, technologized. Lecavalier, onscreen briefly, looks familiar, her look an assemblage of styles familiarized by punk music, cyberpunk genres of fiction and film, and her own work in dance. Taken together, the pair remap the cinematic cliché of the Black male bodyguard, whose typically silent presence exists to convey danger and consolidate the power of the guarded one. Whereas Bassett stays at the heart of the film, Lecavalier's brief appearance seems designed merely to underscore Bassett's model of a powerful physicality for an emergent feminist hero. If it did nothing else, *Strange Days* shows Lecavalier directly taking hold of the figure of the cyborg in performance, in what I take to be a response to the critical paucity of understanding around bodies, identity, and vision.

Yet the film does considerably more. Made shortly after mass unrest in Los Angeles, after LA Police officers caught beating Rodney King on film received a "Not Guilty" verdict—events that surely marked a turning point in the post-truth era, marked by a deterioration of faith in photographic evidence—the film is of particular interest for its development of unusual point-of-view shots. These scenes emulate SQUID technology and, critically, place viewers in the position of the perpetrator in the plot and so challenge their position as viewers of media. Sharply criticized at the time for its gritty depictions of suffering and implied realism, the film is at once an experiment in visual form, an argument for vision as fact, and a critique of visuality as itself oppressive. At best, the film uses its platform to return the public to the King verdict and speak out against white supremacy.

Strange Days ends at a massive outdoor New Year's Party, as Lecavalier backs away from Bassett, refusing to do battle and uttering her only line: "Enjoy the Party." It's an abdication of duty, when duty is on the wrong side of history; Lecavalier gets out of the way, so that Bassett can kick back at the state and corporate forms of control and entertainment that threaten to overtake the real. If the cross-racial kiss between Mace and Lenny prompts a groan as fantasy and (white) millennial hope or for its confines within the frame of heterosexuality, there is simultaneously relief for Mace's survival, amid great precarity, and transversal from good mother to lover whose agency and sexual desire can be realized in popular cinema. For Lecavalier, mistaken as cyborg in and through her danced labor, playing Cindy Minh in *Strange Days* allowed her to grab hold of the cyborg and shape it within the critical space of Bigelow's film (Figure 4.4).

Lecavalier has said that she was moved to do the film by director Katherine Bigelow, who reached out directly; "I wasn't looking to do film but I liked her, and I liked the script." For Lecavalier, the scale of film generally and the thematics of Bigelow's film specifically dovetailed with her own commitment to dance as deeply connected to everyday life; as something that held the potential to be popular and speak meaningfully to audiences. Her research in the form has consistently sought after movement that felt "like her life"—that is, that bore pragmatic relation to the range of experiences, aptitudes, and identities: French-Canadian, Québecois, urban, to mention only a

Figure 4.4 Production still, *Strange Days*. Photo: Merie W. Wallace/Courtesy: Fou Glorieux/20th Century Studios Inc.

few. At the same time, even as images of her proliferated, she avoided reading press reviews; and danced without mirrors as a way to protect the work from the representational economy; of her relation to modes of inscription, she said, "I was doing my own quest in dance, and I was following my own questions … I couldn't explain it …. and in a way it was unexplainable."[67] Her attachment to Lock over a twenty-year career with La La La, and continuing today, remains anchored in his theoretic and poetic engagement with attempts to unform the body—to destabilize the attendant judgments that come with vision, through speed and gesture.

If, as Jennifer González has written, the cyborg appears at moments of anxiety and change "to contain fears and desires of a culture caught in the process of transformation," its hybrid status reveals only what has always been true—the notion of purity as a singular state as an impossibility. Revisiting *Strange Days* alongside a collection of repertoire that circulated across borders and gathered audiences at mass scale, her ongoing commitment to and enactment of bodies as multiple and mutable slips into sharp relief. What, then, did critics and viewers mean when they referred in passing to her frenzied or wild gestures? Or when they described the company as violent or dangerous? Perhaps asking about how they felt might be more apt. Anxiety, tension, excitement, pleasure, and more—a complex and confusing set of responses, a collection of "shared emotional repertoires"[68] involving an expanded set of possibilities for embodied identities, wherein binaries like Black/white, man/woman were surely befuddled. If Lecavalier's dancing and dreadlocks signaled disruption to the categories, and La La La's repertoire enacted through hybrid codes and heightened speed a productive bodily abstraction, reception to them signed anxiety, tension, excitement, and pleasure—and a rehearsal towards an expanded facility in heterogeneity.

---

[67] Lecavalier (2010).
[68] Hurley, *National Performance*, 6.

Conclusion

Dancing, Glorious Expenditure

Dance has many layers, that's what makes it interesting to me—if not, I'd be bored or maybe leave ... it can be ugly, it can be beautiful, it can create, it can destroy.

—Louise Lecavalier[1]

If the system can no longer grow, or if the excess cannot be completely absorbed in its growth, it must necessarily be lost without profit; it must be spent, willingly or not, gloriously or catastrophically.

—Georges Bataille

Then—leaving La La La

One of Lecavalier's final dances with La La La Human Steps was *2* (1995), made around the time of Édouard Lock's father's illness and passing; and Lecavalier's own confrontation with the limits of mortality, after the potentially career-ending injury to the hip in 1994 at age 36. The dance contrasted the company's by-now familiar virtuosic physicality with an accompanying film narrative that focused on aging, memory, and loss. Lock's film, projected at gigantic scale in the theater, at times shows a split-screen, where Lecavalier appears in one frame as a young woman; and, simultaneously, in a second frame as an old woman. The two characters appear on film side-by-side, often performing in parallel simple everyday

---

[1] Lecavalier (2024).

movement sequences like eating breakfast or falling sleep, occasionally noticing each other, smiling in recognition. They are characters and yet they remain Lecavalier, of course, rendered double through the unique qualities of performance, which at once collapses and explodes the link between subject/object and which creates doppelgangers and hauntings via fused temporalities of here and there. For Lecavalier all the more so, as her particular qualities as a dancer, her iconic visual style, and her familiarity to audiences sharpen the performativity of dance, puncturing the theatrical frame all the more easily.

One particularly challenging clip—both in its production and in reception—features Lecavalier as an older woman, observing her younger self preparing to go out. Young Lecavalier chooses which dress to wear, dances around her bedroom, puts on her make-up, bursts into tears as she leaves her apartment—a portrait of youth's drama, and the intensity of lives in formation. As an old woman, she watches her younger self with a benevolent kind of interest, radically slows down her own movement, shows the tic and flutter of the aged body. If the portrayal evidenced a new mood of fragility and vulnerability for the company, it also risked deferring to age as travesty/tragedy rather than as the accrual and deepening of experience. For some, the portrait felt abject—both for how it viewed aging, and for how it asked Lecavalier to represent her own bodily deterioration. The work drew considerable emotional response, deemed unexpected within a repertoire that had always seemed to privilege the spectacular; one critic described audience members leaving the theater in tears.[2]

Lock recalled the considerable range and dexterity the piece required from Lecavalier as an actor, as well as her patience through the lengthy and arduous make-up process required to transform her features. The shooting involved working with an improvised script wherein he ran the film recording of the younger character while simultaneously shooting the sequence for the older character. Lecavalier worked in the here and

---

[2] Kim Coghill, "Pas de 2: Édouard Lock and La La La Steps Find New Maturity." *Uptown*. Winnipeg, MB: February 22–March 6, 1995.

now, with an eye on the film playing and an ear to Lock's direction playing live through an earpiece. Lock remembered her focus amid the chaotic, lengthy shoot, in a crowded space with a large production crew and distractions all around. And he remembered the shock of the first time he saw her in full make-up as an older version of herself:

> I had to walk out, compose myself and walk back in. And when she walked onto the set, it was really weird to see the reaction—some people started to cry, some just picked up their bags and left, and others kind of moved back into the shadows. Nobody talked to her; and at the end of the day, she said, "I've figured out what it's like to be old: nobody wants to be with you."[3]

The mood was somber, and the imagery of the film placed a lens on public discomfort with aging bodies. Whereas the work drew accolades for a newfound sense of "maturity," lyricism, and affective power for the choreographer,[4] it also drew speculation about Lecavalier's age and ability, begging questions anew about her agency and about possible retirement[5] (Figure 5.1).

Reactions of this order testify to the limits of a culture that prizes youth generally and a theatrical dance milieux that quickly anticipates the inability of professional dancers to perform beyond the age of 35 or so, whether due to accrued injuries or through aging, wherein it is presumed that "dancers' bodies become increasingly unable to cope with the physical demands of performing."[6] Yet within modern, contemporary, and movement forms outside of ballet, exemplary performers have long exceeded these expectations, bringing astonishing skill and knowledge to bear on their dancing—for example Kazuo Ohno (1906–2010); Yvonne Rainer (1934–); Germaine Acogny (1944–); Malou Airaudo (1948–); and, closer to home in Montréal, Margie Gillis (1953–) and Angélique Willkie (1963–).

[3] Ibid., n.p.
[4] Ibid., n.p.
[5] Liz Warwick, "Wild Thing." *Montreal Gazette*, October 2, 1995, E3.
[6] Liz Schwaiger, "Performing One's Age: Cultural Constructions of Aging and Embodiment in Western Theatrical Dancers." *Dance Research Journal*, 37 (2007): 107–20; 107.

Figure 5.1 *2* (1995) Louise Lecavalier. Photo: Édouard Lock.

Recent scholarship on aging in dance suggests that, within experimental forms, there is more room for experienced performers, who find revised techniques for moving in light of real physical change and new physical limits.[7] One notable exemplar here might be American choreographer Yvonne Rainer, who danced in reperformances of *Trio A* as *Convalescent Dance* (1967), made while recovering from surgery; and, more recently, *Trio A: Geriatric with Talking* (2010), at age 76.[8] As one of the founders of the Judson Dance Theater, she challenged the nature of technique within theatrical dance and in works such as these, by Risa Puleo's account, suggests the spectrum between ability and disability, problematizing (again) normative readings of virtuosity in concert dance. More recently, dance scholar Bailey Anderson finds that histories and experiences of aging, injury, and other forms of bodily difference have long been "symbiotic" to dance, often unnamed but always "part of our collective dancing."[9]

---

[7] Ibid.
[8] For a discussion of diversity and debility, see Risa Puleo, "Sitting Beside Yvonne Rainer's *Convalescent Dance*." *Art Papers* (Winter, 2018/2019).
[9] Bailey Anderson, "Overcoming and Denial: Disability and Modern Dance in the United States." *Dance Research Journal* 52, no. 3 (2020, December): 58–75; 60, 71.

To raise the question of age and ability in dance is to once again return to notions of virtuosity, understood as partly a function of spectatorship: a narrative, as per Hamera and Osterweis, between dancer and spectator and a way to describe dancing that extends beyond familiar codes. At the same time, there is no virtuosity without technique, though the decision to apply the term virtuoso is more ambiguous than precise, less about "mastery" than about a kind of difference read as more.[10] Recently, many young performers and choreographers eschew virtuosity as movement technique, reading it as spectacular, compliant, anti-conceptual, conservative, and ultimately harmful; and echoing Rainer's earlier critique, as well as the concerns of feminist performance criticism circa the 1980s.[11] That much-needed questioning both of systems of performance training—with their long histories of abuse and violence—and the tyranny of artistry misunderstood as technical perfection has brought about healthier approaches to dance pedagogy and performance. Yet the kind of theatrical dancing Lecavalier aims for takes work: daily, arduous effort to attain a version of bodily strength and mobility that can enable the sort of exact and exacting physicality that most interests her. Here, virtuosity is not a static artifact—a problem of enforced labor or, worse, a demonstration of superiority—but at once perceived excess *and* skill as evidence of labor—that is, educated and trained over time as required in order to do particular styles of movement.

---

[10] Mastery as a term offers contrast to virtuosity. Whereas the figure of the master relates explicitly to land—and the ownership, maintenance, and surveillance of production on such land—the figure of the virtuoso holds no such claim or perch. Whereas the call to discipline is real in both cases, the virtuoso performs along a horizon of technical excellence that may never be achieved. While mastery invokes a history of colonial violence, the perceived virtuoso may engage with a range of techniques—with histories that vary—or, in the case of Lecavalier, invent nuances or new techniques that challenge Western aesthetic ideals—for example, of "uprightness." For more on mastery as a problematic, see Dalie Giroux, *The Eye of the Master: Figures of the Québécois Colonial Imaginary* (Montréal and Kingston, London, Chicago: McGill-Queen's University Press, 2023).

[11] See Danjel Andersson, Mette Edvardsen, and Mårten Spångberg, Eds., *Post-Dance* (Stockholm: Stiftelsen Moderna Dansteatern (MDT), 2017); Yvonne Rainer, "No Manifesto." In *Posthumanism in Art and Science: A Reader*, ed. Giovanni Aloi and Susan McHugh (New York: Columbia University Press, 1965/2008), 97.

In interviews from the time of *2*'s production, Lecavalier was reported to have asked for a shift in the intensity of the repertoire: "I wanted to know what a show was like where I didn't feel like I was dying every time."[12] Elsewhere, she noted,

> You start a show, and it's like a huge mountain. The earlier shows were so physically demanding I would wonder whether I could actually get through this. Now this show is different: its demanding but in another sense—I'm wondering if I can do it well, right to the end.[13]

Yet the dancing remains physically demanding, with the refined technique, intense speed, and partnering that grew more pronounced in the company's later years as Lock's interest in classical ballet developed. A *pas de deux* for Lecavalier with Rick Gavin Tija, himself in recovery from an injury at the time of the project's creation, documents the rapid-fire *off-axis* jumps; precision gestural details; and close partnering that at times borders on the claustrophobic. Though there are reflective pauses, gestures of prayer, moments of surrender, the dancing remains challenging—extreme in its physical and mental requirements. In an interview shortly after this production was in circulation, responding to a question about age, Lecavalier says, "My body is in the best shape it's ever been … yes, I've had a small injury but I've been lucky. And if my mind keeps in shape, my body will too … I hope I can say the same in twenty more years."

More than twenty years later, at the time of press, Lecavalier is indeed still dancing—with the same vigor and intensity that has driven her career. If questions of age and ability activate the realms of possibility and normativity as shaped by the social bearing down on the individual, virtuosity moves us to excess, surplus, expenditure—of labor and something else. Watching *2*, there is a sense of loss not simply tied to the story being told; or to the expenditure of effort on view in the dancing. The technique has solidified, smoothed and polished with time and classical line. Lecavalier performs no lifts, the sneakers are

---

[12] *Chatelaine*, February 27, 1997.
[13] Nadine Meisner, "Superwoman." *Sunday Times*, October 26, 1996, 10:15.

long gone. With the company touring internationally and playing to huge crowds, the work was no longer forged in a craft-like way with a small group in the studio, and Lock—himself a brilliant dancer who moved with quicksilver fluidity in ways unmarred by formal dance training—no longer performed within the work. When "retirement" came finally four years later in 1999, it was a stepping away from La La La and the pressures of the company as an international touring structure. The dancing—transgressing the perceived and real limits of the body—kept going.

Now—*Fou glorieux*

Whereas choreography has more recently been understood as authorship, tool kit and methodology, structuring device and apparatus of capture, a mode of writing at once normative and violent,[14] it has at least since the 1990s served as a mechanism through which to access state and private funding wherein choreographers lead independent projects. For Lecavalier, long uninterested in assuming the role of choreographer, the creation of her production company *Fou glorieux* (glorious madness) has enabled an unusual level of control over her working life and her material. As well, it has enabled her to balance that via collaboration with a surprising range of local and international choreographers, notably Tedd Robinson, Benoît Lachambe, and Lloyd Newson before finally turning to her own craft to develop a series of works including *So Blue* (2012), *Milles batailles* (2016), and *Stations* (2020). She felt the stature that had come with La La La was an obstacle to her own growth and the need to find new ways of dancing:

> I tried not to go to the obvious choreographers, the big big names, because I thought those people would try to give me movement like Édouard's, to maybe keep me in the same kinds of roles—like big,

[14] Foster, Lepecki, Spångberg, Roux.

crazy whoa! So, in the end, I was in the studio. And I started making my own movement.

The interim period, between La La La and *Fou*, proved critical in the turn to authorship, both because it ensured new ways of working—experimental, emergent, bound to dancing knowledge in the studio; and because it enabled her to make movement within the frame of her own physical reality and body schema. The collaboration with dancer/choreographer Benoît Lachambre, who had danced with Les Ballets Jazz de Montréal, Toronto Dance Theatre, and Marie Chouinard before collaborating with European avant-gardists Meg Stewart and Boris Charmatz, proved especially generative. With Lachambre, Lecavalier creates two dazzlingly original new works: *Is You Me* (2008) and *"I" Is Memory*, which dramatically reconfigure the scale, speed, and image of her dancing in what constituted a radical reframe of audience expectations. There are micro-gestures, choreographies of the face, inversions, and stage illusions that continue to challenge the limits of sight and the contours of the body. There is costuming that alters the shape of the body and plays with the hiding and revealing of the face, of bodily identity and technical skill. Building on the throughline of her time with Lock, her post-La La La work plays with perception, something *"déroutant"* for the eye[15] (Figure 5.2).

Her first choreography in thirty years comes immediately after the Lachambre works. I've seen *So Blue* three times, and viewed filmmaker Marlene Millar's documentary many times. The work is structured as a series of phases, bound by shifts in movement, light, and sound. There's a shuffling run for Lecavalier at opening, facing the audience and criss-crossing the stage, arms slicing and teetering through the air, back and forth at shoulder level, as if to maintain balance. There's a sustained inversion with Lecavalier in a shoulder stand, wherein her legs and feet shift form and start to take on the expressivity of the face; suddenly, down is up. And there's a long duet with Frédéric Tavernini, at times

---

[15] Lecavalier (2024).

Figure 5.2 Louise Lecavalier and Frédéric Tavernini in *So Blue* (2012). Photo: Carl Lessard. Courtesy Fou Glorieux.

intimate, hands and arms sculpting the immediate space around and between them; at times, two strangers, arms pulsing, dancing in a club as per the suggestion of Mercan Dede's pounding score. Yet it isn't the choreography I remember, if we understand choreography in its simplest term as a summative mode of composition. Rather, it's the dancing—its material strangeness, illusory qualities, viral affectiveness, and projection of energy.

So Blue offers an eclectic set of gestures that reach for meaning but remain unfixed: for example, in the first phase she raises her finger to the temple and winds. For a second, it's a coo coo gesture but no. The finger drops to tap the heart, the former only a filigree on the way to some other place. Hands come together like a bird in shadow play. Or else she appears transfixed in one spot, watching her hand rotate, her head following as if by compulsion. There are air punches, as if in the club or at a concert; and brush-off gestures, as if from childhood battles.

There's a swagger, slowed down, deconstructed. There are runs, crawls, leaps, and falls. Extreme in terms of performance—the sheer energy required from the performers; extreme in terms of its repetition and accrual of gestures; and extreme in its tightening and release of various psychic states. The work at times points to familiar registers—mimetic body-language, or a partner hold that reminds one of the *pas de deux* structure—then it's gone. No longer bound by *off-axis* vocabulary or iconic costuming, unanchored by specific dance schools save perhaps expressionism, *So Blue* is also unanchored by choreographic teleology. Lecavalier remains above all a dancer, dancing, generating an excess of act and image (Figures 6.3 and 6.4).

Mårten Spångberg has recently sought to distinguish between dance as raw, non-organized pure expression, and choreography as a kind of non-specific disciplining of movement, used commonly to refer to composition, scores, algo rhythms, and strategic planning, to name only a few of the activities. The task at hand, held by the term

Figure 5.3 Louise Lecavalier and Frédéric Tavernini in *So Blue* (2012). Photo: Carl Lessard. Courtesy Fou Glorieux.

Figure 5.4 Louise Lecavalier and Frédéric Tavernini in *So Blue* (2012). Photo: Carl Lessard. Courtesy Fou Glorieux.

post-dance, is to "liberate oneself from the violence of choreography and iterate oneself as a dance-maker,"[16] which may in effect involve any number of activities, spaces, and audiences. For Spångberg, if performance meant "a subject performing subjectivity," dance means "a subject performing form." Provocative, contradictory, manifesto-like, Spångberg nevertheless raises an important question.

That is, it's the working, not the work, that counts. Contrasting the scholarship's wrestling with what constitutes a work—whether authorial signature, as per Laurence Loupp; or a "public and shareable object," as per Pouillaude; or "a politics of emancipation," as per Jérôme Bel in Siegmund—to focus on dancing is by no means to undermine choreography, nor is it to engage in expansive claims for what dancing,

---

[16] Mårten Spångberg, "Post-Dance, An Advocacy." In *Post-Dance*, ed. Daniel Andersson, Mette Edvardsen, Mårten Spångberg (Stockhold: MTD/Moderna dansteatern, 2017), 349–93; 372.

and art more broadly can do.[17] Celine Roux, for instance, describes an "unframing" of the choreographic within French dance during the 1990s. Grappling with the difficulty of making choreography within a market system that celebrates and circulates particular bodies and imagery, Roux sees artists working as "on one hand, a space that reflects on its own existence, and, on the other, a space for a reflexive discourse on the world."[18] The job of dancing, then, is to show and work the gap between hegemonic discourse and marketable forms that emphasize technical virtuosity and/or digestible representations. Roux advocates, as does Spångberg, for an expansive understanding of what constitutes dancing, but sees the elimination of technique as something "everybody seems to agree on."

In fact, no one agrees. There are no unmarked bodies, and the technical is always present, in shifting, multiple, and stylized forms. As Mauss noted in the 1930s, all movement is highly technical, bound by training and tradition, marked by biology, sociology, and psychology. Whereas the claim to virtuosity resides in questions of perception and belief—a culturally inflected mindset that measures gaps between technique and something more than technique—it equally resides in the doing, not as mastery or perfection, but in the pursuit of skill as a function of action and effort. Dancing as *parcours* and pathway.

Susan Leigh Foster, in her study on dance's value as an economy of exchange, distinguishes between dance as commodity and dance as gift: she notes, "commodification of dance's energy, which is presumed to be precious and scarce, entails the careful monitoring of energy followed by strategic expenditure to achieve a maximum effect."[19] The gift, instead, aligns with community, abundance, and "mutual

---

[17] See Laurence Louppe, *Poetics of Contemporary Dance* (Contredanse, 2010); Frédéric Pouillaude, *Unworking Choreography: The Notion of Work in Dance* (London: Oxford University Press, 2017), 54; Gerald Siegmund, *Jérôme Bel: Dance, Theatre and the Subject*, (Springer, 2017), 177. See too Hetty Blades, "Projects, Precarity and the Ontology of Dance Works." *Dance Research Journal* 51, no. 1 (April 2019): 66–78.

[18] Céline Roux, "Performative Practices/Critical Bodies #2: What Makes Dance." In *Danse: An Anthology*, ed. Noémie Solomon (New York: Les presses du reel, 2014), 261–74; 270.

[19] Susan Leigh Foster, *Valuing Dance: Commodities and Gifts in Motion* (Oxford: Oxford University Press, 2019), 18.

indebtedness." Whereas her study notes the movement and overlaps between these modalities and issues a critical call to examine the "why?" of dance, especially within a culture that prioritizes utility and commodification; my interest in thinking about labor is to embrace models that demonstrate an effort that might be considered irrational, foolish even, or outside strict understandings of results or "returns."

The message of Lecavalier and, to my mind, of all those who dance in ways that strike us as exceptional *is* the display of effort as just more and possibly too much, as taboo and transgressive to the extent that it surpasses linguistic meaning and may not be readily assimilated into capital-driven value. Dancing as craft and effort, motivated as much by desire—not as lack but as inquiry—and the rights of the imagination as to the pragmatisms of survival and the rent, never guaranteed for lives in art. Less about notions of freedom or emancipation, a seductive metaphor that writers so often turn to for the form, dance involves profound obligation—as a kind of binding rather than duty—in potentially positive and negative ways, to do and do better. *What does it mean to try this hard?* To spend energy, for sweat and adrenalin, for the feeling of being in effort, against the odds of "meaning" and value. *Fou glorieux.*

Future—*the sun gives without receiving*

In 2023, as the world emerged from the Covid-19 pandemic, Lecavalier worked on a small production with Chinese visual artist Lu Yang entitled *Delusional World*. First performed as a live-stream with dancer Qin Ran in Shanghai, the dance is a thirty-minute motion capture *pas-de-deux* for one dancer with avatars, sound, and game controller. An iterative project, at times live-streamed, Lu invites dancers to animate characters who wander through a nightmarish gamescape shaped by anima, corpses, strange machines, and Buddhist imagery of death and renewal. Lecavalier's iteration, produced for Elektra 2023, found her dancing live in front of a giant video screen, before a live audience crammed into the corner of a warehouse space in the St-Henri neighborhood of Montréal.

Lecavalier described her initial draw to the work:

> I was between *Stations* and the new work I'm making now, and I thought, this world makes me laugh—there's so much humor in it, and after *Stations*, which was so serious, I said yes right away.... When you work with other people, you lose a bit of control—not that I'm so in control all the time in my own work but I can control the environment, the schedule, life—but being in another person's work helps me turn the page, it's like diving into another world.[20]

Moving the give-and-take of agency to the center of the creative process, Lecavalier discussed her approach to the work in a recent interview. She worked primarily on the dance alone in her studio, watching canned films of the game landscape between making new moves.

> I thought, it's a mistake to go for what the setup is proposing ... to interpret the characters and the storyline. If I did that, I knew I'd disappear. The interest wouldn't be the performance, it would just be to watch these characters on the screen ... I had to make them follow me.
>
> I worked against the characters as fate—like for the character in the tutu, it would have been easy to go with ballet, but I tried to make it strange, unusual, to give the contradiction. I made small movements ... down on the ground on all four limbs.[21]

But the work is also, urgently, suggestive—a meditation on the pervasiveness of media circa 2024, the nature of presence, and the rise of networked relations. The screen dominates over Lecavalier's tiny figure as she casts movement on to giant avatars via seventeen mo-cap sensors positioned on her body. There are three different avatars and environments that mark the transitions from one level to the next as in gaming: there is a post-apocalypse graveyard, with a multi-limbed

---

[20] Lecavalier (2024).
[21] Lecavalier (2024).

dancer wandering amid the bodies; there's an insane amusement park, with a male avatar in a tutu—head emerging from his butt; and finally there's a cityscape with a giant roaming girl avatar—the face of Lu herself—peeking around buildings and moving through a city in flames. Amid the spectacular, rapid-fire cuts and shifting scenes played by the game controller Emma Forgues, digital bodies proliferate: images of moving bodies and corpses, body parts and limbs rearranged and in multiple, bodies as multiple, monstrous (Figures 5.5 and 5.6).

Amid these assemblages, the live dancing is, as you might imagine, intensely demanding physically—unorthodox gestures that repeat and pulse, as if to explore and deepen their reach. Because she never aligned with any singular dance technique—studying modern, ballet, boxing, among others—she has felt free to explore new paths. She says,

> Sometimes I try to do things like "contemporary dance," because I still come from there. And this is a part of me so maybe give it a try. And then I look at it and it looks like I'm taking myself seriously, like I'm a serious "contemporary" dancer and I'm analyzing space ... And it's

Figure 5.5 *Delusional World* (2023). Photo: François Blouin. Retouch: Luc Lavergne. Courtesy Fou Glorieux.

Figure 5.6 *Delusional World* (2023). Photo: François Blouin. Retouch: Luc Lavergne. Courtesy Fou Glorieux.

not that I want only lightness, or that I'm against meaning. I trust that, because I've worked so long … that I keep searching with the body all the time, it opens up new discoveries, new stuff … real stuff.

Just as a gesture becomes legible—say, arms low and palms out as if to say "Come on," the movement adjusts, pulses into a series of postures suggesting attitude, strength, rage. She begins with intimate space but gradually moves outward from her body, claiming more space as the work develops. While Lecavalier remains at the center of the piece, the occasional glitch and the barely perceptible lag of the avatars' movements remind viewers of the technology underpinning the dance. Her head tilts, the neck roles, her eyes shift and make direct contact with the audience: alert in the storm of action and light, asking questions. Her hoodie is pulled tight over stacked braids that make strange the shape of her head. Her costuming choice uses layers of ordinary clothing, to be peeled away during the performance to suggest multiple identities within the single figure. Her identity, finally, is ambiguous. *What are we seeing?*

Conceptually and materially, *Delusional World* marks Lecavalier's explicit return to the figure of the cyborg—activating the tension between the organic and inorganic, between body and technology, between performer and avatar as hybrid assemblage. If the cyborg of the 1980s—on view in science-fiction films like *Bladerunner* (1982) and in Haraway's classic manifesto—tended to envision a posthuman utopia bound by shared affinities and a revised feminist ethics, more recent work and times remind us of the continuing political contexts that structure oppression. Dance scholar Hilary Bergson has observed that notions of a hybrid, distributed agency for the body often erase the political categories of gender as well as class and race,[22] an erasure made problematic by legacies of violence and the remaining work required to ensure equities of opportunity, housing, legal treatment, and more. Yet, if Lecavalier's dancing makes strange the nature of a body, it makes strange all manner of categories assigned to bodies, including those of race and gender. What a relief.

Beth Coleman defines avatars as representational proxies for the self that function to magnify agencies; she writes, "it is the avatar's role to aid us in expressing this agency."[23] And agency, following Carrie Noland's understanding, is a matter of kinesthetics wherein "learned techniques of the body are the means by which cultural conditioning is simultaneously embodied and [my emphasis] *put to the test*."[24] In the case of *Delusional World*, we see agencies in plural, augmented and multiplied: from Lu's remarkable photorealistic visual universe, a remix of cultural forms writ through the frame of the popular to game controller Forgues' shifting scenes, avatars, and fields of view, unfolding with the jagged, swinging movement of the gamescape. Then there are the avatars, whose fantastic bodies dance and glitch and lag behind

[22] Hilary Bergen, "Animating the Kinetic Trace: Kate Bush, Hatsune Miku and Posthuman Dance." *Public* 30, no. 60 (2020): 188–207; and Hilary Bergen, "Not a Girl Dancing: Gender, Spectacle and Disembodiment in the Work of Loïe Fuller and Freya Olafson." *Archée*, March 4, 2019.
[23] Beth Coleman, *Hello Avatar: Rise of the Networked Generation* (Cambridge, MA: MIT Press, 2011), 4.
[24] Noland, *Agency and Embodiment*.

Lecavalier's, messing with strict notions of past, present, and future to function ultimately as archival traces—digital bodies and movement records cast into the future as residues of performance. At the intersection, Lecavalier dances—a fury of poetic energy, the storm at the center, her mo-cap sensors carefully sewn by hand [hers] into her costuming. Here, Lecavalier literally draws herself into the cyborg assemblage: act, image, technology, biodata.

Mersch et al. have noted the "asymmetry of relations" between human and non-human actors, wherein technologies threaten to overtake us even as they abstract the phenomena associated with the real.[25] The threat of being overtaken in *Delusional World* is real and equally the point; the artistic team has produced a largesse and abundance through dance, typically felt and seen as an economy of scarcity. Amid a surge of high-resolution, fully dimensional dancing, surrounded by pounding techno-music and rapid-fire digital imagery, there's a risk of sensory overload. Watching from the side, I needed to look away, readjust my eyes, wonder at what was happening. If the content of the dance questions presence and agency in the post-Covid world of pervasive networked relations, the material performance produces a kind of override that is, to borrow from French surrealist Georges Bataille, *insubordinate* in character. I'm not sure that the power of *Delusional World* lies strictly in what can be described through formal strategies of interpretation or the requirements to *mean*. A central facet of Lecavalier's contribution, as I see it, sits in what is perhaps the most important element of her story and what is certainly central to this work as a meditation on technologies of the body within the networked world—that is, at once simply and not simply, dancing. Dancing as energy, developed and made tangible through labor; to be in, with, and full of energy: exacting, time-based, laborious, and writ through with courage and love.

---

[25] Dieter Mersch, Anton Rey, and Thomas Grunwald, "Introduction," in *Actor & Avatar: A Scientific & Artistic Catalogue*, ed. Dieter Mersch, Anton Rey, Thomas Grunwald, Jörg Sternagel, Lorena Kegel, and Miriam Laura Loertscher (Transcript Verlag/Swiss National Science Federation, 2023), 5–21; 12.

A brief reading of Bataille's theory of expenditure and transgression may prove interesting here. Shifting the terms of engagement, Bataille produces an analysis of capitalism, not as exchange nor as a narrative of production and acquisition. His account focuses, instead, on *spending*.[26] In an astonishing turn of phrase, he observes, "the sun gives without receiving." Offering up a wholistic understanding of economy, bound by extremes of terror and death, he writes:

> Classical economics imagined that primitive exchange occurred in the form barter; it had no reason to assume, in fact, that a means of acquisition such as exchange might have as its origin not the need to acquire that it satisfies today but the contrary need, the need to destroy and to lose.[27]

In making his arguments, dance constitutes a core example of "real expenditure;" that is, the literal casting out of surplus energy, unbound by strict understandings of utility or use; and against societal taboos that ensure restraint or modesty. Whereas Bataille emphasizes loss, I'll emphasize expenditure—and by extension, models of expenditure without guaranteed returns—as profound need, pleasure, and resistance. Yes, dance makes objects: choreographies, archival remains, ticket sales. And yes Lecavalier is a star, with considerable access, privilege, and power. Yet expenditure is different than virtuosity as excess, and different too than readings of energy as a regulated commodity or freely circulating gift.[28] Expenditure indexes energy without taking into account a politics of exchange or obligation. To turn to expenditure is, in a sense, to follow Lecavalier's lead; less about the dance, more about the dancing, and what it means to try so hard, with failure and glory always, beautifully, hanging in the balance.

---

[26] Here, I am especially indebted to Michael Taussig's reading of Bataille, in his essay: "The Sun Gives Without Receiving," in *Walter Benjamin's Grave* (Chicago, London: The University of Chicago, 2006), 69–95.
[27] Georges Bataille, "The Notion of Expenditure." In *The Bataille Reader*, ed. Fred Botting and Scott Wilson (Oxford, UK: Blackwell Publishers, 1991), 167–81; 172.
[28] Foster, *Valuing Dance*, 150–1.

A Partial Timeline: Fragments for a Life in Dance

1958   Lecavalier born October 3 to parents Jean Guy and Jaqueline Leblanc; she will be the oldest of four children, with brothers Denis, Luc, and Donald.

1973   Begins taking dance classes with Helena Voronova in Cartierville; and Erik Hyrst on St-Catherine's Ouest.

1974   Parascolaire dance classes at CEGEP Bois-de-Boulogne

1975   First sees and is struck by Édouard's work, *Temps volé* (1975); later, she will see *Remous* (1977) and *Le Nageur* (1978); they will begin working together in 1981 and later become a couple (1984–9).

1977   Accepted to McGill University to study Physical Education; declines, in order to pursue dancing; begins with Pointépiénu, a Bejart-influenced company and studio offering mixed techniques including classes in Dalcroze technique (Figure 6.1).

1978   Joins Groupe Nouvelle Aire, studying Graham and Limon technique as well as with Martine Époque and working with myriad, formative choreographers.

1980   Sees the Min Tanaka performance in Montréal (November 25, Musée des beaux arts/Musée d'art contemporain); impressed by the extreme speed and slowness of the dancing and an aesthetic so unlike the dance happening in the city at the time; "it was a shock, like being on another planet."

1981   Joins Lock Danseurs, for *Oranges*
           Premiere: November 14, 1981, Musée d'Art Contemporain, Montréal
           Performers: Louis Guillemette, Louise Lecavalier, Michel Lemieux, Édouard Lock, Miryam Moutillet

Figure 6.1 *Fantasie sur quatre notes.* Choreography by Louise Latreille, Lecavalier at right. Photo: René De Carufel/Bibliothèque de la danse Vincent-Warren.

       Study trip to New York, stays with Pooh Kaye, performs with Michel Lemieux and Édouard Lock in a benefit for the Kitchen

1981–2 First solo choreography, *Non Non Non je ne suis pas Mary Poppins.*
Montréal, QC: Véhicule Art (307 Ouest Rue Ste. Catherine); November 25–8 and December 16–19, 1982

1981–2 Teaches part-time at CEGEP Ahuntsic; receives a two-year contract, shared with another teacher, to lead class, hire musicians and produce a final show.

1983 *Businessman in the Process of Becoming an Angel*
Premiere: April 13, 1983 Brigantine Room, Harbourfront Toronto

Performers: Claude Godin, Louis Guillemette, Louise Lecavalier, Michel Lemieux, Édouard Lock, Miryam Moutillet

1984 Sees the Nina Hagen show at the Spectrum in January; she recalls, "There was not a minute of cuteness, it was very powerful."

1984 Attends concert of Einstürzende Neubauten outside of London, UK; the show is stopped after 15 minutes because of fire onstage. "I loved the energy—it was so tough, it felt like us, in the way that we were at war with dance. Not dance really, but the soft ways it was still happening …." Later, they will perform together at the Spectrum in Montréal (1990) during a festival of industrial music; and the band will compose music for *Infante*.

1984 Performs at the Rialto Theatre on Avenue du Parc; the company self-produces in what are the last four performances of *Businessman*. Later, after ten years in the Cooper Building on St-Laurent (1983–94), the company will relocate to rehearsal spaces at the Rialto (Figure 6.2).

1985 *Human Sex*
Premiere: April 3, 1985; East Cultural Centre, Vancouver
Performers: Marc Béland, Carole Courtois, Claude Godin, Louise Lecavalier, Édouard Lock, Randall Kaye
Wins Bessie Award for her performance of *Businessman*, New York
Begins taking ballet class with Reynald Rabu (choreographer and dancer with Les Grands Ballets Canadiens, artistic director of the Pacific Ballet and rehearsal director with La La La Human Steps).

1986 Visits Japan in advance of company tour; with Édouard Lock and Marc Béland, she works on a commercial for the department store chain Parco; she will return for tours and for longer, leisure trips over six times in the coming years.

A Partial Timeline 203

Figure 6.2 At the Rialto after the final performance of *Businessman*. Photo: Jack Udashkin.

1987 *Human Sex Duo No. 1*
Director Bernar Hébert
Performers: Marc Béland, Louise Lecavalier, Édouard Lock
New Demons
Premiere: September 19, 1987; Théâtre du Nouveau Monde, Festival International de nouvelle danse Montréal (125 performances, 49 cities)
Dances at Rendez-Vous 87, a two-game hockey series between Canada and Russia held in Quebec City in February; soloists from the Bolshoi Ballet perform a classical duet from *Sparticus* by Aram Katchatourian; at the last moment, Édouard suggests that she and Marc perform their duet to the same music; the four dancers take bows together

1988 "Look Back in Anger," with David Bowie
Performance: Institute of Contemporary Arts (ICA) Benefit, London, UK
Sat-Arts III: *Wrap Around the World*, Nam June Paik, New York, NY

1989 "Danse Avant de Tomber" (Save the Las Dance for Me), Carole Laure
Music Video

1990 Guest artist with David Bowie's "Sound and Vision" Tour; Édouard Lock, Artistic Director and Choreographer. Performs at the Love-In Protest July 29, Parc Lafontaine, organized by Lesbian and Gays Against Violence (LGV) in response to the police raid on the after-hours dance club Sex Garage on July 15, 1990.

1991 *Infante, c'est destroy*
Premiere: April 17, 1991, Théâtre de la Ville, Paris
Performers: Bernadus Bartels, Pim Boonprakob, Louise Lecavalier, Édouard Lock, Marito Olsson-Forsberg, Donald Weikert, Sarah Williams

1992 *The Yellow Shark*, Frank Zappa and Ensemble Modern. Concerts in Frankfurt and Berlin, Germany; and Vienna, Austria.
Performers: Bernadus Bartels, Pim Boonprakob, Louise Lecavalier, Édouard Lock, Marito Olsson-Forsberg, Donald Weikert, Sarah Williams

1994 Hip injury at chiropractor's office
She plays the role of Cindy "Vita" Minh in Katherine Bigelow's *Strange Days*.
Performs in Lock's film, *Velazquez's Little Museum*. ZDF/ARTE.
Begins boxing classes with former-Pro boxer, ballet dancer and trainer Milford Kemp in Los Angeles and Montréal.

1995 *2*
Premiere: April 28, 1995, Théâtre de la Ville, Paris
Performers: Michael Dolan, Liza Kovacs, Sara Lawrey, Louise Lecavalier, Francine Liboiron, Fabien Prioville, Rick Gavin Tija, Donald Weikert

1996	Louise and Édouard appear in Michael Apted's *Inspirations*.
1998	*Salt/Exaucé* Premiere: October 22, 1998, Saitama Arts Theatre, Saitama, Japan (Figure 6.3)
1999	Retires from the company in May Receives the Jean A. Chalmers Award
2000	Lives in Paris for the year, with musician friends in the Kremlin-Bicêtre neighborhood.
2001	Birth of twin daughters, Romie and Janne
2003	Returns to the stage in "Reclusive Conclusions and Other Duets," an evening of choreography by Tedd Robinson, featuring Lecavalier (*Lulu and the Sailor*), Mako Kawano (*Kurosango*) and Margie Gillis (*The Insistent Echo of Reclusive Conclusions*). March 20, National Arts Centre, Ottawa
2005	Reads Virginia Woolf's *Orlando*, which becomes source material for *Cobalt Rouge* (2005, choreography by Tedd Robinson). Hip replacement at the Jewish General Hospital, Montréal
2006	Presents an evening of short solo works by Tedd Robinson (*Lulu and the Sailor*); Crystal Pite (*Lone Epic*, Premiere: August 18, 2006 at Tanz im August—Internationales tanzfest, Berlin); and Benoît Lachambre *("I" is Memory*, Premiere: May 6, 2006, Chiasso, Switzerland—Cinema Teatro). France Bruyère joins on as rehearsal director, following many years of collaboration in the Montréal dance community and with La La La Human Steps.
2006	Founds *Fou glorieux* as a vehicle for her performance work and the development of new choreography, dance and collaborations

Figure 6.3 Extending the body: Louise Lecavalier and Rick Tija. Photo: Édouard Lock.

2008 *Is You Me*, a collaboration with Benoît Lachambre
Premiere: May 23, 2008; Festival TransAmériques, Montréal
Named Officer of the Order of Canada

2009 Two new works: *Children*, choreography by Nigel Charnock; and *A Few Minutes of Lock*, choreography by Édouard Lock
Premiere: September 3–4, Oriente Occidente Festival, Italy

2011 Prix de la danse de Montréal

2012 *So Blue*; Premiere: December 7, 2012, Tänzhaus NRW, Dusseldorf

A Partial Timeline   207

2013 Leonide Massine Dance Prize, "Most Outstanding Female Dancer of the Year on the Contemporary Scene."

2014 Dances in *Reverse_Me* (with Fabien Prioville, Goethe Institute, Montréal); and *Le Délire domestique* (Deborah Dunn, Choreographer; October 20–5, Agora de la danse, Montréal); Governor General Performing Arts Award for lifetime artistic achievement.

Fou glorieux receives the 29th Grand Prix of the Conseil des arts de Montréal.

Moves into White Wall Studio, on Rue Laval in the Plateau; "I think its part of our history, Édouard and me, to not want to impose a big company or establishment; we'll leave dance but not a building."

2015 Companion of the Ordre des arts et des lettres du Québec

2016 *Milles batailles*; Premiere: February 13, 2016, Tänzhaus NRW, Dusseldorf; the work is partly inspired by her reading of Italo Calvino's *The Nonexistent Knight*
(Figure 6.4)

2017 Prix Denise-Pelletier, ACFAS
Honorary Doctorat, Université du Quebec à Montréal

2018 Choreographs and performs in *Les Marguerit[e]s*; directed by Denis Marleau and Stéphanie Jasmin; Espace Go, Montréal

2020 *Stations*; Premiere: February 14, 2020, Tänzhaus NRW, Dusseldorf
(Figure 6.5)

2023 *Delusional World*, with Lu Yang; Premiere: January 26–8, Elektra Montréal, 6th International Digital Art Biennial, Arsenal Contemporary Arts

2023 Officière de l'ordre des arts et des lettres, La Ministre de la Culture, République Francaise

2024   Creates *Ether* for Gauthier Dance; Premiere: February 29th, Stuttgart, Germany; it is her first commission for a company *Minutes around late afternoon* (solo); Premiere: April 10th, Sadler's Wells Theatre/Elixir Festival, London

Figure 6.4 Photo: Carl Lessard. Courtesy Fou Glorieux.

Figure 6.5 Photo: Dieter Wuschanski. Courtesy Fou Glorieux.

Bibliography

Ahmed, Sara. *Living a Feminist Life*. Durham, NC and London: Duke University Press, 2017.

Aikens, Nick, Teresa Grandes, Nav Haq, Beatriz Herráez, and Nataša Petrešin-Bachelez, Eds. *The Long 1980s: Constellations of Art, Politics and Identities*. Amsterdam: Valiz with the Internationale, 2018.

Anderson, Bailey. "Overcoming and Denial: Disability and Modern Dance in the United States." *Dance Research Journal* 52, no. 3 (December 2020): 58–75.

Andersson, Danjel, Mette Edvardsen, and Mårten Spångberg, Eds. *Post-Dance*. Stockholm: Stiftelsen Moderna Dansteatern (MDT), 2017.

Asselin, Suzanne. "Solos entre la folie et la réel." *Le Devoir*, November 30, 1982, 6.

Austin, David. "Narratives of Power: Historical Mythologies in Contemporary Quebec and Canada." *Race and Class*. Institute of Race Relations 52, no. 1 (2010): 19–32.

Baillargeon, Denyse. *A Brief History of Women in Québec*. Waterloo, ON: Wilfred Laurier Press, 2014.

Balsamo, Anne. "Reading Cyborgs Writing Feminism." In *The Gendered Cyborg: A Reader*, edited by Gill Kirkup, Linda Janes, Kath Woodward, and Fiona Hovenden, 148–58. London and New York: Routledge, 2000.

Banes, Sally. *Dancing Women: Female Bodies Onstage*. New York: Routledge, 1998.

Banes, Sally. *Souvenir Program, Festival international de nouvelle danse*. Montréal, Québec: Parachute Editions, 1985.

Bardo, Susan. *Unbearable Weight: Feminism, Western Culture, and the Body*. Oakland, CA: University of California Press, 2004/1993.

Bartky, Sandra Lee. *Femininity and Domination: Studies in the Phenomenology of Oppression*. New York: Routledge, 1990.

Bataille, Georges. *The Accursed Share. Volume 1: Consumption*. New York: Zone Books, 1991.

Bataille, Georges. "The Notion of Expenditure." In *The Bataille Reader*, edited by Fred Botting and Scott Wilson, 167–81. Oxford, UK: Blackwell Publishers, 1982.

Baudrillard, Jean. *America*. London, New York: Verso, 1988.

Beaulieu, Marie. "Accueillir la modernité avec Mary Wigman." In *Chroniques des arts de la scene à Montréal durant l'entre-deux guerres (Danse, Théâtre, Musique)*, edited by Marie-Thérèse Lefebvre. Québec: Septentrion/Cahiers des Amériques, 2016.

Beheils, Michael, and Matthew Hayday, Eds. *Contemporary Quebec: Selected Readings and Commentaries*. Montréal, Québec: McGill-Queen's University Press, 2011.

Berardi, Franco. "Communism Is Back but We Should Call It the Therapy of Singularization." Generation on-line, 2009. https://www.generation-online.org/p/fp_bifo6.htm

Bergen, Hilary. "Animating the Kinetic Trace: Kate Bush, Hatsune Miku and Posthuman Dance." *Public* 30, no. 60 (2020): 188–207.

Bergen, Hilary. "Not a Girl Dancing: Gender, Spectacle and Disembodiment in the Work of Loïe Fuller and Freya Olafson." In *Archée: arts, médiatiques & cyberculture*. March 4, 2019. Montréal, QC. http://archee.qc.ca/wordpress/not-a-girl-dancinggender-spectacle-and-disembodiment-inthe-work-of-loie-fuller-and-freya-olafson/

Berger, Maurice, Ed. *The 1980s: A Virtual Discussion. Issues in Cultural Theory 10*. Georgia O'Keefe Research Centre/Santa Fe and Centre for Art, Design and Visual Culture/University of Baltimore, MD, New York: Distributed Art Publishers, 2007.

Bhabha, Homi K. *The Location of Culture*. London, New York: Routledge, 2004/1994.

Blades, Hetty. "Projects, Precarity and the Ontology of Dance Works." *Dance Research Journal* 51, no. 1 (2019): 66–78.

Blais, Melissa, and Francis Dupuis-Déri. "Masculinism and the Anti-Feminist Countermovement." *Social Movement Studies: Journal of Social, Cultural and Political Protest* 11, no. 1 (2011): 21–9.

Boon, Marcus. "On Appropriation." *The New Centennial Review* 7, no. 1 (2007:) 1–14.

Bowen, Christopher. "Bodily Charmed." *The Scotsman*, October 22, 1996.

Braidotti, Rosi. *Nomadic Subjects: Embodiment and Sexual Difference in Contemporary Feminist Theory*. 2nd edn. New York: Columbia University Press, 2011.

Brooks, Lynn Matluck. *Women's Work: Making Dance in Europe Before 1800*. Madison, WI: University of Wisconsin Press, 2007.

Bunsell, Tanya. *Strong and Hard Women: An Ethnography of Female Bodybuilding*. New York: Routledge, 2013.

Burness, Edwina, and Jerry Griswold. "The Art of Fiction LXXIII: PL Travers." *The Paris Review* 86 (1982): 210–29.

Burt, Ramsey. "New Dance in Canada: Report from Le Festival international de nouvelle danse à Montréal." *New Dance* No. 35 (1986): 14–17.

Butler, Judith. "Performative Acts and Gender Constitution: An Essay in Phenomenology and Feminist Theory." *Theatre Journal* 40, no. 4 (1988): 519–31.

Casemajor, Nathalie, and Will Straw. "The Visuality of Scenes: Urban Cultures and Visual Scenescapes." In *Imaginations: Journal of Cross-Cultural Image Studies* (2017). http://imaginations.glendon.yorku.ca/?p=9152

Chude-Sokei, Louis. *The Sound of Culture: Diaspora and Black Technopoetics*. Middleton, CT: Wesleyan University Press, 2015.

Colin, Noyale, and Stefanie Sachsenmaier. *Collaboration in Performance Practice: Premises, Workings and Failures*. London: Routledge, 2016.

Cooper Albright, Ann. *Engaging Bodies: The Politics and Poetics of Corporeality*. Middletown, CT: Wesleyan University Press, 2013.

Cooper Albright, Ann. *Choreographing Difference: The Body and Identity in Contemporary Dance*. Middletown, CT: Wesleyan University Press, 1997.

Copeland, Roger, and Marshall Cohen, Eds. *What Is Dance? Readings in Theory and Criticism*. Oxford, UK: Oxford University Press, 1983.

Critchley, Simon. "Rummaging in the Ashes: An Interview with Simon Critchley." *Punk is Dead: Modernity Killed Every Night*, edited by Richard Cabut and Andrew Gallix, 39. Winchester, UK; Washington, DC: Zero Books, 2017.

Cvejić, Bojana, and Ana Vujanović. "Exhausting Immaterial Labour," in *Exhausting Immaterial Labour in Performance*, a joint issue of *TkH Journal for Performing Arts Theory* and *Le Journal des Laboratoires*, No. 17 (October 2010): 4–5.

Cvetkovich, Ann. "Introduction." *An Archive of Feelings: Trauma, Sexuality and Lesbian Public Cultures*, 1–14. Durham, NC: Duke University Press, 2003.

Daly, Ann. *Done into Dance: Isadora Duncan in America*. Middletown, CT: Wesleyan University Press, 2002.

Daly, Ann. "Theorizing Gender." In *Critical Gestures: Writings on Dance and Culture*. Middletown, CT: Wesleyan University Press, 2002.

Davis, Tracy C. *Actresses as Working Women: Their Social Identity in Victorian Culture*. London: Routledge, 1991.

Dickinson, John, and Brian Young. *A Short History of Québec*, 4th edn. Montréal, Québec: McGill-Queens University Press, 2008.

Diederichsen, Diedrich. "From Anti-Social Liberal Punk to Intersectional AIDs Activism: Sub-Culture and Politics in Eighties Europe." In *The Long 1980s: Constellations of Art, Politics and Identities*, edited by Nick Aikens, Teresa Grandas, Nav Haq, Beatriz Herráez, and Nataša Petrešin-Bachelez. Valiz, Amsterdam: L'Internationale, 2018.

Dixon Gottschild, Brenda. *Digging the Africanist Presence in American Performance and Other Contexts*. Westport, CT and London: Greenwood Press, 1996.

Dodds, Sherril, and Colleen Hooper. "Faces, Close-ups and Choreography: A Deleuzian Critique of So You Think You Can Dance." *The International Journal of Screendance* 4, no. 1 (2014): 93–113.

Dodds, Sherril. *Dancing on the Canon: Embodiments of Value in Popular Dance*. Basingstoke, UK: Palgrave Macmillan, 2011.

Dodds, Sherril. "Slamdancing With the Boundaries of Theory and Practice: The Legitimization of Popular Dance." In *The Routledge Dance Studies Reader*, 2nd edn., edited by Alexandra Carter and Janet O'Shea, 405–14. New York; London: Routledge, 2010.

Dolan, Jill. "Feminist Performance Criticism and the Popular: Reviewing Wendy Wasserstein." In *Theatre Journal* 60, no. 3 (2008): 433–57. http://feministspectator.princeton.edu/articles/feminist-performance-criticism/

Draper, Ellen, and Jenny Koralek, Eds. *A Lively Oracle: A Centennial Celebration of PL Travers, Creator of Mary Poppins*. New York: Larson Publications, 1999.

Duncombe, Stephen. *Notes from the Underground: Zines and the Politics of Alternative Culture*. Portland, OR: Microcosm Publishing, 2017.

Durepos Jr., Fernand. "Die frau von Berlin: Nina Hagen." In *Pop Rock Montréal* 10, no. 2 (February 21, 1981): 15.

Elswit, Kate. "The Micropolitics of Exchange: Exile and Otherness After Nation." *The Oxford Handbook of Dance and Politics*, 417–38. New York: Oxford University Press, 2017.

Elswit, Kate. *Watching Weimar Dance*. New York: Oxford University Press, 2014.

Enfield, N. J., and Paul Kockelman, Eds. *Distributed Agency*. Oxford, UK: Oxford University Press, 2017.

Federici, Silvia. "Precarious Labor: A Feminist Viewpoint." *Variant* 37, Spring/Summer (2010): 23–5.

Federici, Silvia. *Calaban and the Witch: Women, the Body and Primitive Accumulation*. Brooklyn, NY: Autonomedia, 2004.

Foster, Susan Leigh. *Valuing Dance: Commodities and Gifts in Motion*. New York: Oxford University Press, 2019.

Foster, Susan Leigh. *Choreography and Narrative: Ballet's Staging of Story and Desire*. Bloomington, IN: Indiana University Press, 1998.

Foster, Susan Leigh. "The Ballerina's Phallic Pointe." In *Corporealities: Dancing Knowledge, Culture, Power*, edited by Susan Leigh Foster, 1–26. London: Routledge, 1995.

Foster, Susan Leigh. *Reading Dancing: Bodies and Subjects in Contemporary American Dance*. Berkeley, CA: University of California Press, 1986.

Foucault, Michel. *The Archeology of Knowledge and the Discourse on Language*, translated by A. M. Sheridan Smith. New York: Pantheon Books, 1972.

Frank, Kevin. "'Whether Beast or Human': The Cultural Legacies of Dread, Locks and Dystopia." *Small Axe* 11, no. 2 (June 2007): 42–62.

Franko, Mark, and Alessandra Nicifero, Eds. "Dance, the De-Materialization of Labor, and the Productivity of the Corporeal." In *Choreographing Discourses: A Mark Franko Reader*. London: Routledge, 2018.

Franko, Mark, and André Lepecki, Eds. "Editor's Note: Dance in the Museum." *Dance Research Journal* 46, no. 3 (2014): 1–4.

Frith, Simon. *Music for Pleasure: Essays in the Sociology of Pop*. New York: Routledge, 1988.

Frith, Simon. "Punk 77: The Politics of Punk." New York: The *Village Voice* (October 24, 1977).

Fung, Richard. "Working Through Appropriation." *FUSE* Magazine XVI, no. 5+6 (Summer 1993): 16–24.

Gil, José. *Metamorphoses of the Body*, translated by Stephen Muecke. Minneapolis, MN: University of Minnesota Press, 1998.

Gonzalez, Jennifer. "Envisioning Cyborg Bodies: Notes from Current Research." In *The Gendered Cyborg: A Reader*, edited by Gill Kirkup, Linda Janes, Kath Woodward, and Fiona Hovenden, 58–73. London and New York: Routledge, 2000.

Gradinger, Maeve. "Dances of Disillusion." In *Ballett International/Tanz Aktuell*, 24–8, October 1995.

Graeber, David, and Loretta leng Tak. "Bullshit Jobs: A Conversation with David Graeber." *Built in China Journal* no. 2. Acton: ANU Press, 2019.

Graeber, David. "The Sadness of Post-workerism, or Art and Immaterial Labour Conference—A Sort of Review." 2008. https://theanarchistlibrary.org/library/david-graeber-the-sadness-of-post-workerism

Greenaway, Kathryn. "La La La Dancer Undaunted …." *Montreal Gazette*, March 7, 1990.
Griswold, Jerry. "'Mary Poppins' Creator P.L. Travers Is Even More Fascinating than Her Fiction." *Washington Post*, December 14, 2018.
Hall, Stuart. "Narrating the Nation: An Imagined Community." In *Modernity: An Introduction to Modern Societies*, edited by Stuart Hall, David Held, Don Hubert, and Kenneth Thompson, 613–15. Malden, MA: Wiley-Blackwell, 1996.
Hall, Stuart. "Signification, Representation, Ideology: Althusser and the Post-Structuralist Debates." In *Critical Studies in Mass Communication* 2, no. 2 (1985): 91–114.
Hamera, Judith. "The Labors of Michael Jackson: Virtuosity, Deindustrialization and Dancing Work." *PMLA*, Special Topic: Work, 127, no. 4 (2012): 751–65.
Hamera, Judith. "I Dance to You: Reflections on Irigaray's I Love to You in Pilates and Virtuosity." *Cultural Studies* 15, no. 2 (2001): 229–40.
Hamera, Judith. "The Romance of Monsters: Theorizing the Virtuoso Body." *Theatre Topics* 10, no. 2 (2000): 144–53.
Hanhardt, John G., Gregory Zinman, and Edith Decker-Phillips, Eds. *We Are in Open Circuits: Writings by Nam June Paik*. Cambridge, MA: MIT Press, 2019.
Haraway, Donna J. *Simians, Cyborgs and Women: The Reinvention of Nature*. New York: Routledge, 1991.
Harris, Cheryl. "Whiteness as Property." *Harvard Law Review* 106, no. 8 (1993): 1707–91.
Hart, Lynda. "Introduction." In *Acting Out: Feminist Performances*, edited by Lynda Hart and Peggy Phelan, 1–12. Ann Arbor, MI: University of Michigan Press, 1993.
Harvey, David. *A Brief History of Neoliberalism*. Oxford, UK: Oxford University Press, 2005.
Hawes, Leonard C. "Becoming-Other-Wise: Conversational Performance and the Politics of Experience." In *Opening Acts: Performance in/as Communication and Cultural Studies*, edited by Judith Hamera. Thousand Oaks, CA: Sage Publications, 2005/1998.
Hebdige, Dick. *Subculture: The Meaning of Style*. London, New York: Routledge.
High, Steven. *Deindustrializing Montreal: Entangled Histories of Race, Residence and Class*. Montréal, Québec: McGill-Queens University Press, 2022.

High, Steven. "The Normalized Quiet of Unseen Power: Recognizing the Structural Violence of Deindustrialization as Loss." *Urban History Review* 48, no. 2 (2021): 97–115.

Householder, Johanna, and Tanya Mars, Eds. *Caught in the Act: An Anthology of Performance Art by Canadian Women*. Toronto: YYZ Books, 1979.

Howe-Beck, Linde. "Lemieux Upstages Dancers." *Montreal Gazette*, November 27, 1982, D6.

Hurley, Erin. *National Performance: Representing Quebec from Expo 67 to Celine Dion*. Toronto, Buffalo, London: University of Toronto Press, 2011.

Ireland, Susan, and Proulx, Patrice J., Eds. *Textualizing the Immigrant Experience in Contemporary Quebec*. Westport, CT, London: Praeger, 2004.

Irving, Dan. "Normalized Transgression: Legitimizing the Transexual Body as Productive." In *The Transgender Studies Reader 2R*, edited by Sandy Stone and Aren Aizura. New York: Routledge, 15–29, 2013.

Iseli, Christian. "Double Trouble: Digital Avatars on Stage." In *Actor & Avatar: A Scientific & Artistic Catalogue*, edited by Dieter Mersch, Anton Rey, Thomas Grunwald, Jörg Sternagel, Lorena Kegel, and Miriam Laura Loertscher, 114–122. Bielefeld: Transcript Verlag/Swiss National Science Federation, 2023.

Iskander, Natalie, and Nichola Lowe. "The Transformers: Immigration and Tacit Knowledge Development," edited by K. Elsbach and B. Bechky. *Qualitative Organizational Research—Volume 3*. Charlotte, NC: Information Age Publishing, 2016.

Jameson, Fredric. "Periodizing the 60s," *Social Text* no. 9/10 (Spring/Summer, 1984): 178–209.

Järvinen, Hanna. *Dancing Genius: The Stardom of Vaslav Njinsky*. New York: Palgrave Macmillan, 2014.

Jermyn, Deborah, and Sean Redmond. *The Cinema of Kathryn Bigelow: Hollywood Transgressor*. London, New York: Wallflower Press, 2003.

Jowitt, Deborah. "Step Quickly, Don't Fall Off the World." *ArtsJournal: Arts, Culture, Ideas*. September 15, 2015. https://www.artsjournal.com/dancebeat/2015/09/step-quickly-dont-fall-off-the-world/

Jowitt, Deborah. "Honk if You Love Dogs." In *The Village Voice*, October 9, 1984.

Katz, Barbara. "Concert Lures the 'unbelievable.'" *Montreal Gazette*, February 7, 1984, D8.

Kisselgoff, Anna. "Mixed Media for Rock Music Lovers." *The New York Times*, October 2, 1991, C21.

Kisselgoff, Anna. "Dance: Edouard Lock's Punk Style." *The New York Times*, October 6, 1985, Section 1, 73.

Klein, Gabriele. "Dancing Politics: Worldmaking in Dance and Choreography." In *Emerging Bodies: The Performance of Worldmaking in Dance and Choreography*, edited by Gabriele Klein and Sandra Noeth, 17–27. Bielefeld: Transcript Verlag, 2011.

Kostrin, Hannah. "Jewish Dance Migrations: Margalit Oved's and Barak Marshall's Travelling Aesthetics." Presentation for Dance Studies Colloquium, Institute for Dance Studies, Temple University, 2022. https://www.youtube.com/watch?v=BcyynARycUc

Kunst, Bojana. "Dance and Work: The Aesthetics and Political Potential of Dance." In *Emerging Bodies: The Performance of Worldmaking in Dance and Choreography*, edited by Gabriele Klein and Sandra Noeth, 47–59. Bielefeld: Transcript Verlag, 2012.

Kuppers, Petra. *Disability and Contemporary Performance: Bodies on Edge*. New York, London: Routledge, 2023.

La Berge, Claire Leigh. *Wages Against Artwork: Decommodified Labour and the Claims of Socially Engaged Art*. Durham, NC: Duke University Press, 2019.

Lee, Sook-Kyung, and Susanne Rennert, Eds. *Nam June Paik*. London: Tate Publishing, 2010.

Leffingwell, Randy. "La La La Human Steps Brings Extravaganza to Wiltern." *Los Angeles Times*, March 26, 1994, F8.

Lindgren, Allana. *From Automatistes to Modern Dance: Francoise Sullivan with Franziska Boas in New York*. Toronto: Dance Collection Danse, 2003.

Louppe, Laurence. *Poetics of Contemporary Dance*. Bruxelles: Contredanse, 2010.

Low, Stephen. "The Speed of Queer: La La La Human Steps and Queer Perceptions of the Body." *Theatre Research in Canada* 37, no. 1 (2016): 62–78.

Lynes, Krista Genevieve, and Katerina Symes. "Cyborgs and Virtual Bodies." In *The Oxford Handbook of Feminist Theory*, edited by Lisa Disch and Mary Hawkesworth, 122–42. New York: Oxford University Press, 2016.

Maillé, Chantal. "Intersectionalizing Gender Policies: Experiences in Quebec and Canada." *French Politics* 16, no. 3 (2018): 312–27.

Maillé, Chantal. "Transnational Feminisms in Francophonie Space." *Women: A Cultural Review* 23, no. 1 (2012): 62–78.

Maniura, Robert. "Persuading the Absent Saint: Image and Performance in Marian Devotion." *Critical Inquiry* 35, no. 3 (2009): 629–54.

Manning, Susan. "Dance History." In *The Bloomsbury Companion to Dance Studies*, edited by Sherril Dodds, 303–26. London, New York, Oxford, New Delhi, Sydney: Bloomsbury Academic, 2019.

Manning, Susan, and Lucia Ruprecht, Eds. *New German Dance Studies*. Urbana, IL: University of Illinois Press, 2012.

Manning, Susan. *Ecstasy and the Demon: The Dances of Mary Wigman*. Minneapolis, MN: University of Minnesota Press, 2006.

Martin, Randy. "Dance and Its Others: Theory, State, Nation and Socialism." In *Of the Presence of the Body: Essays on Dance and Performance Theory*, edited by André Lepecki, 47–63. Middletown, CT: Wesleyan University Press, 2004.

Mauss, Marcel. *A General Theory of Magic*. New York and London: Routledge, 2001.

McKenzie, Jon. *Perform or Else: From Discipline to Performance*. London, New York: Taylor & Francis, 2001.

Meisner, Nadine. "Superwoman." *The Sunday Times*, Dance: 10–15, October 20, 1996.

Mercer, Kobena. "Black Hair/Style Politics." *New Formations* No. 3 (Winter 1987): 33–54.

Mersch, Dieter, Anton Rey, and Thomasand Thomas Grunwald. "Introduction," in *Actor & Avatar: A Scientific & Artistic Catalogue*, edited by Dieter Mersch, Anton Rey, Thomas Grunwald, Jörg Sternagel, Lorena Kegel, and Miriam Laura Loertscher, 5–21. Bielefeld: Transcript Verlag/ Swiss National Science Federation, 2023.

Mills, Sean. "Quebec, Haiti, and the Deportation Crisis of 1974." *The Canadian Historical View* 94, no. 3 (2013): 405–35.

Mills, Sean. "*Québécoises deboutte!* Nationalism and Feminism in Québec, 1969–1975." In *Contemporary Québec: Selected Readings and Commentaries*, edited by Behiels and Mayday, 319–37. Montréal, Québec: McGill-Queens University Press, 2011.

Molesworth, Helen. "Work Ethic." In *Work Ethic*, edited by Helen Molesworth, 25–52. Baltimore, MD: Baltimore Museum of Art, 2003.

Mondzain, Marie-José. "Image, Subject, Power: An Interview with Marie-José Mondzain." *Inter-Asia Cultural Studies*, translated by Briankle G. Chang and Nefeli Forni Zervoudaki, 22, no. 1 (2019): 83–99.

Mondzain, Marie José. *Image, Icon, Economy: The Byzantine Origins of the Contemporary Imaginary*. Stanford, CA: Stanford University Press, 2005.

Morrison, Paul. *The Explanation for Everything: Essays on Sexual Subjectivity.* New York: New York University Press, 2001.

Moten, Fred. Lahey Lecture: "And: A Reply to Daniel Tiffany's Cheap Signaling." Writers Read/Department of English, Concordia University, Montreal. September 29, 2017.

Muñoz, José Esteban. *Cruising Utopia: The Then and There of Queer Futurity.* New York: New York University Press, 2019/2009.

Muñoz, José Esteban. *Disidentifications: Queers of Color and the Performance of Politics.* Minneapolis, London: University of Minnesota Press, 1999.

Muñoz, José Esteban. "The White to Be Angry: Vaginal Davis's Terrorist Drag." *Social Text* 52/53, 15, no. 3/4 (1997): 80–103.

Nemiroff, Diana. "A History of Artist-Run Spaces in Canada, with Particular Reference to Véhicule, A Space and the Western Front." MA Thesis, Concordia University, 1985.

Noland, Carrie. *Agency and Embodiment: Performing Gestures/Producing Culture.* Cambridge, MA: Harvard University Press, 2009.

Odom, Selma L. "Delsartean Traces in Dalcroze Eurhythmics." *Mime Journal* 23 (2005): 137–51.

Odom, Selma L., and Marie Jane Warner, Eds. *Canadian Dance: Visions and Stories.* Toronto: Dance Collection Danse Press, 2004.

Osterweis, Ariel. "Disavowing Virtuosity, Performing Aspiration: Choreographies of Anticlimax in the Work of Yve Laris Cohen, Narcissister, and John Jasperse." In *Futures of Dance Studies*, edited by Susan Manning, Janice Ross, and Rebecca Schneider, 431–48. Madison, WI: University of Wisconsin Press, 2020.

Pelgram, Scooter. *Choosing their Own Style: Identity Emergence in Haitian Youth in Québec.* New York: Peter Young, 2005, 45–6.

Pentcheva, Bissera. "Performing the Sacred in Byzantium: Image, Breath, and Sound." *PRI Performance Research International* 19, no. 3 (2014): 120–8.

Pentcheva, Bissera. "The Performative Icon." *The Art Bulletin* 88, no. 4 (2006): 631–5.

Phelan, Peggy. *Unmarked: The Politics of Performance.* New York, London: Routledge, 1993.

Podmore, Julie. "Gone Underground? Lesbian Visibility and the Consolidation of Queer Space in Montréal." *Social and Cultural Geography*, 7, no. 4 (2006): 595–25.

Pouillaude, Frédéric. *Unworking Choreography: The Notion of Work in Dance.* London: Oxford University Press, 2017.

Puleo, Risa. "Sitting Beside Yvonne Rainer's *Convalescent Dance.*" *Art Papers* (Winter 2018/19); https://www.artpapers.org/tag/risa-puleo/

Rainer, Yvonne. "No Manifesto." In *Posthumanism in Art and Science: A Reader*, edited by Giovanni Aloi and Susan McHugh, 97. New York: Columbia University Press, 1965/2008.

Rancière, Jacques. *Dissensus: on Politics and Aesthetics*. New York, London: Continuum, 2010.

Randall, Tressa. "Hanya Holm and an American Tanzgemeinschaft." In *New German Dance Studies*, edited by Susan Manning and Lucia Ruprecht, 79–98. Urbana, IL: University of Illinois Press, 2012.

Renaud, Jeanne, with Denis Marleau. "La Danse modern au Québec; autour d'un temoinage de Jeanne Renaud." *Jeu: cahier de revue de théâtre* 32, no. 3 (1984): 43–8.

Roach, Joe R. "It." *Theatre Journal* 56, no. 4 (2000): 555–68.

Roediger, David R. *The Wages of Whiteness: Race and the Making of the American Working Class*. New York: Verso, 2007.

Roediger, David R. *Coloured White: Transcending the Racial Past*. Berkeley, CA: University of California Press, 2003.

Roediger, David R. "Guineas, Wiggers, and the Dramas of Racialized Culture." In *American Literary History* 7, no. 4 (1995): 654–68.

Rothfield, Philipa, and Thomas F. DeFrantz, Eds. "Relay: Choreography and Corporeality." In *Choreography and Corporeality: Relay in Motion*, 1–12. London: Palgrave Macmillan, 2016.

Roux, Celine. "Performative Practices/Critical Bodies #2: What Makes Dance." *Danse: An Anthology*, edited by Noémi Solomon, 261–73. New York: Les presses du réel—New York series, 2014.

Schneider, Rebecca. "In Our Hands: An Ethics of Gestural Response-Ability." *Performance Philosophy* 3, no. 1 (2017): 108–25; 110.

Schneider, Rebecca. *Performing Remains: Art and War in Times of Theatrical Reenactment*. New York, London: Routledge, 2011.

Schwaiger, Liz. "Performing One's Age: Cultural Constructions of Aging and Embodiment in Western Theatrical Dancers." *Dance Research Journal* 37 (2007): 1107–20.

Siegel, Marcia B. "Dance Analysis—Lock's Duo." Unpublished Notes from a Presentation at the Department of Performance Studies, New York University. New York: October 4 1990.

Siegmund, Gerald. *Jérôme Bel: Dance, Theatre and the Subject*, Springer, 2017.

Simon, Sherry. *Translating Montreal: Episodes in the Life of a Divided City.* Québec, Montréal: McGill-Queen's University Press, 2006.

Simon, Sherry. "Culture and its Values: Critical Revisionism in Québec in the 1980s." In *Canadian Canons: Essays in Literary Values*, edited by Robert Lecker, 167–79. Toronto, Buffalo: University of Toronto Press, 1991.

Sinclair, Sara, Ed. *Robert Rauschenberg: An Oral History.* New York, NY: Columbia University Press, 2019.

Solomon, Noémie, Ed. *Danse: A Catalogue.* New York: Les presses du réel, 2015.

Solomon, Noémie, Ed. *Danse: An Anthology.* New York: Les presses du réel, 2014.

Sorell, Walter. *The Mary Wigman Book: Her Writings Edited and Translated.* Middletown, CT: Wesleyan University Press, 1975.

Stahl, Geoff. "Tracing out an Anglo Bohemia: Musicmaking and Myth in Montreal." *Public: Cities/Scenes* 22-3 (2001): 99–121.

Stahl, Geoff. "The Quest for Metropolis." *City* 5, no. 2 (2000): 257–9.

Straw, Will and Casemajor, Nathalie. "The Visuality of Scenes: Urban Cultures and Visual Scenescapes." In *The Visuality of Scenes/Special Issue—Imagination: Journal of Cross-Cultural Image Studies* 17, no. 2 (2017): 4–19.

Straw, Will. "Some Things a Scene Might Be: Postface." In *Cultural Studies* 29, no. 3 (2014): 476–85.

Straw, Will. "Scenes and Sensibilities." *Public*, no. 22/23 (2002): 245–57.

Stychin, Carl F. "Queer Nations: Nationalism, Sexuality and the Discourse of Rights in Québec." *Feminist Legal Studies* 5, no. 4 (1997): 3–34.

Taussig, Michael. "The Sun Gives Without Receiving," in *Walter Benjamin's Grave*, 69–95. Chicago and London: The University of Chicago, 2006.

Taussig, Michael. *Mimesis and Alterity. A Particular History of the Senses.* New York: Routledge, 1993.

Tembeck, Iro Valaskakis. "Flexible Identifies and the Necessity of Adaptability: The Case of Ruth Abramovitsch Sorel." *Canadian Dance Studies Quarterly.* Toronto: Dance Collections Danse, 2004.

Tembeck, Iro Valaskakis. "Politics and Dance in Montreal, 1940s to 1980s: The Imaginary Maginot Line between Anglophone and Francophone Dancers." In *Canada Dance: Visions and Stories*, edited by Selma Landen Odom and Mary Jane Warner, 271–86. Toronto: Dance Collections Danse, 2004.

Tembeck, Iro Valaskakis. "Walking the Tightrope: Acrobatics and Athleticism on the Montreal Stage." In *Canada Dance: Visions and Stories*, edited by Selma Landen Odom and Mary Jane Warner, 377–87. Toronto: Dance Collections Danse, 2004.

Tembeck, Iro Valaskakis. "Dancing in Montreal: Seeds for a Choreographic History." *Studies in Dance History* V, no. 2 (1994).

Tembeck, Iro Valaskakis. "La La La Human Steps" *Banff Letters*, 58–60. Banff, AB: Banff Centre for the Arts, 1986.

Thomas, Helen. *The Body, Dance and Culture*. New York: Palgrave Macmillan, 2003.

Thompson, M. J. "Two-Way Street: The Icon and the City." In *Performance Studies Canada*, edited by Laura Levin and Marlis Schweitzer, 287–315. Montréal, Québec: McGill-Queen's Press, 2017.

Thurner, Christina. "Affect, Discourse and Dance Before 1900." In *New German Dance Studies*, edited by Susan Manning and Lucia Ruprecht, 17–30. Urbana, IL: University of Illinois Press, 2012.

Traue, Boris, Mathias Blanc, and Carolina Cambre. "Visibilities and Visual Discourses: Rethinking the Social with the Image." *Qualitative Inquiry* 25, no. 4 (2018): 327–37.

Travers, P. L. *Mary Poppins*. New York: Clarion Books, 2006/1934.

Triggs, Teal. "Alphabet Soup: Reading British Fanzines." *Visible Language* 29, no. 1 (1995): 72–87.

Triggs, Teal. "Scissors and Glue: Punk Fanzines and the DIY Aesthetic." *Journal of Design History* 19, no. 1 (2006): 69–83.

Vacante, Jeffery. "Liberal Nationalism and the Challenge of Masculinity Studies in Quebec." *Left* 11, no. 2 (2006): 96–117.

Virno, Paolo. *A Grammar of the Multitude: For an Analysis of Contemporary Forms of Life*. New York, Los Angeles: Semiotext(e), 2004.

Werbner, Pnina, and Tariq Modood. *Debating Cultural Hybridity: Multicultural Identities and the Politics of Anti-Racism*. London: Zed Books, 2015.

Willett, John. *Art and Politics in the Weimar Period: The New Sobriety 1917–1933*. New York: Pantheon Books, 1978.

Winship, Lyndsey. "Cyberpunk Dervish: Louise Lecavalier on *So Blue*, Her First Work as a Choreographer." *Evening Standard*, July 1, 2014.

Whitney, Allison. "Etched with Emulsion: Weimar Dance and Body Culture in Expressionist Cinema." *Seminar: A Journal of Germanic Studies* 46, no. 3 (2010): 240–54.

Wyman, Max. "Edouard Lock: Showman or Shaman?" Presentation, Royal Society of Canada, Ottawa; November 19, 2004.

Recorded Oral History Interviews

Gallant, Jackie: Montréal, January 2020.
Guillemette, Louis: Montréal, November 2014.
Lecavalier, Louise: multiple dates in New York: 1997; Montréal: November 1999; May 2010; February 2011; May 2012; June 2013; October 2016; June 2020; January and March 2024.
Lock, Édouard: Montréal, October 2022.
Lemieux, Michel: Montréal, October 2020.
Moutillet, Miryam: New York, September 2020.
O'Neil, John: Montréal, February 2020.
Skalkogiannis, George: Montréal, January 2021.
Szporer, Philip: Montréal, November 2014.

Media

"Adrienne Clarkson Presents." (1991–2) Interview with Édouard Lock. Canadian Broadcasting Corporation. https://www.youtube.com/watch?v=9Cby3kCnAAw
Blais, Roger, Dir. (1949) *Ballet Festival*. 11 min. National Film Board. https://www.nfb.ca/film/ballet_festival_en/
Paik, Nam June. *Wrap Around the World* (1988) 47 min, colour, sound. Electronic Arts Intermix. See too: "Wrap Around the World" (1988), with Al Franken as Dr. Mobius; www.youtube.com/watch?v=9Vb63Blefpk
Racicot, Yves. (1981) *Oranges: ou la recherche du paradis*/chor. Édouard Lock. Université du Québec à Montréal, service de l'audio-visuel. Bibliothèque Vincent Warrant: Videodisc (NTSC); 58 min, sd, col.
Société Radio-Canada. (1994) *Infante c'est destroy*. DVD. Collection: Bibliotèque de la danse Vincent-Warren.
Radio-Canada. (2016) "Louise Lecavalier: Libérée par la dance, adulée par Edouard Lock." March 29, https://ici.radio-canada.ca/ohdio/premiere/emissions/les-grands-entretiens/segments/entrevue/11632/louise-lecavalier-danse-franco-nuovo

St-Jean, Raymond. (2017) *Louise Lecavalier: Sur son cheval de feu*. 102 min. Ciné Qua Non Média. Filmoption International.

Toutant, Paul. (1983) "Téléjournal," Radio Canada (May 18, 1983). https://ici.radio-canada.ca/nouvelle/1166221/la-la-la-human-steps-compagnie-danse-edouard-lock-archives

Video D Studios (1984). *Businessman in the Process of Becoming an Angel/* chor. Édouard Lock. Bessie Schoenberg Theatre, Dance Theater Workshop, New York. NYPL: 2 streaming video files (NTSC); 83 min., sd., col.

Index

Acogny, Germaine 183
ACT-UP 18, 156
Ahmed, Sara 21
AIDS crisis 10, 11, 14, 18, 35, 156
Airaudo, Malou 183
Albright, Ann Cooper 29, 86, 92
Anderson, Bailey 184
Anderson, Benedict: *Imagined Communities* 2
Anderson, Laurie 72
Anthony, Mary 138
apartheid in South Africa 10, 156
Armitage, Karole 19, 20
Asexuals 114
Asselin, Suzanne 83
Ausdruckstanz 115, 122, 138, 140, 141, 142, 144, 146, 167
Austin, David 164
awards
    Europe's Leonide Massine Dancer of the Year (2013) 38
    Companion of *l'Ordre des arts et lettres de Québec* (2015) 100, 163
    Grand Prix de la danse de Montréal (2011) 38
    Officer of the Order of Canada (2008) 38

Bamboozled (film) 158
Banes, Sally 76, 145
Barthes, Roland 23
Baryshnikov, Mikhail 132
Bataille, Georges 181, 198–9
Baudrillard, Jean 136
Bausch, Pina 131
Beaulieu, Marie 137
Bédard, Frédérik 119
Bel, Jérôme 191
Béland, Marc 109, 119, 125, 148, 152, 153, 154

Berardi, Franco 12
Berger, Maurice 10
Bergson, Hilary 197
Berlin Wall, fall of (1989) 10, 156
Bhabha, Homi K. 149, 153
Bigelow, Katherine 174, 178
Blade Runner (1982) (film) 172, 197
Boomtown Rats 114
Borduas, Paul-Émile 123
Boum, Aomar 170
Bourassa, Robert 12, 149
Bowery, Leigh 19
Bowie, David 43, 147, 148, 152, 153, 154
Brooks, Lynn Matluck 77
Bunsell, Tanya 92
Businessman in the Process of Becoming an Angel (1983) 12, 30, 38, 80, 100, 108, 111, 115, 116, 118, 121, 124, 129, 168
Butler, Judith 2, 27

Cameron, Dan 10
Canadian Ballet Festival (Winnipeg) (1948) 138
Cantsin, Monty 52, 114
Casemajor, Nathalie 37
Centre des femmes 10–11
Championship Wrestling After Roland Barthes 20
Chaput, Benoît 64
Charmatz, Boris 188
Chitty, Elizabeth 85
Chladek, Rosalie 142
Choréchanges 48
Chouinard, Marie 52, 85, 188
Chude-Sokei, Louis 156, 158, 160
Cirque du Soleil 147
Clark, Lygia 110
Clark, Michael 19, 20

Coleman, Beth 197
Colin, Noyale 109
Convalescent Dance 184
Cooperberg, Morris 34
Copeland, Roger 7
Crawford, Matthew: *Shop Class as Soul Craft* 16
Critchley, Simon 132, 134, 135
Cunningham, Merce 151
Cvetkovich, Ann 8
cyborg 18–19, 75, 164, 172–9

Daly, Ann 27
Dancer as Relay 37, 43
Danse dans la neige 138
Davida, Dena 53, 83, 109, 121
Davis, Tracy C. 27
Dede, Mercan 189
DeFrantz, Thomas 24
Deleuze, Gilles 24
Delusional World 22, 193, 197, 198
Derrida, Jacques 2
Devo 114
Dion, Céline 147
discourse 2, 7, 9, 10, 20, 21, 27, 28, 31–3, 36, 38, 39, 42, 140, 153, 156, 158, 159, 163, 192
Dishes 84
Diva (film) 118
Dodds, Sherril 106, 126–7
Drastic Classicism 20
dreadlocks 150–3, 157–63, 176, 179
Du Bois, W.E.B. 165
Duncan, Isadora 9, 27, 31, 64
Duplessis, Maurice 139
DV8 Physical Theater 105, 144

Einstürzende Neubauten 133
Eisler, Lee 121
Elswit, Kate 124, 140, 142
Eurocrash movements 144
European dance theatre 144
eurythmics 140
expenditure 186, 192, 198–9

Fabre, Jan 131
Federici, Silvia 100
feminism 10, 11, 18, 19, 89, 150, 155
feminist performance 8, 87, 89, 144, 185
Flemish New Wave 105, 144
Forgues, Emma 195, 197
Forti, Simone 81
Fortier, Paul-André 78, 133
Foster, Susan Leigh 92, 192
Fou glorieux 28, 187, 188
Foucault, Michel 24, 32, 33
Frank, Kevin 157, 160
Franken, Al 148
Franko, Mark 16
Freud, Sigmund 145
Frith, Simon 115
Front de libération des femmes du Québec (1969–71) 10
Fuller, Loïe 9, 26
Fung, Richard 158

Gallant, Jackie 55, 134
Gert, Valeska 142
Gertz, Clifford 42
gestures 129–30
Gillis, Margie 91, 183
Glasnost (1986–91) 10
Godin, Claude 119, 125
Goldin, Nan: *Witnesses: Against our Vanishing* (exhibition) 10
González, Jennifer 147, 179
Gottschild, Brenda Dixon 165, 166
Gould, Glenn 104
Graeber, David 16, 17
Graff, Ellen 16
Grimes, Sabela 171
Groupe de la Place Royale 59, 123
Groupe Nouvelle Aire (GNA) 48, 59, 76, 78, 80, 82, 122, 133, 139, 140, 167
Guillemette, Louis 47, 67, 78, 80, 100, 101, 108, 109, 111, 116, 121, 125, 130, 155, 168

Hagen, Nina 60, 113, 114
Hall, Stuart 29, 164
Hamera, Judith 103, 104, 185
Hammond, Linda Dawn xvi, 4, 6, 44, 62, 72, 73, 107, 134
Haraway, Donna J. 18–19, 17, 173, 197
Hart, Lynda 87
Hemingway, Nora 166
Holm, Hanya 138
Hooper, Colleen 106
Houston-Jones, Ishmael 20
Howe-Beck, Linde 82
Human Sex 63, 96, 97, 100, 114, 116, 144, 148, 168
Hurley, Erin 150
hybridity 21, 26, 32, 35, 149, 153, 158, 172, 174, 222

"I" Is Memory 188
Infante, c'est destroy 39–40, 92, 111, 125–6, 157, 161
Is You Me 188
Iskander, Natasha 143

Jameson, Fredric 11
Jooss, Kurt 123, 141, 142
Jowitt, Deborah 12, 13, 173
Judson Dance Theater 102, 184
junk bonds crash (1990) 12

Kantor, Istvan 114
Kaye, Pooh 81, 84, 85
King, Rodney 177
Kisselgoff, Anna 12, 136
Klein, Gabriele 7–8, 16–17
Kraftwerk 114
Kunst, Bojana 16
Kvietys, Yoné 139

L'École de danse modern 138
La Berge, Clare Leigh 97
La Gaspésienne 139
la grand noirceur 139
La Patrie 137

Laban, Rudolph von 123, 141
Lacan, Jacques 25
Lachambre, Benoît 187, 188
Lapointe, Paul 133
Laurin, Ginette 133
Le Groupe de la place royale 123
Leese, Elizabeth 141
Legault, François (Premier of Québec, 2018–) 143
Lemieux, Jacqueline 119
Lemieux, Michel 37, 50, 78, 80, 84, 110, 111, 116, 132, 133
Lepage, Robert 147
Lepecki, André 16
Les Ballets Jazz 59, 188
Les Grands Ballets Canadiens 59, 133
Lesage, Jean 34
Létourneau, Jocelyn in Erin Hurley, 163
Leung, Simon 20
Léveille, Daniel 78
Lily Marlene in the Jungle 116
Littler, Bill 57
Lock, Édouard 3, 9, 12, 20, 37, 40, 42, 75, 77–9, 82, 84, 93, 97, 99, 101, 108, 109, 114, 116, 119, 121–2, 125, 128, 130–1, 132–4, 140, 152, 154, 156, 159, 164, 165, 166, 168–70, 172, 179, 181, 182–3, 186, 187, 188
Lock Danseurs 77, 79, 80
"Look Back in Anger" 148, 203
Low, Stephen 170
Lowe, Nichola 143
Lu Yang 22, 193, 195, 197
Lynes, Krista 173
Lyon, Lisa 92

Maniura, Robert 40, 41
Manning, Susan 124, 141, 142
Mapplethorpe, Robert 92
Martin, Randy 5–6
Époque, Martine 140
Mary Poppins (film) 85

Mauss, Marcel 192
McKenzie, Jon 102
Men Without Hats 35, 114
Mercer, Kobena 162, 163
Mersch, Dieter 198
Millar, Marlene 188
Milles batailles 187
Mills, Sean 36, 159
mimetic vertigo 31
Mobius, Dr. 148
Mondzain Marie-José 23, 41–2, 43
Monroe, Marilyn 54
montage 130–1
Montreal Gazette 114, 137
Montréal Modern Dance Company 139
Mooney, Paul 158
Morris, Mark 20
Morrison, Paul 95
Moten, Fred 110
Moutillet, Miryam 47, 48, 77, 78, 80, 96, 97, 100, 109, 111, 116, 121, 125, 129, 133, 168
Mulroney, Brian 12, 121, 149
Muñoz, José Esteban 8, 88

Nagys, Birouté 139
New Demons 147, 151
New Puritans (Clark) 19
Newson, Lloyd 187
Noland, Carrie 108, 110, 197
Nomi, Klaus 72
Non Non Non je ne suis pas Mary Poppins 3, 75, 79, 81, 82–3, 84
nouveau bouger 105, 123, 142, 145

O'Neil, John 62
Odom, Selma 140
off-axis 124–5, 127–8, 136, 153
Ohno, Kazuo 183
Olympics
    Montreal (1976) 34, 35
    Seoul (1988) 148, 150–1

Oranges: ou la recherche du paradis (1981) 37, 38, 57, 78–9, 80, 84, 96, 115, 116, 118, 121, 124, 129
Osterweis, Ariel 86, 102, 185

Paik, Nam June 43, 147, 148, 151, 152, 156
parascolaire dance classes 5
Parts of Some Sextets (Rainer) 102–3
Patenaude, Guy 118
Pavlova, Anna 9, 31
Payette, Lise 11
Phelan, Peggy 14, 15, 25, 26
Piazzolla, Astor 81
Pirates of the Caribbean (film) 160
Pittman, Robert 131
Pointépiénu 76, 80, 140
Poitras, Robin 85
Pop Rock, Montreal 113
Pouillaude, Frédéric 191
Predator (film) 160
Puleo, Risa 184

Qin Ran 193
Quiet Revolution 34, 115, 139

Racine, Rober 134
Rainer, Yvonne 102–3, 183, 184, 185
Rational Youth 114
Reagan, Ronald 10, 12, 97, 121, 149
Refus Global generation 123, 138, 142, 146
Remous 122
Renaud, Jeanne 123, 138, 141
Riopelle, Françoise 123, 138
Roach, Joe 43
Robinson, Tedd 187
Roediger, David 157, 165
Rothfield, Philipa 24
Roux, Celine 192
Ruth Sorel Dance Group 138–9

Sachsenmaier, Stefanie 109
Sakamoto, Ryuichi 151

Salomons, Elsie 123, 141
Savings and Loans crisis 12
Schneider, Rebecca 87
Schoop, Trudi 141
Sex Pistols 136
Shils, Edward 42
Siegel, Marcia 128
Simon, Sherry 36
Skalkogiannis, George 57, 97, 99, 100, 108, 121
So Blue 13, 110, 187, 188, 189, 190
Solomon, Noémie 142
Sorel, Ruth Abramovitsch 138, 142
Spångberg, Mårten 190, 191, 192
Spivak, Gayatri 2
Stahl, Geoff 36
Staples, Brent 158
Stations 187, 194
Stewart, Meg 188
Strange Days (film) 174–8, 179
Straw, Will 33, 37
Streb, Elizabeth 85
Sullivan, Françoise 123, 138
Susskind, Daniel 16
sweaty concepts 21
Symes, Katerina 173
Szporer, Philip 55

Tanztheater 141, 167
Tate, Greg 158
Taussig, Michael 31
Tavernini, Frédéric 188
Tembeck, Iro 122, 131, 139, 167, 172
Temps volé 122
Thatcher, Margaret 12, 149
Them 20
Thurner, Christina 140
Tija, Rick Gavin 186
Toutant, Paul 121
Travers, P. L. 85
Trio A: Geriatric with Talking 10, 184
Turning Point, The (film) 133

Udashkin, Jack 89, 91, 95, 105, 110

Vandekeybus, Wim 144
Viau, Annie 25
Village Voice 12
Virno, Paolo 104, 108
virtuosity 22, 82, 86–8, 98, 101–5, 135, 141, 173, 184–6, 192, 199

Whitney, Allison 144
Wigman, Mary 123, 137, 138, 142
Willkie, Angélique 183
Wenders, Wim 40
Wings of Desire (film) 40
Wrap Around the World 147–8, 150–1, 153, 156
Wyman, Max 122

Yvette incident 11

Zappa, Frank 43
Zilon 52, 63

About the Author

MJ Thompson is Associate Professor at Concordia University, Canada. She has written for a wide variety of publications, including *Ballettanz, Border Crossings, The Brooklyn Rail, Canadian Art, Dance Current, Dance Ink, Dance Magazine, The Drama Review, Women and Performance,* and more. Her academic work is funded by the Social Sciences and Humanities Research Council in Canada and her essays have appeared in several anthologies, including *Performance Studies Canada* (2017). More recently, she received the National Park Service Arts and Sciences Residency (Cape Cod National Seashore) where she worked on a long-form essay about the body in landscape.